Library Services for Children and Young People
Challenges and opportunities in the digital age

Edited by
Carolynn Rankin and Avril Brock

facet publishing

Published by Facet Publishing,
7 Ridgmount Street, London WC1E 7AE
www.facetpublishing.co.uk

Facet Publishing is wholly owned by CILIP: the Chartered Institute of
Library and Information Professionals.

British Library Cataloguing in Publication Data
A catalogue record for this book is available from the British Library.

ISBN 978-1-85604-712-8

First published 2012

Text printed on FSC accredited material.

Mixed Sources
Product group from well-managed
forests and other controlled sources
www.fsc.org Cert no. SA-COC-1565
© 1996 Forest Stewardship Council
FSC

Typeset from editors' files by Flagholme Publishing Services in 10/13 pt
University Old Style and Chantilly.
Printed and made in Great Britain by MPG Books Group, UK.

Contents

Contributors

Tricia Adams

Tricia Adams, BA MCLIP, has worked in several sectors, including government libraries, and as a self-employed information specialist, but came back to her favourite role - working with children - in various guises, which she has done for the last 19 years. This has included a period as a primary school librarian, before moving back to public libraries in her home county of Northamptonshire, where she was Head of Children's and Young People's Public Library Services and the manager of the Schools' Library Service - Learning Resources for Education. She has been Director of the School Library Association - an independent charity - since 2008.

Briony Birdi

Briony Birdi (née Train) is a Lecturer in Librarianship and the Director of the Centre for the Public Library and Information in Society (CPLIS) at the Information School, University of Sheffield. Her research interests include public libraries and librarianship, youth and school libraries, libraries and social inclusion, reading research and the promotion of minority genre fiction. Briony has been at Sheffield University since 2002, prior to which she was a Research Fellow in the Centre for Information Research at the University of Central England in Birmingham (now Birmingham City University). Before that, she worked in marketing for both Dillons and Waterstones booksellers. She completed an MA in Librarianship at Sheffield University in 1997.

Carolyn Bourke

Carolyn's work as Outreach and Marketing Co-ordinator at Fairfield City Library Service allows her to be involved in researching, planning, marketing, implementing and evaluating the outreach services and programmes, including those for babies, children, youth and adults, from a huge range of cultural and socio-economic backgrounds. As well as library qualifications, she holds a Master of Education degree, specializing in literacy, and is interested in expanding the current thinking on emergent literacy and numeracy, in order to encourage parents to help prepare their children for life-long learning. Working in a highly multicultural environment, Carolyn is passionate about demonstrating that public libraries provide opportunities to build social capital in their communities, through the processes of connecting and engaging with local government, community groups, schools, businesses, families and individuals.

Avril Brock

Dr Avril Brock is a Principal Lecturer in the Carnegie Faculty at Leeds Metropolitan University, lecturing on Early Childhood Education and Childhood Studies. Her current research interests include professionalism and reflective practice, children's early language and literacy development and supporting bilingualism and story play.

Avril comes from a family of readers. At the age of 81 her father was still reading a book a day, albeit in large print and normally a crime or mystery novel. The library was both a rich resource and a haven for her – a place that has offered many delights, since her father first took her there at four years old. Avril began reading Enid Blyton's vast range of stories and then gravitated towards C. S. Lewis, Laura Ingalls Wilder, Mary Norton and hundreds of other authors. An avid reader from the age of seven onwards, her reading would often continue far into the evening. To escape detection by her parents, who would object to late nights on a weekday evening, a torch under the bedclothes helped the reading process immeasurably. Radio Luxembourg provided accompaniment in the background.

Alix Coughlin

One of Alix's earliest memories is being told off for not coming to dinner, because of always having her head in a book, and that hasn't really stopped since. Trained as a primary school teacher, she also got into trouble in this role, for encouraging children to read books that were not in the set reading scheme and for letting her class out late, so as to finish the last chapter of the latest Alex Rider. After teaching in the UK and Australia, Alix is now Lecturer at Craven College, Skipton, on both the BA and Foundation Degree in Young Children's Learning and Development, where she continues to encourage early years' practitioners to introduce high quality literature into their settings. She is currently completing an MA in Childhood Studies at Leeds Metropolitan University, with research interests in children's literature and film.

Mel Gibson

Dr Mel Gibson is a Senior Lecturer at the University of Northumbria, working in the area of Childhood Studies. She trained as a librarian and specialized in work with children and young people, in school and public library services. In addition to this, Mel has also run training and promotional events about comics and graphic novels for libraries, schools and other organizations since 1993, when she contributed to *Graphic Account*, edited by Keith Barker, which focused on developing graphic novel collections for 16 to 25 year olds and was published by the Youth Libraries Group. A National Teaching Fellow, she has used that award to develop a website - www.dr-mel-comics.co.uk - and thus support a range of comic collection, promotion and scholarship activities.

Lucy Gildersleeves

Lucy Gildersleeves is a Chartered Librarian and Lecturer on the MA Library and Information Studies degree at the Department of Information Studies, University College of London (UCL). She is also Programme Director for the department's Master in Research degree. Her teaching and research interests are in the areas of school and public libraries, evaluation, information literacy, library design and management. From 2011 to 2012, she is running a UK-wide school library impact study - *Do School Libraries Make A Difference?* Before joining UCL, Lucy worked in various children's librarian posts, as a deputy branch public librarian, as a library advisor in secondary schools and as the leader of an Essex Libraries area team of professional librarians. She is actively involved with CILIP's youth and schools work, in particular, with the joint CILIP and School Libraries Assocation information literacy taskforce.

Edward Halpin

Edward Halpin is a Professor in the Faculty of Arts, Environment and Technology at Leeds Metropolitan University and has a background in politics, community development and social informatics/information management. For his PhD, he studied 'the use and application of information and information technology for human/child rights'. He describes himself as a political scientist, with a particular interest in human rights, child rights, peace and conflict resolution and the use of information in the pursuit of these issues.

Edward has worked as an expert for the European Parliament Scientific and Technical Options (STOA) Unit; he is also a Member of the Chartered Institute of Library and Information Managers and a Fellow of the Royal Society for the Arts. He is Chair of the Geneva-based Human Rights Information and Documentation Systems International (HURIDOCS) – an international non-governmental organization (NGO), helping human rights organizations use information technologies and documentation methods to maximize the impact of their advocacy work.

Christine Irving

Christine Irving was the Scottish Information Literacy Project Researcher/Project Officer from 2004 to 2010. She researched information literacy skills and competencies in early years' education, schools, university, the workplace, public libraries and adult literacies agendas. Christine worked on the development of a National Information Literacy Framework (Scotland), with cross-sector partners linking primary, secondary and tertiary education to life-long learning, including the workplace and adult literacies agendas. She is a strong advocate of information literacy, dedicated to researching and promoting the understanding and development of information literacy in all aspects of life, from the cradle to the grave. She was involved in petitioning the Scottish Parliament for the recognition of information literacy in the Scottish school curriculum. Previous projects include co-authoring post-16 online information literacy materials and a Scottish Qualifications Authority (SQA) information skills qualification. She holds a BA (Hons) in Information Management from Queen Margaret University, Edinburgh, and an MSc in Life-long Learning and Development from Glasgow Caledonian University.

Sandra Miranda

Sandra Miranda recently retired after 23 years as Director of the White Plains Public Library, New York, USA. Her time there afforded many wonderful opportunities for capital and service improvements, most notably The Trove children's area. She was inspired throughout her career by many colleagues, as well as by her community. She still marvels at the freedom given to her during The Trove project, but credits that trust to a shared conviction that libraries and literature are critical in our lives, and that serving children and families in powerful new ways is possible and truly exciting. Sandra trained as a librarian and holds a second Masters in English. She served as Library Director in two other communities prior to White Plains, and held leadership positions in various professional associations, including that of President of the New York Library Association in 1994.

Carolynn Rankin

Carolynn Rankin worked for 20 years in special and academic library and information services before moving into professional education in 2000, most recently as a Senior Lecturer in the Faculty of Health and Social Sciences at Leeds Metropolitan University. She is Deputy Chair of the CILIP Library and Information Research Group and External Examiner for the CILIP Qualifications Board. Carolynn's research interests are interdisciplinary, exploring the connections between civil society and social justice and access to literacy and learning via libraries. She has undertaken research on the social impact of the National Year of Reading in the UK and is currently evaluating the development of the *Sister Libraries* programme of the International Federation of Library Associations.

By chance Carolynn met Avril Brock during a coffee break about five years ago and as research partners they have now co-authored and edited four books including *Delivering the Best Start: a guide to early years libraries* for Facet Publishing, and *Professionalism in the Interdisciplinary Early Years Team*, published by Continuum.

Laura Topping

Laura Topping's first school report said 'Laura's reading is excellent. I wish I could say the same about her behaviour!' She has been breaking boundaries ever since. She is a radical librarian, who pursues social justice and believes in the power of the professional to make a difference. She works in Huddersfield Library in West Yorkshire and considers herself a 'story time' veteran. Her background includes working as a children's bookseller and as a teacher. She is a passionate believer in the rights of the child and is an activist, of the quiet variety, in areas such as feminism and LGBTQ rights. Her dissertation on stock selection was produced for her Masters in Information Studies, with the vision of an equal society and making a difference through public libraries. Her research interests include childhood, ethics, feminism, learning styles and unschooling, parenting, education, children's and young adult literature, politics and dystopias.

Philippa Trevorrow

Dr Philippa Trevorrow is a Research Fellow and Lecturer at Leeds Metropolitan University. She has a BSc/BEd (Hons) in Mathematics and Education and a PhD from the University of Exeter. Her current research interests include youth participation and the use of new technology by young people, and the use of new technology in sport. She has co-edited two books and published in a number of journals and conference papers.

Rachel Van Riel

Rachel Van Riel is Director of Opening the Book – the library design and training company that she founded in 1991, after discovering that libraries offered the best possible context for the work she wished to do. Sometimes challenging as a 'critical friend' to libraries, Rachel is a passionate advocate for public and school libraries in the wider cultural and educational sector. Rachel introduced the concept of reader development, which has changed the way public libraries in the UK engage with their customers. Starting from the reader viewpoint has led Opening the Book into developing training, promotions, collections policies, websites, library furniture and new library designs.

Rachel has taken reader-centred ideas to European countries, from Norway to Hungary, to Australia, Canada and New Zealand. She has designed and installed more than 80 library interiors in the UK and has given consultancy advice on library design in Norway, Sweden, Ireland and the Netherlands.

Carol Webb

Carol Webb is co-author of the book *The Innovative School Librarian: thinking outside the box*, published by Facet Publishing. A CILIP Fellowship was awarded to her in 2007, particularly noting her work in reader development. Carol began her career in health and public libraries, before specializing in school libraries. As part of developing her expertise in the education field, Carol has completed a Masters' degree and is now studying for a Doctorate in Education. She has also designed and provided professional training to both librarians and teachers.

Foreword

Annie Everall OBE

As a child, I was regularly taken to the children's library in Gloucester, by my parents. It was in a separate building to the main library, and I have very strong memories of those visits and the impact that they made on me, as I chose, and then proudly carried home, my books. At the time, you couldn't join or use the adult library until you reached the age of 12, and how excited I was on the day that I was finally old enough. We had a ceremonial visit for me to join the adult library. As a school student, both the public library and my school library were vital in enabling me to access the range of books and information resources that I needed for my studies. As a teenager, I started working one evening a week in my local community library, in order to earn some pocket money, but, in fact, I got much more than this. While working there, an inspirational librarian showed me the vital place that a good library has in its community and taught me what 'being a librarian' really meant. He made me realize where I wanted my career path to take me. Today, some 40 years later, spanning a career spent working in the field of children and young people's library services, my belief in the value of library services - the role they have in their local communities and the impact they can have on the lives of children and families - is as strong as ever.

Communities need libraries, and, in difficult times, libraries are needed more than ever, because they provide safe and trusted spaces for communities, as well as resources that can be used and borrowed, instead of having to be bought. In this digital age, this is a time of great change for libraries. The pace of change is rapid, with many challenges affecting how library services continue to shape and deliver their services. In the UK, the Government's agenda for public sector reform, combined with ongoing budgetary restraint, has seen changes and cuts in many library services, with new models of service delivery starting to emerge, which will redefine the role of library services and librarians in this country. The needs of children and young people are also changing, in terms of what they read, how they read, how they access information, and how they use and access library services. While the debate over the direction of library services is ongoing, children's and school librarians must deal with 'what is' now and be able to respond proactively, innovatively and imaginatively to the many challenges that they are facing in their local libraries.

This book provides a timely and insightful look at the role of libraries in this changing world and draws on case study evidence from the UK and internationally, to show how they can, and are, continuing to make a difference in the lives of the children and communities they serve. Carolynn Rankin and Avril Brock have taken a thematic approach to help readers quickly identify their target areas of interest. However, the overall chapter structure also provides a natural framework and narrative, which encourages a progressive exploration of the key themes at play. Following this path through the book will reward the reader with a much deeper understanding of the connections and interdependencies between the government policy agendas that shape the delivery of library services: the ways in which we connect and engage with our communities, design libraries fit for purpose in this digital age and seek to maintain high, professional standards. All of these aspects have an important bearing on the future development of library services. I believe that these outstanding contributions from leading professionals, from the UK and internationally, supported by the wealth of bibliographic references, will give the reader insight, stimulation and, hopefully, support - especially to those librarians facing the pressure of maintaining high quality services in the challenging times ahead.

Throughout my career, like many other children's and schools librarians, I have always believed in the principle of 'getting the right book, to the right child, at the right time' (the children's library service version of Ranganathan's third principle of library science - 'every book its reader'). For librarians trying to deliver innovative and quality services for children and young people, this is the right book, and with all the uncertainty and change that we are currently experiencing, this is very much the right time to read it.

Annie Everall OBE, BA (Hons) Lib, MCLIP

Acknowledgements

Thanks are due to the contributing authors and to all the librarians, children and young people who willingly shared their viewpoints and experiences of both libraries and reading; the ever-helpful staff in the reading room at the British Library in Boston Spa; and our families – thanks, again, for your patience.

All photographs on the front cover and in Chapter 12 are copyright Opening the Book, photographer Richard Battye, and are reproduced with thanks.

Introduction and vision for the book

Carolynn Rankin and Avril Brock

> Libraries are treasure houses of stories, poems, essays, from every country in the
> world and from all times, and literature shades off into history and magic and
> mystery and religion, into sociology and anthropology – into nearly every subject
> you can think of, and it is there for everyone. There for the trouble of finding
> someone who loves books ready to make suggestions. A public library is the most
> democratic thing in the world.
>
> (Lessing, in Fraser, 1992, 47)

This book demonstrates how libraries and library services are essential for
supporting children and young people's development and celebrates the range
of library and information services (LIS) that offer accessible learning opportunities.
Throughout the book we reflect upon good practice in both local public libraries
and school-based provision, drawing on a range of examples from within the UK
and internationally. The importance of books and reading is central to the book,
but we also focus on the electronic learning age, which is now very appealing to
children and young people.

This is an edited book, with invited contributions from nationally and internationally known practitioners and LIS academics. The book is organized into
four parts, each covering key themes. Parts 1 to 3 include an introductory chapter
by one or both of the editors, followed by further chapters by invited contributors
from the USA, Australia and the UK; these each finish with a case study, to
illustrate themes drawn out in the preceding chapters. The chapters develop the
vision for the future and discuss opportunities and challenges for children's
librarians and policy-makers in the digital age.

This book is timely, and through drawing on current policy and practice it
will prepare LIS practitioners for the challenges of learning and reading in an

electronic world; challenges which are pushing the boundaries of library services. We believe this book is an innovative and valuable text for anyone working in the fields of library services, information services and education. It establishes a sound background in various aspects of library provision for five to 18 year olds. It provides professional insight for those who have to strategically plan or deliver library services and programmes at either a local community level or in schools. Our aim is that this book is an accessible, informative and inspiring text, which offers practitioners the knowledge, ideas and confidence to work in partnership with other key professionals in delivering services and programmes. The case studies, scenarios and vignettes, drawn from UK and international sources, show that the key issues have an international dimension, and the similarities and differences in service provision will be of interest to many. The use of vignettes is intended to help focus and give particular insight into a setting, an event or an experience. Innovative initiatives are used to present diverse views of library services across the primary and secondary age groups and include qualitative and quantitative evidence of effective practice. Examples from best practice – what others have tried and what works well – permeate the book.

The book provides an evidence base, which promotes and encourages the development of effective library services for children and young people. This book provides a vision for children's library services for the future and engages with the challenges and opportunities for children's librarians and policy-makers in the digital age. Experienced practitioners share their knowledge about strategies to maximize access to services, and the book considers how children and young people of tomorrow will be provided with relevant and accessible services, resources and programmes.

Part 1 introduces the themes of policy, people and partnerships. The opening chapter, written by the editors – Carolynn Rankin and Avril Brock – sets the scene, by discussing why public libraries are important for children, for society and for families in supporting literacy. The key message is that libraries change children's lives, but they also need to support the needs of digital natives. To compete with other information and entertainment sources, libraries must meet, or even exceed, the high expectations of today's technologically savvy young people when it comes to library services. School libraries are also introduced as powerful agents of learning, and the role of the school library as a place for learning is picked up by Tricia Adams, of the School Library Association, in Chapter 2. Partnerships are a recurring theme throughout the book, and the opening chapter discusses how they add value and the role of this concept in the literacy challenge. Literacy and reading are key themes, and in Chapter 3 Briony Birdi addresses the changing shape of reading as a 21st-century challenge. She provides practical suggestions how both public and school libraries can meet some of these challenges head-on. The power of collaborative partnerships is demonstrated in the case study by Christine Irving, as she describes the Scottish Information Literacy Project. Cross-sectorial partnership working was essential to the project's success, and influencing policy concerning information literacy was achieved by using the Scottish e-petition system. This is a good example of advocacy in action.

Part 2 of the book takes the theme of connecting, engaging and reaching your audience and, importantly, catching the latest wave (thus acknowledging the role of technology). The editors, supported by Alix Coughlin, develop an overview of libraries, literacy and popular culture in Chapters 5 and 6. Chapter 5 discusses the links between social capital and literacy, and the specific skills involved in the reading process are explored in some detail. This chapter also raises the issue of the child's right to information – again, this is a strong theme throughout the book and is discussed in depth later, in Chapter 15. Chapter 6 looks at what's cool to read, considering a range of genres, favourite books, classic tales, and diversity and intercultural material. The chapter concludes by considering e-books and the future of reading. Carol Webb then picks up this issue in Chapter 7, by discussing the creative integration of information technology in the school classroom. The challenge she identifies is the use of professional expertise within specific school cultures to create the library service that each particular school needs. Success is determined by an approach to information literacy that is both teaching- and learning-centred, as opposed to curriculum-centric. Carol was presented with the School Librarian of the Year Award in 2011, by the School Library Association, for her outstanding work.

The seemingly complex world of manga, comics and graphic novels is clearly explained and described by Mel Gibson in Chapter 8. Guidance is provided on how to go about developing, selecting and promoting a collection aimed at teenagers and young people. Mel flags up issues concerning common stereotypes of the medium and suggests resources to draw on, to develop knowledge about the material. There is enormous potential for outreach and partnership, working around manga, comic and graphic novels. Carolyn Bourke's work as Outreach and Marketing Co-ordinator at Fairfield City Library Service in Australia means that she is involved in all aspects of the outreach services for her public library service. In Chapter 9, Carolyn provides suggestions for strategies and approaches to outreach and marketing for children and young people and looks at a number of successful Australian projects as case studies. The message from the southern hemisphere strikes a chord with the UK perspective – namely, that each local community differs in many ways, but the need for partnerships and networks remains a constant. This notion is further developed in the next chapter by Carolynn Rankin, based on the National Year of Reading (NYR). The NYR was designed as a social marketing campaign, and the case study chapter provides a description of the planning, promotion and delivery of the NYR, in order to present the attempts to reach specific target groups. The discussion focuses on the role of public libraries as key partners in delivering the campaign and comments on findings from a case study in Yorkshire, which used the generic social outcomes' framework to look at the impact of NYR in two public library authorities.

Part 3 focuses on buildings, design and spaces. The introductory chapter by Carolynn Rankin looks at library place and space transformation and the challenge of designing for digital natives. The case for place is made by presenting an overview of the place of the library in the community and taking a brief look at design trends. The importance of good design is stressed, along with emphasis on the importance of consultation. The chapter includes examples of designs for children and teenagers and provides practical guidance. Although there is much written about library design, there is not a great deal of material specifically on the design of libraries for children and young people; this is the specific focus of the next chapter, Chapter 12, by Rachel Van Riel. Rachel introduced the concept of reader development, and the information in this chapter is based on her experiences of designing over 80 library interiors. She argues that radical shifts in thinking and practice are needed, in order to keep UK children's libraries relevant and valued in the 21st century, and that the library of the future should be able to integrate digital and print resources much more successfully than we do at present. In Chapter 13 Sandra Miranda describes The Trove Library in White Plains, New York, which is a successful, multisensory, multimedia space. As the Director, she wanted to recreate the library for a new generation that is used to being entertained, engaged and active, and she and her staff looked at museums, playgrounds and bookstores for ideas on how to achieve this. The result exemplifies an unusual trend in public library design for children - a theatrical space that is more like a bookstore or children's museum than a library. The goal of offering a learning environment layered with opportunity seems to have been helped, by designing with technology.

Part 4 consists of two chapters that focus on professional practice. Evaluating the impact of library services for children and young people is a key aspect of provision - taking the development cycle full circle. Practitioners need to use evidence systematically to inform the development of services. Lucy Gildersleeves - an experienced researcher in impact studies - provides an overview of evaluation, emphasizing that it helps to understand the context within which we operate, to see patterns in performance and to make decisions on priorities; crucially, it enables us to show how our activity makes a difference to our communities. In the final chapter, Chapter 15, a team of colleagues, and a former student from

Leeds Metropolitan University, tackle the difficult issue of professional ethics and the rights of the child. They consider some of the key legal codes outlining children's and human rights, offer a framework on youth citizenship and give some examples of professional practice, relating to the library setting, when selecting stock and providing services. Censorship and issues of information access and intellectual freedom are discussed in detail.

Carolynn Rankin and Avril Brock

Note

A number of chapters comment on school provision in the UK. In the UK, the National Curriculum is divided into four key stages through which children progress during their school life. The four key stages are as follows:

Key Stage 1	Ages 5-7	Years 1 and 2
Key Stage 2	Ages 7-11	Years 3, 4, 5 and 6
Key Stage 3	Ages 11-14	Years 7, 8 and 9
Key Stage 4	Ages 14-16	Years 10 and 11

Reference

Fraser, A. (ed.) (1992) *The Pleasure of Reading*, Bloomsbury.

PART 1

Children's library services – policy, people and partnerships

Library services for children and young people – an overview of current provision, future trends and challenges

Carolynn Rankin and Avril Brock

Introduction

This introductory chapter sets the scene, by exploring how library services for children and young people endeavour to meet the changing needs of their communities in the 21st century. It will consider the UK policies that have shaped current provisions and reflect upon the cultural and economic influences that inform the future direction for these services. Policy-makers are concerned about educational attainment and future employment prospects, therefore literacy levels and reading skills for the youth of the information age are receiving a high profile. The primary focus for the discussion is the UK, but as the public library is an international phenomenon, the discussion also extends to include librarians across the world, who are working to provide appropriate services for their communities. This chapter discusses the work of librarians who specialize in providing services and resources to support the needs of children and young people, from five to 18 years. These practitioners will usually be employed in the public library service or in school libraries. They may have a variety of different career titles, for example, children's librarian, school librarian, community librarian, teen or youth librarian, outreach librarian or literacy development officer. In this introductory chapter, the term 'librarian' includes all practitioners who are active intermediaries in providing library services for children, young people and their families. Perspectives from library practitioners are included, as they are actively involved in planning and delivering services and resources. Viewpoints from children and young people are also included, as their needs and desires should be recognized by adults. In sum, this chapter provides authentic, rich evidence about the benefits of partnership.

Library practitioners are at the forefront of promoting children's rights. They play a key role in disseminating information about the importance of literacy and reading to children, for parents, educators, children's advocates and political decision-makers. Libraries and librarians are vital aides to literacy development, and the generally held message is that reading with children is important, irrespective of first language, heritage or cultural background (Rankin and Brock, 2009). Koren (2011, 154) reminds us that the United Nations Convention on the Rights of the Child (CRC) offers support to develop library policy and practice, related to children and young people. School libraries and children's libraries should be committed to human values and human rights, and children should be able to rely on libraries to provide them with their right of access to information and education. Librarians who work with children and young people 'are some of the most vital professionals in the library and information profession' (McMenemy, 2008, 70). This belief is echoed by McKee, who promotes professional librarians, as being an important part of the school's and children's workforce: 'librarians give children a love of reading and also help develop their information skills' (McKee, 2009, 5). The case for reading for pleasure has been thoroughly and extensively set out in research, by bodies such as the Organisation for Economic Co-operation and Development; the 'Reading for Change' report showed that reading for pleasure is more important for a child's educational success than their family's socio-economic status (OECD, 2002). Improvements in literacy, at any point in life, can have a profound effect on an individual.

This chapter is divided into four sections. The first and second sections discuss the shared common-purpose services provided for children and young people, through public libraries and school libraries. The third section considers the role of partnerships in delivering that provision. Finally, the concluding section reflects on the future challenges for children's libraries in the digital age.

Part 1: The public library – a worldwide phenomenon

Public libraries have traditionally encouraged children and young people to make use of their resources and services. Koontz and Gubbin (2010) remind us that public libraries are a worldwide phenomenon, occurring in many different cultures and at various different stages of development. The public library manifesto of the International Federation of Library Associations and Institutions (IFLA) and UNESCO is provided in over 20 languages on the IFLA website. First published in 1994, this manifesto lists the mission of the public library, including a particular responsibility to meet the needs of children and young people. There is a strong, inherent message about 'creating and strengthening reading habits in children from an early age, 'and stimulating the imagination and creativity of children and young people' (IFLA, 2004).

The manifesto was updated in 2009 by the IFLA Public Library Section, with additional recommendations, so that public libraries can place their services in the 21st century, with use of new information technologies, which have become available since 1994 (IFLA, 2009a, 135-6, Appendix 5). This revision included developing public library buildings as community and cultural spaces, not just as physical stores of knowledge, and it acknowledges the challenges that have been brought about, through the growing impact of developments in technology.

Why public libraries are important for children – society, family and literacy

Communities give purpose to libraries, and library provision reaches out to the local community, beyond the library walls. There is growing interest in the social impact of what libraries can offer and how they can contribute to the social cohesion and development of their communities (Johnson, 2010; Varheim, 2009; Bourke, 2005). Children grow up in a particular social and cultural environment, shaped by a variety of influences, including home life, family, friends and community. Race, ethnicity, culture, diversity and language all play a part in forming an individual's identity, aspirations and life prospects. Socio-economic status, geographical location, early childhood education and care settings all affect the context and the environment in which a child grows up and evolves (Brock, 2011). Opportunities to develop language and literacy are important for the young child, and the children's library has a key partnership role to play in helping to develop these skills, by providing access to resources and services for children and their families (Blanshard, 1997; Fasick and Holt, 2008). Here is the view of Katherine, a development librarian, in interview:

> I am a development librarian, which means that I do work with all sections of the community - so one day I will be in the town centre library doing reading with the visually impaired, then out to a children's centre the next. When you are working with children you realize they are at an age when you can have an influence in their lives.
> (Katherine, development librarian)

Effective library services will put the community at the heart of matters, when they are developing and delivering services, engaging with people and responding to their needs. The IFLA guidelines for libraries for multicultural communities state that in reflecting the needs of the population they serve, libraries greatly impact upon people's lives as learning centres, cultural centres and information centres (IFLA, 2009b). Libraries give identity to a community and should provide opportunities for everyone within that community. Libraries are a social leveller and, compared with some other types of cultural activity, can reach a much broader range of age groups, genders, and ethnic and social backgrounds. As Feinberg et al. observe, libraries 'provide opportunities for people who do not necessarily travel in the same occupational, social, political, or economic circles to meet and greet each other' (2007, 22).

The period of the New Labour government, from 1997 to 2010, was generally seen as an opportunity for public libraries to be placed back on the political agenda, as combating social exclusion was at the heart of the political mission. The role of the public library was identified, in aiding this mission (McMenemy, 2008). The first-ever national public library strategy - Framework for the Future - provided a long-term strategic vision that public libraries in England could aspire to by 2013; this included the core role of the service in the promotion of reading and informal learning (DCMS, 2003). The public library is also seen as a trusted community resource, providing a universal entitlement to the skills and joy of reading, essential information, learning and knowledge at all stages of life and involvement in the social, learning and creative life of the community (Dolan, 2007; MLA, 2008; MLA, 2010b).

Research by the MLA investigated the reasons why people choose to use libraries, looking at factors that differentiate public libraries from other sources of similar services (e.g. commercial bookshops). There are a number of 'incentives' for use, which represent library strengths - libraries are cheaper than alternatives, and there are aspects of library services that are unique. The research emphasized the opportunities provided for children to get involved in activities and to help them develop a love of reading:

> Libraries have elements of a strong brand that they should be able to build on: good awareness of the core offer; high levels of trust and loyalty; and they are viewed affectionately by much of the population. Libraries should see their ability to reach across the social spectrum as an asset, particularly in building partnerships with other public services.
> (MLA, 2010a, vii)

The contribution of the public library – generating social capital

Public libraries were originally established to produce social change, and the evidence shows that many library services and outreach work has a real and valuable role to play in community development (Matarasso, 1998a; Pateman and Vincent, 2010). There is considerable academic debate about the concept of social capital, which has been influential in policy circles. The concept is contested and used for varying purposes, largely by social theorists (Sullivan, 2010). It has been described as the complex web of relationships between organizations, communities and groups, which make up civil society. This particular concept is used to describe social relationships, networks and community strength, including reciprocity, good neighbourliness and trust. There is a view that public libraries have the potential to act as generators of social capital, as they are open to all and provide community meeting spaces and a safe place for people to meet (Johnson, 2010; Varheim, 2009; Aabo, 2005; Bourke, 2005). Research by Matarasso (1998a) into the impact of libraries on a wide range of personal and community development issues found the wider, often unseen, importance of libraries to their communities. Public libraries are complex institutions, but they offer a place where individual people and families alike can become part of the community and can effectively connect with local services:

> . . . most of the people whose lives may be affected by library facilities or special initiatives remain largely invisible. One of the strengths of a library is the freedom it offers people to determine the terms and nature of their own use of it.
>
> (Matarasso, 1998a, 4)

Social capital is considered important in the building of an individual's human capital. Dex and Joshi (2005) are undertaking the longitudinal UK Millennium Cohort Study of babies born in the year 2000. Children will have levels of capital stock from their parents' financial circumstances and wealth, from their parents' human capital as education and knowledge, from their parents' and wider family's social and relationship capital, and from the neighbourhood's social capital and infrastructure of services. Governments have been recognizing the crucial importance of understanding these intergenerational and intragenerational relationships and transmission processes. Each generation passes on to the next some of the wealth and knowledge that it has accumulated, and the transfers take different forms at different stages of the life course (Brock, 2011). This has implications for the role of libraries in supporting family learning, and Pateman and Vincent (2010) provide a well-argued justification for extending the social justice role of the public library and the provision of needs-based services.

Libraries and the literacy challenge

Librarians know that reading to babies and young children is one of the most effective ways of enhancing language development in a child (Brock and Rankin, 2008; Walter, 2009). There are a number of great 'selling points', when encouraging parents and carers to bring their children to the library, as they provide free access to books and other crucial resources. Effective public library services are central to supporting literacy development at all ages:

> If children can be inspired by the excitement of knowledge and by works of the
> imagination at an early age, they are likely to benefit from these vital elements of
> personal development throughout their lives, both enriching them and enhancing
> their contribution to society.
>
> (Gill, 2001, 6)

It is never too early to start encouraging the development of a love of books and
reading. Most cultures have their own long-established rhymes and songs, and
singing in different home languages can promote bilingualism and provide an
important cultural link to the children's heritage.

There is considerable evidence to show that low literacy levels are a barrier to
social justice. Low literacy levels produce social, economic and cultural exclusion
that can scar communities and undermine social cohesion. Literacy is not just
about reading ability, but is a skill that is central to many facets of today's life. In
2007, a US perspective on the wider benefits of literacy was reported in *To Read
or Not to Read* (National Endowment for the Arts, 2007). The National Literacy
Trust (NLT) compiled an equivalent document for England; the report *Literacy
Changes Lives* draws on a number of longitudinal studies that have tracked their
subjects from birth, including the National Child Development Study (NCDS)
and the British Cohort Study. This research presents evidence that literacy has a
significant relationship to a person's happiness and success, gives a clear indication
of the dangers of poor literacy and outlines the benefits of improving literacy for
the individual, the community, the workforce and the nation (Dugdale and Clarke,
2008, 6). Children's libraries, with their welcoming presence in communities,
are well placed to help address the literacy challenge (Sim, 2001), and this
potential will be discussed further in Chapter 5.

Libraries change children's lives

Public libraries in the UK have been at the centre of their local communities since
the 19th century, providing services for children and young people and reflecting
the diversity of the population that they serve (Black, Pepper and Bagshaw, 2009;
McMenemy, 2008; Brophy, 2007; Goulding, 2006). The Public Libraries and
Museums Act 1964 came into force in April 1965, and the provision of a public
library service is still a statutory duty for local councils. In order to meet key legal
requirements, a local library service must serve both adults and children and
provide value for money, working in partnership with other authorities and
agencies. The Arts Council England states that access to knowledge, experiences
and treasures within libraries is every child's birth right (Arts Council England,
2011).

Public libraries make a measurable and substantial contribution to local economies and help to bridge social divides. They support well-being, encourage reading, spread knowledge, contribute to learning and skills, and help to foster identity, community and a sense of place for people of all ages, backgrounds and cultures (MLA, 2008; Matarasso, 1998a). In *A Place for Children*, Elkin and Kinnell (2000) attempted to assess the significance of the public library service in the UK, in supporting the reading development of children and young people, from birth through to 16. Elkin and Kinnell write that '[e]very child needs the library: children are the future movers and shakers of the nation. Reading has a value in children's personal, social and imaginative development' (2000, 118). This research found that libraries supported children's development, improved their reading skills and offered a welcoming, safe, socially inclusive place in which to read and a neutral ground for those disaffected from school.

Start with the Child (CILIP, 2002) also recognized the contribution that libraries can make in delivering government policies on life-long learning, combating social exclusion and improving the quality of life of children and young people in the UK. At the centre of advocacy activity, this report argues that libraries can change children's lives:

> Reading is a hugely important part of children's and young people's development. Books inspire their imagination, help them to grow emotionally, and develop their understanding of the world and their place in the local and global community, past and present. Libraries are a hugely important part of children's and young people's lives because they bring books and children together; they provide reading opportunities free of charge, and so they encourage experimentation and learning.
>
> (CILIP, 2002, 9)

More recently, CILIP has produced guidelines and extensive advice on what should be provided at a local level, by the public library service. A good library service should provide a positive experience for local people and help deliver:

- key policy objectives, by providing a positive future for children and young people
- strong, safe and sustainable communities
- equality, community cohesion and social justice
- health improvements and well-being.   (CILIP, 2009, 3)

Access to library services can provide educational and cultural enrichment for the young and help to inspire the imagination. There are many heart-warming anecdotes of early visits to the public library. Doris Lessing (in Fraser, 1992, 47) writes of libraries as treasure houses of stories, poems and essays from every country in the world and from all times. Alex (aged ten) is a regular user at his local branch library, and here are his views on the library experience:

> When you first start a library you get books and I've been going for eight years. When you go to the library there's no charges – you can get the books for free instead of having to buy a book for £8 at WH Smith. You get these library cards . . . We've done the Reading Challenge twice before. . . .   (Alex, interviewed in 2010)

This young library user is experiencing the library as a treasure house and a familiar, welcoming place to visit, recognizing that what is on offer is important in everyday life. Public libraries are free and open to all, but there is still an issue concerning encouraging all sections of the local community to make use of the services on offer. Teenagers and young people of the digital natives' generation are a particularly challenging target group to attract and satisfy.

Economic challenges for the public library

At the time of writing this chapter, the prevailing financial climate, under the Coalition government, presents very difficult challenges for public library funding. Rooney-Browne (2009) discusses the role that public libraries play in times of economic crisis; a scrutiny of preliminary statistics and anecdotal evidence from library communities in the UK and the USA suggests that public libraries in both of these countries have coped with huge increases in visitor numbers, shifts in societal expectations and increasingly complex demands for specific resources and services. Rooney-Browne suggests that it has taken a global financial crisis for public libraries to receive the credit they deserve for the invaluable role that they play in society, providing an essential public service. In these challenging economic times, public libraries are emerging as 'recession sanctuaries' (Jackson, 2009), because they promote an ethos of borrowing over buying, thus offering citizens access to innumerable free resources, such as books, newspapers, magazines, information, advice, workshops and entertainment.

Public libraries are relevant to 21st-century communities, but are still at risk; the UK public library sector is currently facing library closures and severe cuts to budgets. Durcan sees this time of imminent new austerity as:

> a good time to reinforce our traditional role and to drive and exploit our potential as the free street-corner, village, town and city-centre access points to positive activity, recreation, skills support, information and knowledge.
>
>   (Durcan, 2011, 328)

The current recession has created opportunities for public libraries to rise to the challenges that are facing them, but the economic climate is presenting a difficult reality for services that are funded by the public purse.

Children's librarians – professional intervention

Children's librarians present themselves as well-rounded professionals, who have a good knowledge of their client groups, understand theories of children's learning and development and work to support the needs of their diverse communities. They are recognized for being good at managing to reach 'hard-to-reach' groups, successfully building partnerships, based on reading and family learning. The core business services involve maintaining and developing a lively and attractive stock, which reflects current needs, and promoting their resources, by means of accessible displays and booklists (Esson and Tyerman, 1991). This raises the ethical challenge of collection development and methods of choosing materials that reflect a variety of values and opinions for the local community culture. Some UK public library authorities leave book selection up to commercial suppliers, while others still rely on the decisions of professional librarians. In the process of collection development, many of the choices that selectors make have strong ethical implications (Hauptman, 2002; Brock, Rankin and Swiniarski, 2011). Ethical issues relating to library services for children and young people will be discussed further in Chapter 15 of this volume.

Internationally, library practitioners have collaborated to provide guidance, in order to help public libraries implement high quality children's services. It is widely recognized that the demands of the information age have reshaped librarianship and the use of technologies to acknowledge and enhance the economic, cultural and communication revolution in today's world. The Guidelines for Children's Library Services, published by the IFLA Libraries for Children and Young Adults Section, provide an implementation tool for libraries of all sizes and economic levels. The goals for children's library services are:

- to facilitate the right of every child to information; functional, visual, digital and media literacy; cultural development; reader development; lifelong learning; creative programs in leisure time
- to provide children with open access to all resources and media
- to provide various activities for children, parents and caregivers
- to facilitate families' entry into the community
- to empower children and to advocate for their freedom and safety
- to encourage children to become confident and competent people
- to strive for a peaceful world.   (IFLA, 2003, 9)

Librarians play a key role as reading champions and information brokers, supporting the digital natives of the 21st century. They provide active intervention in reader development, by increasing confidence and an enjoyment of reading and opening up reading choices (Elkin, Train and Denham, 2003). In public libraries and school libraries, librarians are often involved in helping to promote reading programmes, such as the Summer Reading Challenge, Chatterbooks and World Book Day. The rise in the number of children's fiction issues is encouraging news for UK librarians (CIPFA, 2010).

The library profession does, perhaps, still experience the 'shushing' stereotyping – the misconceived expectation that the library space and its books will be guarded by someone determined to maintain this as a silent domain. However, proactive and innovative library professionals have a vocation for an occupation that brings satisfaction, enjoyment and a commitment to others. Higgins (2007) writes that the personal touch that children's librarians bring to their communities sets the stage for life-long reading. Because so many children visit the library with their parents, children's librarians can generate the highest profile of service within the community, providing positive professional intervention for children and their families. Katherine talks about her experiences of running library skills sessions for primary school children in a small branch library in Leeds:

> I got involved in helping to deliver some library skills sessions in a small branch library that is part of a joint use centre, based in a shopping and leisure centre. Many families who go to the primary school next door weren't aware of the library, because it is in a recreation centre. This is an area of low literacy and a lot of problems. The branch librarian arranged for the entire primary school to bring a class in every week and to encourage the children to join, so that they were at least borrowing library books through the school. Because most of them had never been in a library, they initially tried to keep quiet and formal, and then the kids were all getting giddy and enthusiastic – they were picking up books and shouting, 'Miss, Miss look at this'. I felt that it was successful session, because the kids really enjoyed it, and you could see that they were getting enthusiastic about reading. They all went back to school with a book and a pack to take home, which included a joiner's form and information about the library service.
>
> After the sessions, I stayed on in the library to finish up some other work, and there were loads of parents coming in with comments like, 'My kid's just given me this from the library and said I have to come in here, so can I do whatever this is for?' And you know, from that uncertain start, they all ended up joining and then going home with books – and you could see that that was really rewarding.
>
> (Katherine, development librarian)

Bronfenbrenner - a co-founder of the USA's Head Start programme (1979; 1989) - is well known for his cross-cultural studies on families and their support systems and on human development and the status of children. Interpersonal relationships are embedded in the larger social structures of community, society, economics and politics. Bronfenbrenner's model of the universal child places her at the centre of concentric circles of influence - the family, the immediate context and the wider cultural context - and so indicates the influences that affect young children's life experiences. The skills of the children's librarian go far beyond storytelling and, in fact, provide professional intervention that reflects Bronfenbrenner's model of concentric circles of influence for the child, the family, the immediate context and the wider cultural context. The evidence from successful library programmes and projects shows creativity, flexibility and professional generosity. Library services for young people are at their most effective and inspiring with enthusiastic, highly skilled staff. The range of skills required to be effective in the role can be overwhelming, and the target user group is incredibly diverse, as young people move through many developmental stages from 0 to 18 years, with huge diversity in their changing interests and needs. It is a dynamic and innovative area of the profession (Blanshard, 1997; Cerny, Markey and Williams, 2006; Joseph, 2007).

Part 2: A shared common purpose - the public library and the school library

School libraries are the other key provider of services for the age group covered by this book. The public library and school library have shared common purposes of introducing children to library services, encouraging children in understanding themselves and their worlds and developing life-long learners. Callison (1997) discusses these common purposes and explores the mutual advantages for information literacy, through public and school library partnerships. There are, however, some significant differences in the settings, in terms of contact with key practitioners and the specific services that are provided. In the public library, there will be transient contact between children, their families and the librarian and other staff; although there may be opportunities to interact on a regular basis. In contrast to this, the school librarian will have a more sustained opportunity for contact and interaction, beyond encouraging a love of reading and providing a community space.

At this point, it is useful to consider the differences between the public library and school library provision for children, although it is important to remember that they share a common purpose, overall. Table 1.1 indicates the differences between school and public libraries, in providing services to children and young people.

The school librarian has an essential, specialist role to play in supporting pupils' learning and development into effective, independent learners and readers (School Library Association, 2006). The interactions provide a direct opportunity to support the information search process – an instructional framework developed by Kuhlthau, which helps guide pupils through the complex and essential stages of inquiry (Kuhlthau, 2010). Further discussions on the role of the school library and the school librarian are provided in Chapter 2, by Tricia Adams, and in Chapter 7, by Carol Webb.

Table 1.1 *Differences between school and public libraries in providing services to children and young people (adapted from Callison, 1997, 39)*

Public library	Differences in:	School library
General public, including babies, young children and their families, school-age children, teenagers and young adults	Users	Specific audience, including pupils, teachers and support staff, parents, parent volunteers, school governors
Based on overall community needs	Collection – physical and virtual resources	Based on curriculum and instructional needs; implements the curriculum and complements course work
Reader recommendations; homework assignments; community networking and outreach; after-school activities (story hour, arts and crafts, summer reading schemes)	Services to users	Instruction in information-research skills and use of information technology; team teaching; curriculum planning; resource and literature recommendations
Providing access to books and information; offering and delivering community activities, reading promotion, services targeted at specific age groups	Primary role of the librarian	A facilitator providing access to resources, teaching information research and retrieval skills; supporting the education programme of the school; supporting the information search process
Operating as a community hub open to all; may be a specialized space designed for the age group or a dedicated area	The physical space	School library space used by the school community; may be a classroom library

School libraries as powerful agents of learning

The school library should provide a wide range of books and multimedia resources to support teaching and learning, and foster a reading and information culture that promotes independent, motivated readers and learners for life. School libraries are unique in their ability to support teaching and learning, equipping all children and young people with transferable skills, but there are many challenges in providing effective services (Markless, 2009). The Ofsted report *Good School Libraries* (2006) emphasized the commitment and support of head teachers, the appointment of specialist library staff, effective monitoring and evaluation and coherent programmes for developing pupils' library skills. Developments in the curriculum have increased the need for a quality school library in every school, run by a skilled, enthusiastic and appropriately trained practitioner. Erin was appointed as a qualified school librarian and used her professional skills to make a difference to the services on offer:

> The school wanted someone to encourage the children to read recreationally – they felt that the curriculum had really limited the amount of external reading, and they wanted children to widen their interests and read for enjoyment. As a result, we spent a lot of money on fiction. The library was manned by me from 10am to 6pm, but children could go in the library between 8am and 8pm. It was a place they could go. We were zoned and had quiet areas for silent study and areas to chat and read together in, which seemed to work well – we had a sixth form collection, an international area and a computer area.
>
> (Erin, school librarian)

There is a growing evidence base which conveys the strong and consistent message that school libraries are powerful agents of learning, central to engaging students in the transformation of information into deep knowledge and understanding, and providing them with life skills to continue living, learning and working in any information- and technology-intense world (Todd and Gordon, n.d.). However, despite the potential offered by school library services, the evidence shows that many schools in the UK have no qualified librarian, and in many parts of the world school librarianship is not even recognized as a skilled profession (Adams, 2011; Marquardt and Oberg, 2011).

Evidence shows that primary schools successfully providing library services and promoting reading provide a print-rich environment, encourage collaboration between library staff and teachers and use evidence to evaluate the effectiveness of the library (Greenwood, Creaser and Maynard, 2008; 2009). However, there is a view that some school libraries, like public libraries, have an image problem. Lockwood showed that schools who had managed to overcome the negative perception of the school or classroom library had used a variety of imaginative ideas. Library loyalty cards rewarded regular borrowers, parents' events and activities were held in the school library, and the collection was expanded to include newspapers, magazines and comics (2008, 38).

School libraries in the UK came under the spotlight in 2010, when a commission examined their future role in the 21st century (National Literacy Trust, 2010). The findings gave cause for concern, reporting that although school libraries have a unique role in raising literacy levels, promoting reading for pleasure and improving access to knowledge, in many schools, the library service is poorly embedded in the infrastructure and largely absent from school development plans. This is a clear message that one of the key agencies that school libraries and school library services could, and should, be working more closely with is the public library. Partnership with the public library service allows the school library to demonstrate the role it plays as a vital resource for the whole community.

Part 3: Partnerships and adding value – current and future opportunities

Library and information practitioners have a tradition of networking with other professional groups and developing communities of practice. Research shows that libraries 'are steeped in the ethos of mutuality, they appreciate partnership; their purpose is flexible enough to allow them to support others while keeping sight of their own aims' (Matarasso, 1998b, iii). Librarians can play an important role as connectors, working in intra-organizational teams in their local communities (Rankin et al., 2007; Rankin, 2011). The research evidence shows how libraries connect with education, youth work, hospitals, social services, local business, arts groups, the voluntary sector and many more organizations, and that they add value throughout each of these sectors (Matarasso, 1998a). Working with community partners will expand the reach of the library to connect with new audiences and partnerships, so as to create new and improved services (Feinberg et al., 2007). Partnership work brings benefits for both the individual practitioner and the organizations that they work for.

Librarians who specialize in providing services to young children are actively involved in taking their provision and resources out to the local community, and much of their time is often spent on outreach work and building partnerships. Libraries are key partners, alongside children's centres, in encouraging family reading, and children's librarians provide collaborative activities, such as story-telling events, toy libraries, family literacy activities, craft activities and puppet shows. There are many models of partnership working and collaboration. In organizational terms, this means working with other professionals and practitioners. Partnerships may be in place at a strategic level, where organizations or agencies have a policy directive to collaborate, in order to achieve shared agendas. The public library is the prime community access point, designed to respond to a multitude of ever-changing information needs (Koontz and Gubbin, 2010), and the key challenge is for librarians to implement policies in libraries and work with partner organizations to deliver effective services.

Partnership – challenges

Professionals working in partnership provide networking and outreach opportunities for many librarians. However, we need to be aware that this way of working can present difficult challenges and ethical dilemmas for professionals, particularly in cross-sector partnerships, where participants from different organizations may have different strategic priorities, differing political drivers and varied levels of knowledge:

> We have recently sent out 'hello' letters to reiterate about libraries and 'count me in' resources to family outreach workers because they are engaging with families. A lot of it is about encouraging partnership working. You will go to a meeting to talk to family outreach workers about something else, and you will get phone calls through after you go to different meetings, as you speak to different people.
>
> (Lorraine, community librarian)

The UK government policy under New Labour required a focus on working across professional and organizational boundaries, as this was seen as a potential way to help complex societal problems. Partnership working and increased interagency working has been promoted, with legislation aimed at increasing this type of co-operation at both strategic and operational levels (Rankin and Butler, 2011). Effective partnership takes time to develop and will have a better chance to flourish, if space and time is devoted to planning. Katherine – a community librarian – has first-hand experience of partnership working:

> We have to be reactive to government initiatives, for example dads are a big issue at the moment, and [we are] also reacting quickly to funding opportunities involving partners. In partnership working we have had discussions about our differing agendas and are there any that we can join up? Because to me that is what partnerships are about – there has got to be something in it for us and something in it for them. Schools are a good example as we have to try and work out what agendas you are sharing. That's the whole point of partnerships. We deal with a lot of people with whom we have shared agendas and limited resources – so if we can team up with the available resources to work on the same agendas, then it is a win-win.
>
> (Katherine, community librarian)

As discussed earlier in the chapter, children's librarians have a good knowledge of their client groups and are good at connecting with 'hard-to-reach' groups, successfully building partnerships, based on reading and family learning. However, there are critical challenges ahead in finding the resources to continue delivering publicly funded library services in times of economic strictures. Librarians may be effective and reliable partners in providing services that the public appreciate, but they are rarely recognized as the lead agency, and, as such, they do not yet have as powerful a political voice in promoting their professional worth (Rankin, 2011, 165).

Partnerships in the literacy challenge

Public libraries have a key role to play as community hubs for supporting child and family development and life-long literacy. For many families, the library is a vital community hub of literacy activity, where reading activities are modelled and reading resources are freely available. School libraries – the other provider for the five to 18 age group – provide a useful hook for encouraging family involvement, as resources borrowed from the school library are taken into the home (National Literacy Trust, 2010).

The Manifesto for Literacy, launched by the National Literacy Trust in 2009, was developed in consultation with over 30 national organizations. It makes specific recommendations for the government to develop literacy support for families, to modernize literacy teaching and to run a national campaign, taking literacy to new audiences (National Literacy Trust, 2009, 8). During the consultation period, the four key themes that emerged all suggested a role for libraries:

- breaking down barriers: the importance of speech, language and communication in the early years
- better literacy begins at home: the role of the family in developing a child's literacy
- literacy is the key to the digital age: the need to modernize literacy in the school curriculum to include new forms of literacy and promote the enjoyment of literacy
- brighter futures: to raise awareness of the importance of literacy skills where they are lowest.

Here are the views of Pauline – a mum, who regularly brings her two sons, aged eight and ten, to visit their local library:

I think that bringing them to this environment is very important. If they get used to it and then go on [to] the secondary school, using a library and handling books, accessing information from textbooks and doing homework won't be so much of a problem. They will be comfortable learning in a library setting. My mum never took me to a library. I can go into Smiths and look at the books there and buy books for the boys, but look at the range of books available here in the library – you couldn't possibly buy them all. The whole concept is fantastic. Jack is fascinated by the non-fiction – I couldn't provide him with all this. These are the building blocks to set him up for later life – using reference books and reading stories.

(Pauline, Alex and Jack's mother)

In reviewing a range of research on reading, Maynard (2011) suggests the role played by libraries and librarians, in providing access to reading material, cannot be over-emphasized, and this applies to all kinds of material, not just books. The National Year of Reading (NYR), in 2008, provided an opportunity to promote the message that all forms of reading count, including books, magazines, comics, newspapers, online and song lyrics (Thomson, 2009). The role of libraries in the NYR campaign is discussed further in Chapter 10.

Partnerships with parents – the importance of family learning

Research and policy have documented the complex and powerful influences that home and community have on young children's educational and social achievement. There is, therefore, an increasing expectation that library professionals will work in partnership with parents. Parents, after all, are in the best position to introduce their children to the world of words. Reading together and sharing books encourages talking, which helps develop speaking and listening skills. We know that fluent readers are more likely to do well in school, and reading and literacy skills will stand them in good stead for life in the 21st century. The benefits of sharing books last longer than a lifetime, since children who are brought up to value reading are far more likely to pass on their love of reading (and their good literacy skills) to the next generation (Rankin, 2011, 185)

An Ofsted (2009) evaluation survey of family learning observed intergenerational family learning provision in a variety of settings. Many public libraries are involved in this family learning provision, offering opportunities for intergenerational learning and learning that helps parents and carers to more successfully engage with, and effectively support, their children. Good partnerships, team teaching and consultation with parents are central to effective delivery.

Part 4: Future trends and challenges
The place of the children's library – the challenge to remain relevant in the 21st century

There are challenges facing public libraries in the digital age; many other activities are competing for family time, and young people have opportunities to access knowledge and resources, without using the library. The needs of targeted audiences have to be met, and librarians can add value, by being aware of educational and social trends and using that evidence base and knowledge to develop effective partnerships. Librarians need to work at reshaping and reviewing services and skills to maintain their relevance and contribution to local community users. Community partnerships can build on traditional services and help to market and promote innovative services, and innovative practitioners are currently doing so, involving children and young people in the design of library spaces and the type of services and activities on offer (Bolan, 2006; Parsons, 2008). The 2020 Mars Express Project in Sweden involved children and young people in the development and design of the library room of their local library (Håkansson, Claesson and Gullstrand, 2008). Based on Howard Gardner's (1993) educational theories about multiple intelligences, the three-year project started by focusing on what public libraries needed to do, in order to develop into more interesting, creative and welcoming spaces for children and young people – in other words, to be perceived as places that stimulate reading. Children's and school librarians have responded to the challenges brought about by the information age.

What of the future for children's library services? Elkin (2011) speculates on the many and varied future needs of the child. Reading still has transformational power; for the older generation, this largely means reading in printed form, particularly for leisure. Media and technology inevitably impact on the child, and the provision of multimedia, audiovisual and computer technology, in addition to the printed word, are the prerequisites for developing library services for children of the 21st century (Elkin, 2011, 241).

Treasure house or store house – what does the digital future hold for children's libraries?

The digital age provides positive opportunities for the library to reaffirm and reassert a position as a cultural and educational resource for the community. The children's library can be seen as a treasure house, providing access to wonderful books and other resources, to stimulate the imagination and delight the sense of adventure. In a technologically reliant future, people will require ever more effective and flexible reading skills, and the fundamental skills of wide, effective reading and early literacy acquisition will remain paramount (Elkin, 2011, 237).

Libraries and reader development agencies seem well placed to take advantage of new technologies to extend their activities. A report on digital futures identifies a new role for libraries, indicating their potential as a physical community hub:

> the explosion in online information means that many readers will entirely bypass these services in favour of Google Books, Amazon and LibraryThing. Increasingly, the advantage of libraries is that they operate as a kind of 'facetofacebook', enabling actual, local, community interaction.
>
> (Harrington and Mead, 2010, 31)

This bodes well for the recognition of the 'place' of the library, building on existing, positive notions of a trusted community space. In the profession, there is a recognition that service providers need to embrace the world of the digital natives – the born digitals – in order to make creative connections (Fasick, 2011). The Reading Agency is working on a development project, using a social network to build links between real-world libraries and distributed online conversations between young readers aged between 11 and 19. This project virtually connects the young people involved in HeadSpaces, which are informal reading spaces in libraries, cafés and community centres, designed for, and by, young people (The Reading Agency, n.d.).

Conclusion

This chapter has extensively discussed how library services for children and young people are meeting the needs of their communities in the 21st century. Public libraries have traditionally encouraged children and young people to make use of their resources and services and have provided trusted community spaces for intergenerational learning and cultural experiences. Librarians play an important role as connectors, working with community partners to expand the reach of the library, thus connecting with new audiences. There are challenges and opportunities ahead for those delivering library services for children and young people. The Reading Agency sets out the challenge eloquently:

> Reading in the UK is changing dramatically. New digital platforms are transforming the ways in which people discover and read their books, while new websites and services are changing their engagement with fellow readers. For those involved in writing, publishing, selling and lending books, these are tumultuous but exciting times, full of both threats and opportunities.
>
> (The Reading Agency, 2011, 3)

The following chapters will explore how children's librarians are rising to the challenge of providing 21st-century services, by using their imagination, skills, knowledge, flexibility and professional generosity.

Bibliography

Aabø, S. (2005) The Role and Value of Public Libraries in the Age of Digital Technologies, *Journal of Librarianship and Information Science*, 37 (4), 205-11.

Adams, T. (2011) SLA: using evidence to move forward in the UK. In Marquardt, L. and Oberg, D. (eds), *Global Perspectives on School Libraries Projects and Practices*, IFLA Publications.

Arts Council England (2011) *Culture, Knowledge and Understanding: great museums and libraries for everyone*, Arts Council England.

Black, A., Pepper, S. and Bagshaw, K. (2009) *Books, Buildings and Social Engineering: early public libraries in Britain from past to present*, Ashgate.

Blanshard, C. (1997) *Managing Library Services for Children and Young People: a practical handbook*, Library Association.

Bolan, K. (2006) Looks Like Teen Spirit, *School Library Journal*, 52 (11), 44-8.

Bourke, C. (2005) Public Libraries: building social capital through networking, *Australasian Public Libraries and Information Services (APLIS)*, 18 (1), 71-5.

Brock, A. (2011) The Child in Context: policy and provision. In Brock, A. and Rankin, C. (eds), *Professionalism in the Interdisciplinary Early Years Team: supporting young children and their families*, Continuum Publishing.

Brock, A. and Rankin, C. (2008) *Communication, Language and Literacy from Birth to Five*, Sage.

Brock, A., Rankin, C. and Swiniarski, L. (2011) Are we Doing it by the Book? Professional ethics for teachers and librarians in the early years. In Campbell, A. and Broadhead, P. (eds), *Working with Children and Young People: ethical debates and practices across disciplines and continents*, Peter Lang.

Bronfenbrenner, U. (1979) *The Ecology of Human Development*, Harvard University Press.

Bronfenbrenner, U. (1989) Ecological Systems Theory, *Annals of Child Development*, 6, 187-249.

Brophy, P. (2007) *The Library in the Twenty-First Century*, 2nd edn, Facet Publishing.

Callison, D. (1997) Expanding Collaboration for Literacy Promotion in Public and School Libraries, *Journal of Youth Services*, 11 (1), 37-48.

Cerny, R., Markey, P. and Williams, A. (2006) *Outstanding Library Service to Children: putting the core competencies to work*, ALA Editions.

CILIP (2002) *Start with the Child*, Chartered Institute of Library and Information Professionals,
www.cilip.org.uk/filedownloadslibrary/groups/ylg/startwiththechild.pdf.

CILIP (2009) What Makes a Good Library Service? Guidelines on public library service provision in England for portfolio holders in local councils, Chartered Institute of Library and Information Professionals, www.cilip.org.uk/get-involved/advocacy/public-libraries/Documents/, What_makes_a_good_library_service_CILIP_guidelines.pdf

CIPFA (2010) *Children's Fiction is Major Growth Area for UK Libraries*, Chartered Institute of Public Finance and Accountancy.

DCMS (2003) *Framework for the Future: libraries, learning and information in the next decade*, Department for Culture, Media and Sport.

Dex, S. and Joshi, H. (eds) (2005) Children of the 21st Century: from birth to nine months, Policy Press.

Dolan, J. (2007) *A Blueprint for Excellence: public libraries 2008–2011, connecting people to knowledge and inspiration*, Museums, Libraries and Archives Council.

Dugdale, G. and Clark, C. (2008) *Literacy Changes Lives: an advocacy resource*, National Literacy Trust.

Durcan, T. (2011) The Future of and for Library and Information Services: a public library view. In Baker, D. and Evans, W. (eds), *Libraries and Society: role, responsibility and future in an age of change*, Chandos.

Elkin, J. (2011) The User of Tomorrow: young people and the future of library provision. In Baker, D. and Evans, W. (eds), *Libraries and Society: role, responsibility and future in an age of change*, Chandos.

Elkin, J. and Kinnell, M. (2000) *A Place for Children: public libraries as a major force in children's reading*, British Library Research and Innovation Report 117, Library Association.

Elkin, J., Train, B. and Denham, D. (2003) *Reading and Reader Development*, Facet Publishing.

Esson, K. and Tyerman, K. (1991) *Library Provision for Children*, Association of Assistant Librarians Publishing.

Fasick, A. (2011) *From Boardbook to Facebook: children's services in an interactive age*, Libraries Unlimited.

Fasick, A. and Holt, L. (2008) *Managing Children's Services in the Public Library*, 3rd edn, Libraries Unlimited.

Feinberg, S., Deerr, K., Jordan, B., Byrne, M. and Kropp, L. (2007) *The Family-Centered Library Handbook*, Neal-Schumann Publishers.

Fraser, A. (ed.) (1992) *The Pleasure of Reading*, Bloomsbury.

Gardner, H. (1993) Multiple Intelligences: the theory in practice, Basic Books.

Gill, P. (2001) (ed.) *The Public Library Service: IFLA/UNESCO guidelines for development*, IFLA publications, 97, Saur.

Goulding, A. (2006) *Public Libraries in the 21st Century: defining services and debating the future*, Ashgate.

Greenwood, H., Creaser, C. and Maynard, S. (2008) *Successful Primary School Libraries: case studies of good practice*, Library and Information Statistics Unit.

Greenwood, H., Creaser, C. and Maynard, S. (2009) Successful Primary School Libraries in Challenging Circumstances, *New Review of Children's Literature and Librarianship*, **15** (2), 89-113.

Håkansson, E., Claesson, L. and Gullstrand, A. (2008) 2020 Mars Express - towards the future children's and young adult's library, *74th IFLA World Library and Information Congress: conference proceedings from an international conference held on 10-14 August 2008, Québec*, IFLA,
www.ifla.org/IV/ifla74/index.htm.

Harrington, M. and Meade, C. (2010) *Read:write: digital possibilities for literature*, Arts Council England,
www.futureofthebook.org.uk/ifbook%20ACE%20report_final.pdf.

Hauptman, R. (2002) *Ethics and Librarianship*, McFarland.

Higgins, S. (2007) *Youth Services and Public Libraries*, Chandos Publishing.

IFLA (2003) *Guidelines for Children's Library Services*, International Federation of Library Associations and Institutions.

IFLA (2004) *IFLA/UNESCO Public Library Manifesto*, International Federation of Library Associations and Institutions,
http://archive.ifla.org/VII/s8/unesco/eng.htm.

IFLA (2009a) IFLA Public Library Manifesto Update. In Koontz, C. and Gubbin, B. (eds) (2010), *IFLA Public Library Service Guidelines*, IFLA Publications 147, Saur.

IFLA (2009b) *Multicultural Communities: guidelines for library services*, 3rd edn, International Federation of Library Associations.

Jackson, D. Z. (2009) The Library - a recession sanctuary, *Boston Globe*, 3 January.

Johnson, C. A. (2010) Do Public Libraries Contribute to Social Capital?: a preliminary investigation into the relationship, *Library and Information Science Research*, **32** (2), 147-55.

Joseph, M. (2007) You'll Pick it Up as you Go Along: professional development in library services for young people. In Bundy, A. (ed.), *Learning Futures: public libraries for the new generations in Australia and New Zealand, conference proceedings from an international conference held in Adelaide on 9-10 March 2007*, Auslib Press.

Koontz, C. and Gubbin, B. (eds) (2010) *IFLA Public Library Service Guidelines*, IFLA Publications 147, Saur.

Koren, M. (2011) School Libraries and Human Rights. In Marquardt, L. and Oberg, D. (eds), *Global Perspectives on School Libraries Projects and Practices*, IFLA Publications.

Kuhlthau, C. C. (2010) Guided Inquiry: school libraries in the 21st century, *School Libraries Worldwide*, **16** (1), 17-28,
http://comminfo.rutgers.edu/~kuhlthau/docs/GI-School-Librarians-in-the-21-Century.pdf.

Lockwood, M. (2008) *Promoting Reading for Pleasure in the Primary School*, Sage Publications.

McKee, B. (2009) Why we are Important - children and young people's librarians in a changing world: turning the key, *Youth Library Review*, **39**, Spring, 5-7.

McMemeny, D. (2008) *The Public Library*, Facet Publishing.

Markless, S. (2009) *The Innovative School Librarian: thinking outside the box*, Facet Publishing.

Marquardt, L. and Oberg, D. (eds) (2011) *Global Perspectives on School Libraries Projects and Practices*, IFLA Publications.

Matarasso, F. (1998a) *Beyond Book Issues: the social potential of library projects*, British Library Research and Innovation Report, The British Library Board.

Matarasso, F. (1998b) *Learning Development: valuing the social impact of public libraries*, British Library Research and Innovation Report, The British Library Board.

Maynard, S. (2011) Children's Reading Habits and Attitudes. In Baker, D. and Evans, W. (eds), *Libraries and Society: role, responsibility and future in an age of change*, Chandos.

MLA (2008), *Framework for the Future MLA Action Plan for Public Libraries - 'towards 2013'*, Museums, Libraries and Archives Council.

MLA (2010a) *What Do the Public Want from Libraries? A practitioner guide*, Museums, Libraries and Archives Council.

MLA (2010b) *What Do the Public Want from Libraries? User and Non-User Research - full research report*, Museums, Libraries and Archives Council

National Endowment for the Arts (2007) *To Read or Not to Read: a question of national consequence*, Research Report 47, National Endowment for the Arts.

NLT (2009) *Manifesto for Literacy*, National Literacy Trust, www.literacytrust.org.uk/assets/0000/2584/manifestoforliteracyfullversion.pdf.

NLT (2010) *School Libraries: a plan for improvement*, National Literacy Trust and Museums, Libraries and Archives Council, www.literacytrust.org.uk/assets/0000/5718/ School_Libraries_A_Plan_for_Improvement.pdf.

OECD (2002) *Reading for Change: performance and engagement across countries*, results from PISA 2000, Organisation for Economic Co-operation and Development.

Ofsted (2006) *Good School Libraries: making a difference to learning*, Office for Standards in Education, www.ofsted.gov.uk/resources/good-school-libraries-making-difference-learning.

Ofsted (2009) *Family Learning: an evaluation of the benefits of family learning for participants, their families and the wider community*, Office for Standards in Education, http://dera.ioe.ac.uk/343/1/Family%20learning.pdf.

Parsons, S. (2008) Live and Loud in Lancashire, *Public Library Journal*, Summer, 2-4.

Pateman, J. and Vincent, J. (2010) *Public Libraries and Social Justice*, Ashgate.

Rankin, C. (2011) The Librarian - a key partner in promoting early language and literacy. In Brock, A. and Rankin, C. (eds), *Professionalism in the Interdisciplinary Early Years Team: supporting young children and their families*, Continuum Publishing.

Rankin, C. and Brock, A. (2009) *Delivering the Best Start: a guide to early years libraries*, Facet Publishing.

Rankin, C. and Butler, F. (2011) Joined up Working: issues and challenges for the interdisciplinary team in supporting the 21st century family. In Brock, A. and Rankin, C. (eds), *Professionalism in the Interdisciplinary Early Years Team: supporting young children and their families*, Continuum Publishing.

Rankin, C., Brock, A., Halpin, E. and Wootton, C. (2007) The Role of the Early Years Librarian in Developing an Information Community: a case study of effective partnerships and early years literacy within a Sure Start project in Wakefield. In Arsenault, C. and Dalkir, K. (eds), *Information Sharing in a Fragmented World: crossing boundaries. Conference proceedings of the Canadian Association of Information Sciences 35th Annual Conference held on 10–12 May 2007, McGill University, Montreal,* Quebec, Canadian Association for Information Science.

Rooney-Browne, C. (2009) Rising to the Challenge: a look at the role of public libraries in times of recession, *Library Review*, **58** (5), 341–52.

School Library Association (2006) *The Role of the School Librarian*, School Library Association, www.sla.org.uk/role-of-school-librarian.php.

Sim, L. (ed.) (2001) *All Our Children – social inclusion and children's libraries*, Youth Libraries Group.

Sullivan, A. (2010) Ethnicity, Community and Social Capital. In Hansen, K., Joshi, H. and Dex, S. (eds), *Children of the 21st Century: the first five years*, The Policy Press.

The Reading Agency (n.d.) *Headspace: the first 3 years*, The Reading Agency.

The Reading Agency (2011) *Libraries and Digital: research into the use of digital media in libraries to develop audiences for reading*, The Reading Agency.

Thomson, A. (2009) *Reading: the future*, National Literacy Trust.

Todd, R. and Gordon, C. (n.d.) *School Libraries, Now More Than Ever: a position paper of the center for international scholarship in school libraries*, Centre for International Scholarship in School Libraries, www.nmm.net/storage/resources/The_Importance_of_School_Libraries.pdf.

Varheim, A. (2009) Public Libraries: places creating social capital?, *Library Hi Tech*, **27** (3), 372–81.

Walter, V. (2009) *Twenty-First-Century Kids, Twenty-First-Century Librarians*, American Library Association.

Websites

Booktrust, www.booktrust.org.uk/.
CILIP, www.cilip.org.uk.

National Literacy Trust, www.literacytrust.org.uk/.
Reading for Life, www.readingforlife.org.uk/.
School Library Association, www.sla.org.uk/.
The Reading Agency, www.readingagency.org.uk/.

2 21st-century school libraries – visionary spaces for learning

Tricia Adams

Introduction

In the 21st century, schools in the UK are going through a huge process of change. There are enormous challenges, in terms of the changes to the curriculum and the impact of the financial recession on resources. There are societal changes that the school – and the library, at its heart – must be able to respond to. The impact of Google, and all the online resources that we use daily, are particularly felt, when budgetary constraints mean savings are inevitable. The library, with its vital but often difficult to prove impact, can seem a luxury. This chapter will discuss how in the 21st century the school library is not a luxury, but a necessity: the bedrock, the head and heart of all learning, offering a place of both relaxation and stimulation in the school setting and in the wider community as a whole.

The 21st-century vision for schools, taken from Building Schools for the Future (a UK Government investment programme in secondary school buildings in England) (DfES, 2003), is that:

> Schools should inspire learning. They should nurture every pupil and member of
> staff. They should be a source of pride and a practical resource for the community.
> They will offer a safe, secure, inclusive and comfortable environment . . . with
> improved areas such as dining areas, libraries and entrances and better accessibility
> and facilities for non-pupil users of the school.

And, as Professor Stephen Heppell (2010), a leader in the fields of learning, new media and technology, stated:

> The school library is incredibly important - much more so than in the past. It's a
> place where everyone comes to share and learn. The evidence continues to
> accumulate that libraries - and their librarians - lie absolutely at the heart of 3rd

millennium learning organisations: a place for scholarship, a place to escape into adventures, a place of discovery, a place to share and explore, a place for deep thought, a place for surprise, and above all else a place absolutely without limits. The best schools have libraries at their centres not as some sad throwback to an earlier age but as a clear and evocative prototype of what ambitious learning might look like in this century of learning.

The current scene

So how do we create the 21st-century school library? As with any utility, we need to assess what the user needs now, what the user will need for the next five years and what they will need for the next 55 years after that, and, from there, we can start to plan. In other words, we must think: 'so, what do our users need?'

Barrett (2010) has identified some interesting research studies on school libraries, including Ontario's school libraries in Canada, Booktrust's research and primary school libraries, the Ohio 2006 report and the Ofsted report *Good School Libraries*. These all include recommendations and evaluations of libraries. The most recent research in the UK, commissioned by the School Libraries Group (SLG) of the Chartered Institute of Library and Information Professionals (CILIP) (2010), showed that there is some wonderful innovative reading and information literacy work being carried out in schools around the UK. However, there is such a variety in provision, particularly in staffing, that the overall picture is very mixed. The findings of this report are also supported by Booktrust research (Greenwood, Creaser and Maynard, 2008), which indicates that the situation between primary school libraries (for ages four to 11) and those in secondary schools (11 to 16 or 18) is very different. Primary schools rarely have a dedicated full-time staff member, and the study found that almost one-fifth of primary school libraries were only open during lesson times. The Office for Standards in Education, Children's Services and Skills (Ofsted) (2006) underlines that free use of the school library helps schools to evaluate children's attitudes towards reading. The SLG research findings also emphasized that too many primary school library lessons focused simply on the exchange of books, rather than reading and library skills. Williams, Coles and Wavell (2002) also identify flexible scheduling to be important, when encouraging children to use their school library. *Exemplary School Libraries in Ontario* (Klinger et al, 2009), *Good School Libraries* (Ofsted, 2006) and *Keeping Young Australians Reading* (Centre for Youth Literature, 2009) all emphasize similar success factors, when creating good school-library provision: support from head teachers is vital, trained staff had a very positive effect on the impact of the library, evaluation was key to monitoring effectiveness, and management was, overall, more important than the size of the budget for the library.

Research by the National Literacy Trust (NLT), relating to linking school libraries and literacy, made over 30 recommendations for securing the future of school libraries (Clark, 2010). There are many echoes of earlier research reports, including the concept of government support for school libraries. Worryingly, the authors reported that nearly 28% of students did not use their school library, while only 3% did not have a school library (Clark, 2010, 4):

> Young people who read above the expected level for their age are twice as likely as young people who read below their age to be school library users (77.7% as opposed to 35.9%). This link is not necessarily causal but it does suggest that if school libraries do not perform to the highest level there will be significant implications for pupil achievement. Cuts to schools library services will exacerbate this problem. What this Commission has established is that in many schools the school library is a wasted resource, poorly embedded in the infrastructure of the school: encouraging reading for pleasure but resistant to 'teaching' literacy and phonics; absent from school development plans, official guidance and inspection frameworks; staffed (in one third of primary school libraries) by people who have no specialist knowledge of children's literature.

The next steps

So, I repeat, how do we create the 21st-century school library? Let's start with the main user – the student. Learning has become significantly more personalized – the learner is now encouraged to learn in the style that best suits them, at the particular time that best suits them – and learning has become a collaborative experience, with students working in groups of varying sizes, using mixed media and a range of skills, in order to produce the specific learning experience that gets them to where they need to be to progress.

The school community may also need access to a library that supports their needs, in creating learning experiences, not only for their school children, but also for the wider community. The concept of the extended school can have a huge impact on the school library. Extended services are additional services and activities that are regularly offered by schools to pupils, their families and the community. These services often take place outside normal school hours and can include access to both childcare and support for learning. There are many models of extended schools under development in the UK at the present moment, from schools opening their premises from eight till eight, to 'villages of schools', where the provision covers 0 to 18 years in a variety of buildings, with a school library based in a community centre on the same site, which is open to all.

The idea of the school library has changed from the popular perception of a dusty, silent room full of books, with a huge, imposing issue counter, often found in older school buildings. So how do we respond? How do we make do and mend in our older buildings? And what do we suggest if we have the option of a new build or a new partnership? Recently, there have been some fascinating developments in the provision of libraries in universities - offering open spaces, no tables, soft seating and refreshment options - and all of these seem to have had a beneficial effect on student engagement and learning, from the responses that have been received so far. School librarians need to look at some of these changes in provision and see what we can learn from them. Dr Ross Todd, Director of the Center for International Scholarship in School Libraries (CISSL) at Rutgers University, has stated that we need 'knowledge space not information space, connections not collections, actions not positions, evidence not advocacy' (2003, 52).

So how do we create our knowledge space? Careful planning is vital, including considerate planning of the physical location, if the library is a new build. This aspect needs to be considered, as, to give one example, sunlight can be a huge benefit or a huge problem in libraries. The variation in lighting in library spaces can create stimulating environments for study, reading or conversation, as well as acting as a stimulant for increased brain activity. Both shape and size are important, access is crucial, but, above all, adaptability is key. We may struggle to envisage the future requirements of the library ten years hence, but the current library must work for its users for at least 25 years. In all this, it is important to remember that health and safety requirements also need to be considered when planning the physical space of the library.

Therefore, as previously mentioned, space in a library is crucial. Generous space tends to give a relaxed atmosphere and reduces stress in learners. But space is not a luxury, as it gives us the opportunity to be flexible - for shelving, display, work spaces - and can make the library more interesting and inviting. Ideally, all libraries should be zoned into areas designated for work and the myriad of other uses. The library has to meet all sorts of different uses during the course of the day and, thus, needs to be able to accommodate a whole class exploring mixed media information sources; sixth form students wanting private study areas; small research groups working collaboratively; ICT users preparing written work; chill-out spaces for comfortable relaxation; game play - chess, scrabble or war gaming; and newspaper and magazine reading. Careful planning and a creative use of space mean that the school library can be all these things to all these users.

However, this enabling provision of space and staff are of no use if there are no resources. So what can we provide, in today's straitened circumstances, that will also fulfil future needs? There is no simple formula or ration of books to student numbers in today's world, but the library support for the school curriculum must be considered. This goes along with the need to actively develop students' wider reading patterns and behaviour; the pleasure and health benefits that they can get from developing a reading habit; the need for an increasing battery of information-handling skills; and how all of this helps to foster students' personal development and interests for the rest of their lives.

In my view, a school library should include:

- books, lots of them, in all formats - paperback, hardback, electronic, audio and large print, fiction, non-fiction, graphic and the frankly frivolous, too
- ICT - preferably, adaptable laptops and Wi-Fi, with lots of software, linked to the school's VLE and intranet and the school library's management system; access to these systems should always be available 24/7; the interactive whiteboard should be provided for whole class interaction or for small groups to collaboratively play or work
- journals, magazines, newspapers, both paper copies and online, for everyone to browse, read, learn from or simply enjoy
- film and music - there will always be a proportion of our students who are visual learners or auditory learners. Therefore, these resources (DVD, CD, MP3/4) will be vital to their success, as well as key in providing extra options for other students.

Necessary considerations to make the library work

So how do we make this work in our zoned library spaces? We are used to having fiction browsing areas, reference sections and non-fiction areas, but perhaps we need to be a little creative, when including a small area for video viewing, having the comfortable seating partway between the fiction browsing area and the newspaper and magazine section. Consider having the quiet study area away from the informal area, the group area being bookable in various configurations (for groups, classes or mentors and mentees). Also important is some space for staff work and library preparation areas for the crucial day-to-day running of the library.

To make this 21st-century school library a reality, there has to be flexibility in the arrangement of shelving, seating and other furnishings and there is a good range provided by library furniture suppliers. Dubber and Lemaire (2007) provide expert advice on library equipment, visiting local schools and sharing ideas with other librarians and teachers. Use the expertise available in the local school library support services and join up with the local public library service. There can be benefits all round from partnering with others, in order to enhance what each school library can offer, both in terms of resources and knowledge about resources.

As a basis for developing school libraries in the 21st century, the School Library Association (SLA) is working on an ongoing advocacy campaign, which deals with the how and the why of school libraries. The *Primary School Library Charter* (SLA, 2010) campaigns in the UK to ensure school libraries are staffed by trained and qualified librarians, emphasizing the need to provide robust school libraries at the point of student need, in order to adequately support their learning and reading. Staffing is paramount in all school libraries, and, again, this needs to be flexible and integrated. The demands of the extended school day means that it is no longer acceptable to have just one librarian – there needs to be a team effort, with a trained librarian as the leader of a team, which is able to cover mixed uses during a long day, as well as be open at all break times and before and after school. The school teaching staff needs to know that their librarian colleagues will use their complementary skills, so as to support them in gathering new material for their particular subjects, as well as partnering in supporting the students to learn and achieve, by delivering specifically targeted activities to help them with assignments.

Use the evidence base

This is also a serious call to provide evidence of the impact of school libraries and to make sure that whatever libraries do – however informal or structured – is evaluated and feeds into the relevant part of the school's self-evaluation. Evaluation doesn't have to be an unwieldy, formal process. Instead, it can be a very simple question-and-answer session involving students, relating to how they feel, what they used, how easy they found it and other useful comments. To take a simple example – evaluation feedback can be a very informal blob chart produced by a student. One chart can be filled out at the start of the activity – detailing how confident the student may feel about using a library, reading a book or finding information. The same blob chart activity, at the end of that student's induction, can show if their confidence has grown. Over time, this becomes a valuable piece of evidence that pupils are benefiting from using the library and, thus, can be used to bid for funds, report to senior managers, and generally gain more buy-in from other staff in the school (Markless, 2009).

This is borne out by Nancy Everhart, who echoed what Ofsted reported in *Good School Libraries* in 2006: that support from senior colleagues, especially the head teacher, is vital in good school-library provision. This links up with the similar recommendations from the School Library Commission (MLA, 2010), concerning the vital importance of inclusion of the library and its staff in all planning and policy developed throughout the school; without this support, it simply will not work. Interestingly, Everhart's article echoes *Good School Libraries* in other respects, too, particularly in that evaluation of all library programmes is seen as key to recognizing the library impact within the school in question. Everhart states that: 'it is crucial that school librarians be cognizant of any and all methods that principals use and of other factors that might influence evaluations because the outcomes of these evaluations have serious professional consequences' (2008, 40). She goes on, further, to quote Ross Todd:

> What's important is that the gathered evidence highlights how the librarian plays a crucial role in boosting student achievement, in shaping important attitudes and values, in contributing to the development of self-esteem, and in creating a more effective learning environment.

Both Ofsted (2006) and Everhart (2008) comment on the crucial elements of a quality school library, using similar phrases relating to the 'library's physical environment, inviting displays, librarian interaction, and feelings of welcome', and that school librarians should be aware that maintaining a positive library climate can promote or enhance positive self-concepts in students and could facilitate learning.

A number of recommendations from *Good School Libraries* and Everhart's article are centred on the teaching of information literacy skills. In 2006, Ofsted recommended that schools should develop high quality, coherent programmes for teaching information literacy, in order to provide better continuity, challenge and progression in pupils' learning. We know that this skill is increasing and improving in many schools. This is evidenced annually, as the SLA evaluates the submissions for the School Librarian of the Year Award; without fail, every school that enters has a developed or developing information literacy scheme in place. The Qualifications and Curriculum Authority (QCA, 2008) has developed a big-picture curriculum, so as to reinforce the concept of the curriculum as the entire, planned learning experience of a young person. This states that learners should be proactively involved in their own learning, with resources well matched to learning needs, for example, use of time, space, people and materials – these are all envisaged in the 21st-century school library. The information literacy case study, in the Specialist Schools and Academies Trust booklet (SSAT), titled *At the Heart of Learning*, from the George Abbot School in Guildford (2008), states: 'the librarians are committed to supporting students in building the skills to work with text: skimming, sifting, assimilating, organizing, understanding and enjoying'.

Here, the librarian's philosophy is summed up as 'the library is about learning. It's not just a warehouse of books'. On this point, I couldn't have expressed it better.

Conclusion

President Barack Obama referred to the library as the 'magic threshold' in his speech to the American Library Association annual conference in Chicago in 2005, when he was a US Senator (Obama, 2005). This, I think, underlines the role of both the library, and vitally, the librarian, namely, that we must never overlook – as the gateway to reading – the informal learning that comes from this reading, but also the well-being and relaxation and recreation that comes from reading. The NLT (Dugdale and Clark, 2008) has published a research document that similarly shows the impact that literacy has on life and life expectations – those with low literacy levels are more likely to live in a non-working household, they are less likely to have children, more likely to live in overcrowded situations and less likely to vote. Librarians can help to provide opportunities for change. As this NLT document heralds, 'Literacy changes lives', and school libraries must have a central role in making that happen.

References

Barrett, L. (2010) Effective School Libraries: evidence of impact on student achievement, *School Librarian*, **58** (3), 136-9.

Centre for Youth Literature, State Library of Victoria (2009) *Keeping Young Australians Reading*, Sue McMerracher for the Centre for Youth Literature, www2.slv.vic.gov.au/about/information/publications/policies_reports/keeping-reading.html.

CILIP (2010) *School Libraries in the UK: a worthwhile past, a difficult present – and a transformed future?* (Report of the UK National Survey for School Libraries Group of CILIP), Chartered Institute of Library and Information Professionals.

Clark, C. (2010) *Linking School Libraries and Literacy: young people's reading habits and attitudes to their school library, and an exploration of the relationship between school library use and school attainment*, National Literacy Trust.

DfES (2003) *Building Schools for the Future: consultation on a new approach top capital investment*, Department for Education and Skills.

Dubber, G. and Lemaire, K. (2007) *Visionary Spaces: designing and planning a secondary school library*, School Library Association.

Dugdale, G. and Clark, C. (2008) *Literacy Changes Lives*, National Literacy Trust, www.literacytrust.org.uk/assets/0000/0401/Literacy_changes_lives_2008.pdf.

Everhart, N. (2008) Principals' Evaluation of School Librarians: a study of strategic and non-strategic evidence-based approaches, *Synergy*, **6** (2), 39–46.

Greenwood, H., Creaser, C. and Maynard, S. (2008) *Successful Primary School Libraries: case studies of good practice*, Library and Information Statistics Unit and Loughborough University.

Heppell, S. (2010) Press Release, CILIP School Libraries in the UK, www.cilip.org.uk/news-media/Pages/news072010.aspx.

Klinger, D. A., Lee, E. A., Stephenson, G., Deluca, C. and Luu, K. (2009) *Exemplary School Libraries in Ontario: a study by Queen's University and People for Education*, Ontario Library Association.

Markless, S. (ed.) (2009) *The Innovative School Librarian: thinking outside the box*, Facet Publishing.

MLA (2010) *School Libraries: a plan for improvement*, Museums, Libraries and Archives Council and National Literacy Trust.

Obama, B. (2005) *Bound to the Word*, American Library Association, http://boulderlibrary.wordpress.com/2008/11/10/bound-to-the-word-by-barack-obama-courtesy-of-american-library-association.

Ofsted (2006) *Good School Libraries: making a difference to learning*, HMI 2624, www.ofsted.gov.uk/resources/good-school-libraries-making-difference-learning

Qualifications and Curriculum Authority (2008) *A Big Picture of the Curriculum*, Department. for Education, http://curriculum.qcda.gov.uk/uploads/Curriculum%20aims_tcm8-15741.pdf.

SLA (2010) Primary School Library Charter, School Library Association, www.sla.org.uk/primary.php.

SSAT (2008) *At the Heart of Learning: the role of the library in the specialist school*, Specialist Schools and Academies Trust.

Todd, R. (2003) Irrefutable Evidence, *School Library Journal*, **49** (4), 52–4.

Williams, D., Coles, L. and Wavell, C. (2002) *Impact of School Library Services on Achievement and Learning in Primary Schools*, DfES and Resource.

Websites

The Hub, http://hubinfo.wordpress.com.

3 The changing shape of reading – the 21st-century challenge

Briony Birdi

Introduction

Experience will have shown the readers of this book that a highly literate child is not necessarily a reading child and, similarly, that not every child with reading difficulties will dislike reading. Our work - to develop literacy and to encourage reading - has changed in recent years, in part owing to developments in the educational curricula, and in part rapidly changing technologies.

This chapter presents six themes through which to consider the challenges facing libraries and the book trade as a whole, making suggestions as to how both public and school libraries can meet them head on.

Reading, the family and the library

Recently, reading research has broadened in scope to consider the way in which social contexts influence reading ability. It is now widely accepted that the development of reading skills occurs not only in the classroom, but also within social settings, at home and in the wider community. Children and family members combine languages, literacies and cultural practices from a variety of contexts. In many examples grounded in 'real world settings', in other words, beyond the school gates, children's learning and their development as readers are supported and, in turn, support those of others, in ways that are not necessarily recognized or understood within the school curriculum (Olmedo, 2004).

The most obvious example of a child or young person's 'real world setting' is the family. The phrase 'family reading' tends to be interpreted in two ways: first, as family members supporting each other in the development of their literacy skills, and, second, as family members sharing their enjoyment of reading and storytelling.

Unfortunately, a number of barriers have been found to prevent effective family reading. These barriers are described below:

1 Lack of early language and reading experiences: where children are not encouraged to talk and take part in extended conversations with those they spend their time with, their understanding of the spoken and written word is poorer than that of their peers.
2 Intergenerational barriers: where parents have not enjoyed reading, or were not read to themselves, they do not necessarily understand its importance. Reading is, consequently, seen as a chore.
3 Poor basic skills: where parents' own basic skills are low, they are less confident and less able to support their children's reading.
4 Economic and financial barriers: in periods of poverty, owing to debt, poor housing, health problems or unemployment, reading becomes a luxury, rather than a necessity.
5 Cultural barriers: for reasons of language, tradition or economic circumstance, some communities do not see the reading habit as part of their culture.
6 Institutional barriers: people's needs may not be recognized by the infrastructure that should support them, because some institutions - schools, libraries, for example - fail to engage effectively with them.

How we can help

In order to break down these barriers, a 'model of effective family reading' could include the following elements:

- reading for pleasure being recognized, at school and in the home, and promoted by the library service, as an important part of the process of learning to read
- providing a safe and fun space for children to feel comfortable to read in
- providing support to families in reading together; reading in the home being encouraged and supported by schools, the library service and the local community.

(National Literacy Trust, 2011)

Realism and children's reading

Titles that we may describe as 'realistic fiction' are often popular with young readers, as they represent an author's attempt to reflect their everyday reality - a reality which may not be sufficiently well represented in popular culture. Although not exclusively, the term tends to be associated with older readers, covering potentially controversial issues, such as religion, alcohol and drug use, friendships and betrayals, first sexual experiences and sexual orientation. What are the benefits of reproducing such issues in narrative form? Critics argue that it can encourage children to consider how they would act in similar circumstances, in theory, to help them to develop into 'responsible adults'. Also, as the narrative is often written in the first person, from the perspective of a young narrator, this, arguably, helps the reader to identify more easily with the characters and situations that are presented.

So, in theory, we have a realistic portrayal of life for the child to read and adapt, using relevant extracts to support his or her personal development. Or do we? Although the majority of titles seen as 'controversial' are intended for 11 to 16 readers, rather than younger children, this issue is, nonetheless, relevant to the primary age group. The bestselling picture book *And Tango Makes Three* (Parnell and Richardson, 2005), which tells the story of two male penguins hatching a penguin egg and successfully raising the young female chick, has been at, or near, the top of the American Library Association's (ALA's) annual list of the most frequently challenged books for four consecutive years. The challenges made are that the book has homosexual themes, it is 'anti-family' and that it is unsuited to the intended age group. In the UK, the reaction to the book has, generally, been less negative than in the USA, and it continues to sell extremely well. For older readers, certain books published from the 1990s onwards have been described as 'über-realistic'; in 1994, Anne Fine wrote about domestic violence and bullying in *The Tulip Touch*, and Melvin Burgess, in the following year, wrote about young heroin users in *Junk*. There were many supporters of these novels and a number of awards made to the authors, but they were not without their critics.

Books such as these can divide public and professional opinion, winning prizes for originality and literary merit, while at the same time being criticized for not protecting children from the harsher realities of life. Two contrasting views of children's authors present both sides of the argument: first, Bel Mooney commented in *The Times* in 2002: 'Human beings can have too much reality and young readers especially require some sort of hope, a promise of redemption.' Second, Paul Jennings suggests: 'We do not do our children a favour if we pretend that everything is easy. We cannot shelter them from the truth that there is pain, hardship and loss in life' (Jennings, 2004, 193-4).

How we can help

Recent research into the censorship of children's books has provided some useful recommendations (Stannard, 2008, 74-5), which can equally be applied to potentially controversial realistic fiction:

1   Collection development policy: as recommended by the Museums, Libraries and Archives Council (MLA, 2009), a written collection development policy should be created for children's materials, made available to the public and used to defend material, if the need arises.
2   Guidance: more staff guidance is felt to be needed, as to what children can borrow and the role that library staff and parents should take in this. Library staff should also have guidance as to how to act, if a parent complains about a book.
3   Staff discussion: potentially controversial materials should be discussed at staff meetings, to increase awareness and enable staff to prepare responses to any complaints that they may receive.
4   Labelling: possible identification and labelling of controversial material should be considered. Although this goes against the recommendation of the ALA (2004), both parents and staff involved in the UK research felt that books and other resources about controversial subjects should be clearly identified. Curry (1997, 142) suggests that effective labelling can be the 'least judgmental and most impersonal way to alert patrons to possible offense'.

Reading and identity

As they develop their awareness of themselves and the world around them, children inevitably begin to explore complex identity issues, such as race and ethnicity, class, disability, gender and sexual orientation. Research, and our own experiences, has shown us that the act of reading fiction can support children, in forming both personal and social identities, helping them to understand who they are, how they relate to others and what roles they can play now and in the future (Cotterell, 1996; Rosenblatt, 1994; Ross, McKechnie and Rothbauer, 2006). As Louise Rosenblatt neatly states: 'Literary texts provide us with a widely broadened "other" through which to define our world and ourselves' (Rosenblatt, 1994, 145).

To take the issue of ethnicity as an example, it is claimed that a child's reading of multicultural fiction can provide a 'route into empathy' (Elkin and Triggs, 1985) and that fiction can be a 'tool', with which to educate children and adults 'about understanding others' (Mar et al., 2006, 708). However, if the act of reading imaginative literature about cultures other than one's own has the potential to increase intercultural understanding, it follows that their portrayal within this literature must be accurate and fair. An inaccurate or unfair representation could, arguably, have a negative effect on readers' views of other ethnic groups. It is felt that identity is shaped by positive recognition – whereby, each identity is appreciated and respected – and that a negative recognition can cause people to '. . . suffer real damage, real distortion, if the . . . society around them mirror[s] back to them a confining or demeaning or contemptible picture of themselves' (Taylor, 1992, 25).

At the same time, an *absence* of references to these issues of identity within stories can have an equally negative effect. Having too few disabled characters in children's fiction, for example, can convey the idea that disabled people are less valued by society, so, to counter this, the inclusion of text and images of disabled children in storybooks enables them to become the norm (Wyatt, 2010).

How we can help

There are many ways in which we can help to bridge the gap and provide sufficient resources for children to consider their selves and identity. To sum up, here are two examples:

1   Making sure that children's fiction is selected with appropriate images and text, relating (in particular) to race and ethnicity, disability, gender and sexual orientation. Guidelines are available from organizations such as Scope – In the Picture (for children with disabilities), and well-researched stock checklists are being compiled, for example, for sexuality (Chapman, 2007).

2   Many of the texts specifically written to address the lack of representation, or misrepresentation, of particular issues are published by lesser-known authors from smaller, independent publishers. As these will not necessarily be selected by library suppliers for purchase, the library collection can be supplemented (where possible) by going directly to the publishers.

Not for loners any more: social reading and the child

Reading has tended to be regarded as a solitary activity, but with the rapid growth of both the internet and activities such as reading groups, reading is, today, seen as increasingly social, facilitating a wide range of social 'connections' between readers of all ages. Of course, for younger readers, the introduction to social reading is generally made automatically, through hearing stories read aloud and by learning to read in a classroom context. As they develop as readers, become able to decode texts and enjoy stories without adult help, children are still engaging in a potentially social activity. To give two of the more obvious, recent examples, J. K. Rowling's Harry Potter series and Philip Pullman's *Northern Lights* trilogy have sparked a seemingly infinite number of social interactions, across the most diverse readership. It is argued that simply reading popular novels such as these enables children to participate in these 'conversations', 'even if one never speaks a word of it to anyone' (Ross, McKechnie and Rothbauer, 2006, 127).

Yet, reading 'communities' do not only arise from the most popular titles; reading audiences can be as mainstream or specialized as necessary, covering books from all genres and drawing together certain kinds of readers, who may not otherwise have an obvious reason or opportunity to socialize.

How we can help

In recent years, we have all become aware of the online communities, which have given children a forum to communicate about all manner of books and reading, but Ross, McKechnie and Rothbauer (2006) suggest that the virtual community is just one of three possible communities of readers. An understanding of the nature of these communities can help us to engage with our young readers and to support them in their social development.

As the name 'local communities' implies, these occur in the child's own neighbourhood and are sustained by face-to-face interactions with people they know or meet on a daily/regular basis, in order to share reading experiences: neighbours, family members, friends, library staff, fellow pupils and teachers, etc. Shared activities might include recommending and sharing books with one another, meeting at the local library to talk about reading experiences or even joining a reading group at their library or at school.

Textual communities, also known as 'fictional communities', are established when readers 'make connections with textual characters', identifying with an experience, feeling or character trait and, thereby, gaining a sense of belonging. A similar process can also occur, when a reader identifies with the author of a text. Authors Jacqueline Wilson and Anne Fine (to give just two examples) have frequently referred to letters or e-mails received from fans, who have clearly identified with characters in their novels, even to the extent that they now feel less alone in their particular situation.

Virtual communities involve members who may never meet in person, but who can, nonetheless, engage in extremely rewarding and enjoyable online discussion and activity, sharing reading opinions and experiences with individuals and groups of all sizes. Some online communities remain local, while others have a truly global scope, which, if appropriately monitored by adults, can improve a child or young person's social skills and connections and can also motivate them to read more.

Complementary or antagonistic: the role of technology in reading

As the title of this section suggests, technology is still viewed both as complementary to, and antagonistic towards, the act of reading, and nowhere is this debate more relevant than in considering the younger reader. Described as 'Generation M' (Roberts, Foehr and Rideout, 2005) for the central role of media in their lives, even very young children are often comfortable and confident with multimedia and technology.

For some, the term 'reading' still only refers to the reading of books and other printed materials, but to fully support children in their development as readers, we must also take into account the other ways in which they may choose to 'read' on a daily basis. Our interpretations of terms such as 'literacy' and 'reading' are far broader today than they have been previously, and they take into account the more interactive processes through which children learn to read and to develop a reading habit. The book that children hold in their hands is linear, read by moving from the beginning to the end, in the order intended by the author. The multimedia text is non-linear, having no set path for the child to follow, and is an interactive text in which he or she can decide where to go. The two activities can be entirely complementary, developing different skills and, arguably, giving children a more rounded reading experience.

How we can help

As Jennings (2004, 188) writes: 'Most problems with computers relate to their over-use', and, certainly, we need to encourage children not to use computers as their only source of reading material, but to see them as a means of supporting and enhancing their printed-book reading. When presented as complementary, rather than antagonistic, research has shown that younger readers can enjoy print and multimedia equally. The world has changed, and we should not be too concerned if our younger readers do not necessarily see book reading as the 'best' and most enjoyable form of literacy. Often the child or young person who says he does not read is later revealed to enjoy a hugely diverse range of texts, and we can reassure him that he is, indeed, an avid reader.

Exploring partnerships in literacy and reading promotion

The rapid growth of reader development in libraries and the impact of initiatives, such as the National Year of Reading, World Book Day and The Reading Agency's Summer Reading Challenge, have resulted in the relatively recent increase in the promotion of reading for pleasure, across the whole of the book trade. All of these initiatives mentioned above have involved partnership working, to a greater or lesser extent.

The growth in reader development activities, in promotional ventures and in partnership working come together to affirm three principles of the book industry (Thebridge and Train, 2002, 139):

1   Books play a central role in public library services, despite fears that they are being marginalized.
2   It is acceptable for library staff to actively encourage reading and to help customers with reading choices.
3   The public is best served when the skills of publishers, booksellers and librarians are combined to develop readers and the reading habit.

Reading activity is now more consistently planned and sustained, with more practitioners looking to incorporate reading promotion into their library strategy. There has been a concerted attempt across the book industry to promote not only the book project, but also the reading experience, from which a market for book buying and borrowing can grow.

The partnership 'offer' of individual members of the book trade

The world of publishing and bookselling has changed dramatically in recent years, because of the market dominance of online bookselling, the rapid growth of e-publishing and the increasing use of e-books and e-book readers by children and young people, combined with the global economic recession. Yet, each potential partner still brings – and stands to gain – a huge amount to any working partnership to promote children's reading.

'Reading is libraries' core business and it has huge partnership potential' (Wyatt, 1998, 86); we know what libraries can offer. In short, they potentially provide access to the entire population, still considered a neutral space at the centre of the local community. Library staff know their readers and actively work with schools and school libraries to encourage children to develop a reading habit, and, as research shows, those who borrow books are more likely to buy them, too; this is an obvious 'selling point' in brokering a partnership.

Ranging in size from small, local, independent organizations to the large multinational publishing houses, publishers provide access to authors and illustrators, publicity materials about specific titles and authors, support for themed promotions and much more. Sometimes the less well-known imprints of larger publishing houses can provide useful titles for partnership, promoting new authors or a specialist interest. The smaller, local publishers are logical partners for work with a community focus.

Although fewer in number than before, there are still a huge number of bookselling outlets. All offer the potential for partnership, providing (for example) venues for events, areas to display promotional materials and bookstalls at library events. Booksellers often work with local schools and their libraries, in order to bring children to the shop to meet authors, participate in storytelling or other positive reading-related activities (Thebridge, 2001).

Conclusion

The reading landscape in the 21st century is, undoubtedly, very different from that of the previous one: new formats and media have emerged, and new practitioner and publisher approaches have developed, in order to use them in creative and imaginative ways. Yet, as this chapter has shown, the basic principle and purpose of reading remains the same, and the role of both public and school libraries, in developing and supporting the reading child, cannot be underestimated.

References

ALA (2004) *The Freedom to Read Statement*, American Library Association.

Chapman, E. (2007) *Provision of LGBT-Related Fiction to Children and Young People in Public Libraries*, University of Sheffield Masters dissertation.

Cotterell, J. (1996) *Social Networks and Social Influences in Adolescence*, Routledge.

Curry, A. (1997) *The Limits of Tolerance: censorship and intellectual freedom in public libraries*, Scarecrow Press.

Elkin, J. and Triggs, P. (1985) *The Books for Keeps Guide to Children's Books for a Multi-Cultural Society*, Books for Keeps.

Jennings, P. (2004) *The Reading Bug . . . and How to Help Your Child Catch It*, Penguin Books.

Mar, R., Oatley, K., Hirsh, J., dela Paz, J. and Peterson, J. B. (2007) Bookworms Versus Nerds: exposure to fiction versus non-fiction, divergent associations with social ability, and the simulation of fictonal social worlds, *Journal of Research in Personality*, **40** (5), 694–712.

MLA (2009) *Guidance on the Management of Controversial Materials in Public Libraries*, Museums, Libraries and Archives Council.

Mooney, B. (2002) Writing Throughout the Ages, *The Times*, 28 August, www.belmooney.co.uk/journalism/writing_ages.html.

National Literacy Trust (2011) *Transforming Lives: families*, National Literacy Trust.

Olmedo, I. M. (2004) Storytelling and Latino Elders: what can children learn? In

Gregory, E., Long, S. and Volk, D. (eds), *Many Pathways to Literacy: young children learning with siblings, grandparents, peers and communities*, Routledge.

Parnell, P. and Richardson, J. (2005) *And Tango Makes Three*, Simon & Schuster.

Roberts, D. F., Foehr, U. G. and Rideout, V. (2005) *Generation M: media in the lives of 8–18 year olds*, Kaiser Family Foundation, www.kff.org/entmedia/upload/Generation-M-Media-in-the-Lives-of-8-18-Year-olds-Report.pdf.

Rosenblatt, L. (1994) *The Reader, the Text, the Poem: the transactional theory of literary work*, Southern Illinois University Press.

Ross, C. S., McKechnie, L. and Rothbauer, P. M. (2006) *Reading Matters: what the research reveals about reading, libraries and community*, Libraries Unlimited.

Stannard, T. (2008) *The Guardians of Children's Literature? A study into the attitudes of public library staff and parents regarding issues of censorship in children's books*, University of Sheffield Masters dissertation.

Taylor, C. (1992) *Multiculturalism and the Politics of Recognition*, Princeton University Press.

Thebridge, S. (2001) *Reading Together, Working Together: guidance for booksellers, librarians and publishers on promoting books and reading*, University of Central England in Birmingham in association with Ulverscroft Large Print Books.

Thebridge, S. and Train, B. (2002) Promoting Reading Through Partnerships, *New Library World*, **103** (1175/1176), 131–40.

Wyatt, A. (2010) *A Portrayal of Disability in Children's Fiction: the availability and promotion of such resources in public libraries*, University of Sheffield Masters dissertation.

Wyatt, R. (1998) Reader Development and Literature Promotion, *Public Library Journal*, **13** (6), 86.

4

Case study. Engaging and influencing policy and the curriculum – the Scottish Information Literacy Project experience

Christine Irving

Introduction

Library and information science (LIS) professionals support learning and teaching in a variety of ways, and this chapter will focus on information literacy (IL) and the key messages that it holds for engaging and influencing policy. Using the Scottish Information Literacy Project as a case study, I will discuss the experience of the project and project partners, in their engagement with IL and their endeavours to influence government policy and the curriculum, based upon my direct involvement in the project, as project officer and researcher. The issues that were faced included the recognition of the term 'information literacy' in its own right, as a key life skill at policy level, in the school curriculum and in the role of the school librarian. Key to the success of the project was collaborative partnership and networking, advocacy, and using research and official reports to develop strategies.

The Scottish Information Literacy Project (SILP) started in October 2004 as an innovative national pilot, aimed towards developing an IL framework with secondary and tertiary partners to link to secondary and tertiary education, which, at the end of the project, could be rolled out to other participants. The aim was to produce secondary school leavers with a skill set, which further and higher education could recognize and develop or which could be applied directly to the world of work. Cross-sectoral partnership working was essential to the project's success, and partners were recruited from relevant library sector contacts, and working relationships were established, with a range of organizations involved in lifelong learning and learning and teaching.

Information literacy: recognition/contextualization

The term 'information literacy' was coined in 1974 by Zurkowski (Crawford, 2011, 257). The term is still used by the LIS profession, and, in 2004, the Chartered Institute of Library and Information Professionals (CILIP) decided that there was a 'need to define the term in a way that [wa]s understandable by all information-using communities in the UK' (CILIP, 2004a), stating that in 'an era of lifelong learning, this effectively means that information literacy has relevance for all ages from primary school to senior citizens' (CILIP, 2004a).

The CILIP (2004b) definition is: 'knowing when and why you need information, where to find it, and how to evaluate, use and communicate it in an ethical manner'. This definition implies several skills (or competencies) that are required, in order to be information literate, which are an understanding of:

- a need for information
- the available resources
- how to find information
- the need to evaluate results
- how to work with, or exploit, results
- ethics and the responsibility of use
- how to communicate or share your findings
- how to manage your findings

The term or, more importantly, the skills and competencies it represents also have gathering international interest. Shigeru Aoyagi, the Chief of the Division of Basic Education at the United Nations Educational, Scientific and Cultural Organization (UNESCO), stated that:

> For all societies, Information Literacy is becoming an increasingly important component of not only literacy policies and strategies, but also of global policies to promote human development.   (UNESCO, 2003)

Despite this international declaration, which also states that IL is a basic right and key to social, cultural and economic development of nations, communities, institutions and individuals (UNESCO, 2003), it is not generally recognized as a term outside the library and information profession.

There are numerous models, frameworks and standards: the Information Literacy website (2010) outlines the different information literacy definitions, models and frameworks, including the 2005 Alexandria High-Level Colloquium, which supports political lobbying and urges 'governments and intergovernmental organizations to pursue policies and programmes to promote information literacy and lifelong learning' (Garner, 2006, 4). The SILP project used the CILIP definition (CILIP, 2004a) of IL skills and competencies, supported by IL examples that related to the individuals' environment. This helps them to contextualize the skills and competencies, as IL means different things to different people and can change, depending on their education and experience and the information environment/ landscape that they find themselves in.

Collaborative partnership and networking is crucial

You can achieve so much more working collaboratively. A network of contacts can often help individuals to gain access to people within organizations who are otherwise difficult to identify or to reach. Partners can also help identify issues and provide a body of evidence. They can circulate news about forthcoming events, publications and policy issues. Based on the experience of the SILP team, the key points for developing collaborative partnerships are to:

- identify organizations and individuals to work with
- identify and work with project partners who are active, strong advocates and believe in your vision
- use personal and professional contacts, network, talk to people at every opportunity
- work cross-sectorally and not just with librarians
- develop a community of practice
- have meetings and involve people in dialogue and discussion.

Advocacy strategies

Influencing policy, whether at local or national level, is not an easy undertaking. Yet, the seemingly impossible can be achieved, with conviction and belief in yourself and what you propose. This belief and confidence is referred to as self-efficacy by Bandura:

> Perceived self-efficacy is concerned with people's beliefs in their ability to influence events that affect their lives. This core belief is the foundation of human motivation, performance accomplishments, and emotional well being.
>
> Unless people believe they can produce desired effects by their actions, they have little incentive to undertake activities or to persevere in the face of difficulties. Whatever other factors may serve as guides and motivators, they are rooted in the core belief that one can make a difference by one's actions.
>
> (Bandura, 2010, 1534)

Perseverance and determination are needed to help drive change. You also need an advocacy strategy, and decisions need to be made concerning who to talk to and who are the key decision makers. It is good practice to review the approaches that have worked for other people and to look at IL advocacy toolkits for guidance and ideas. One example is *Information Literacy Toolkit: securing change through advocacy tools*, produced by the Chartered Institute of Library and Information Professionals Scotland. This toolkit was developed as the task group felt that to 'help drive change' forward, more guidance was required to support librarians, when making the business case for information literacy. Help may be needed in securing political leverage and resources, in order to develop and implement information literacy programmes. Support may be particularly welcome in institutions where embedding a skills programme, involving librarian input into existing activities led or owned by other educationalists, has not been encountered before (Milne, 2007).

The SILP advocacy strategy includes identifying key figures within governmental and non-governmental organizations, advocating the importance of IL and developing strategies and advocacy from existing policies, using research and exemplars of good practice as evidence. We evaluated our actions and took opportunities to communicate and share experiences with others. In order to do this, we needed to network, with a keen eye for creating and using every opportunity that headed our way. It was important to communicate outside our profession in language and terms that could be understand by our intended audience (Andretta, 2009; Bruce, Edwards and Lupton, 2006).

SILP advocacy work at government level – using the Scottish Parliament petition system

The Scottish Executive (which is now known as the Scottish Government) is responsible for most of the issues relating to the day-to-day concerns of the people of Scotland, including education. Staffed by civil servants, it is a separate body from the Scottish Parliament, which houses Scottish Members of Parliament and their staff. The Scottish Parliament has devolved powers within the UK. These cover matters such as education, health and justice, rural affairs and transport.

Tentative contacts with the Scottish Executive Education Department and education bodies indicated there was little awareness about what IL actually is. Most believed either that the issue was being dealt with elsewhere or did not understand what it meant or what could be done. It also became clear that the education bodies were acting on priorities that were emerging from the Scottish Government, which failed to recognize the importance of IL and so had not identified it in the school curriculum. From a practitioner's viewpoint, this was particularly significant, in considering the role of the school librarian. If progress was to be made, it would be necessary to influence Scottish government's policy-making.

The SILP team decided to use the Scottish Parliament's petition system in order to address this issue strategically, rather than approaching individual agencies in a piecemeal fashion. A petition is a formal request to a higher authority, for example, parliament or another authority, signed by one or a number of citizens. Provided it is on an issue that the Scottish Parliament has powers to deal with, any citizen is able to raise an e-petition and have concerns addressed through the formal processes of parliament. The e-petition enables citizens to engage with government and with their elected representatives, through using technology that is specially designed for the purpose (Macintosh, Malina and Whyte, 2008).The petition by the SLIP team called on the Scottish Parliament to urge the Scottish Executive to ensure that the national school curriculum recognizes the importance of IL as a key lifelong learning skill. The supporting evidence included an IL definition, a national declaration on the importance of IL, the collated assumptions made about IL and research findings of pupils' and students' IL skills (or lack of them). It was successful in attracting 710 signatures (about twice the average figure), including some leading figures in the worldwide IL movement. Owing to the high number of signatures, an opportunity was granted for a deputation to present the petition in person, make a short presentation and answer questions from members of the Petitions Committee. After listening to the evidence, the Petitions Committee decided to seek comments and 'agreed to write to the Scottish Executive, Learning and Teaching Scotland, the Scottish Qualifications Authority, Her Majesty's Inspectorate of Education, EIS and Universities Scotland' (Scottish Parliament, 2005). The organizations included a range of educational non-governmental organizations (NGOs), trade unions in the teaching profession and the overarching university body (Universities Scotland). Responses to the consultation were also received from the public sector trade union (Unison) representing school librarians, School Library Association in Scotland (SLA Scotland) and the body for further education/colleges. Most responses were favourable, including those from Her Majesty's Inspectorate of Education (HMIe), Learning and Teaching Scotland, Universities Scotland, SLA Scotland and Unison School Librarians. The process enabled comments to be made on the responses, and several sympathetic bodies also submitted further evidence, including the US National Forum on IL. This international perspective was particularly welcome. Based on the evidence collected, the Committee closed the petition. One Petition Committee member (a Member of the Scottish Parliament) stated:

All the responses seem to support the petitioner. The responses from the Scottish Executive, Her Majesty's Inspectorate of Education, the Educational Institute of Scotland and the Scottish Qualifications Authority in particular clearly support 'A Curriculum for Excellence' as the way forward. The petitioner has therefore been pushing at an open door and no further action on the petition is needed.

(Scottish Parliament, 2006)

The favourable responses were extremely valuable for advocacy work, and the mention of the curriculum as 'the way forward' supported our ongoing advocacy work with the Curriculum for Excellence (CfE). An initial meeting with the CfE team had highlighted a number of issues. There was a need to link IL to the cohesion and progression of an age three to 18 curriculum (which was the direction that the CfE was taking). Clarification was required, in order to clear up the confusion between study skills, library skills, information skills, information-handling skills and IL. Those interested in IL needed to contribute to the curriculum review, raise the profile of IL and lobby for its inclusion in the curriculum.

The discussion in this section of the chapter has highlighted the need to be aware of how policies are made and how practitioners can seek to influence them, by using the systems in place, by providing evidence supported by research findings and by advocating for what you believe in.

Exploit the evidence base – using research and official reports

Advocacy work requires evidence to support it. This could include using your own research and research findings from recognized experts. Official reports are also very useful, as they can be used to support your research or to provide an opportunity to engage or influence policy.

Research was carried out by the SILP, with secondary and tertiary partners, as to what IL skills, if any, students brought to university (Irving and Crawford, 2006). This identified that information literacy skills were generally taught in schools in the first and second year (from the ages of 12 to 13), but were not subsequently reinforced within the curriculum. This resulted in fragmented levels of knowledge and usage for students' remaining years at school. The research at hand found that students arriving at university generally have either poor or very limited information literacy skills. The level of skills varied, depending on the student, the course, the school they came from and their home life. Unfortunately, because of the fragmented approach to IL learning and teaching within universities and the issue of whether a particular discipline recognizes their desirability, these skills are enhanced for some students, but many leave university with the same information literacy skills as when they arrived (Irving and Crawford, 2006).

The SILP findings supported an interim report by Her Majesty's Inspectors of Education (HMIe, 2005, 16), *The Integration of Information and Communication Technology in Scottish Schools*. The report stated: 'Few schools have systematic approaches to developing information literacy to ensure that all pupils acquired this set of skills [information literacy] progressively as part of their passport of core and life skills.' A systematic approach is difficult, if IL is not included in the curriculum, and Williams and Wavell (2006) found that, for many teachers, information literacy was considered as cross-curriculum skills' building and, thus, separate from their subject, rather than as a way of learning and teaching. These findings reinforced our belief that teaching information literacy skills should be part of the curriculum and begin at school (Irving and Crawford, 2006), as it is too late to wait until university to pick up this skillset. This view of the need for information literacy training at a young age was later supported by a report by the Center for Integrated Business Education and Research (CIBER), which stated: 'At the lower end of the information skills spectrum, the research finds that intervention at university age is too late: these students have already developed an ingrained coping behaviour: they have learned to "get by" with Google' (CIBER, 2008, 23). The interim report *Digital Britain* (BERR and DCMS, 2009) also supported early years training in digital and media literacy. Both of these literacies include IL.

The research findings not only supported the development of the National Information Literacy Framework Scotland, but provided evidence for engagement with the Scottish Government and Scottish Parliament, as outlined above, and the CfE teams.

SILP advocacy work with the curriculum

Having the knowledge and understanding of the emerging curriculum, the language and the key messages within the official communications (which included documents, briefings, websites and newsletters) all meant being able to communicate, in terms that the CfE teams (comprising seconded teachers) understood and were committed to. It also helped with demonstrating how IL was a key element of the vision and substance of the emerging curriculum.

Ongoing engagement with the curriculum review included attending Scotland's Learning and Teaching Festival, making contacts and seeking out key decision-makers. The draft National Information Literacy Framework Scotland (Irving and Crawford, 2008) was used to demonstrate how IL was relevant to learning, and teaching and lifelong learning in particular. As a result, the CfE team leader subsequently contacted me in excitement about the field of IL and the fact that we were using similar language to the CfE team in their draft of *Curriculum for*

Excellence. This was followed by a face-to-face meeting and, although the term 'information literacy' was not explicitly used within the CfE draft (nor is it still within the implemented CfE), the CfE literacy team recognized it as a key component; and IL skills and competencies can be found in their Literacy across Learning framework and Experiences and Outcomes documents (CfE, 2009c), most notably within the:

- listening and talking section: finding and using information, understanding, analysing and evaluating
- reading sections: finding and using information, understanding, analysing and evaluating, in order 'to encourage progression in understanding of texts, developing not only literal understanding but also the higher order skills'
- writing section: organizing and using information.

For the SILP, its partners and IL advocates, this recognition of the skills (although not the term IL itself) was an important achievement, achieved through advocacy work. Recognition has also been given to critical literacy:

> In particular, the experiences and outcomes address the important skills of critical literacy. Children and young people not only need to be able to read for information: they also need to be able to work out what trust they should place on the information and to identify when and how people are aiming to persuade or influence them.
> (CfE, 2009b, 20)

For practitioners, it is important to recognize critical literacy within the curriculum and its link to information literacy.

The SILP project's advocacy strategy also identified teachers' continuing professional development (CPD) as an area that should be targeted; however, it had proved difficult to reach. An opportunity presented itself, through research by the University of Glasgow (2008), on the draft of the CfE experiences and outcomes document, which highlighted the concerns of teachers' information and critical literacy abilities, plus their need for CPD activities in connection with the CfE. This information was subsequently used in discussions with the CfE literacy team, resulting in a research and development project, which tackled this issue as linked to another key project aim – namely, to begin IL at a young age. The resulting project, *Real and Relevant – information and critical literacy skills for the 21st century learner (early and first level)* (SILP, 2009a), aimed to create a quality CPD information literacy resource pack (SILP, 2010), containing background information about information literacy, learning and teaching approaches and supporting resources:

The project identified exemplars of practice which demonstrated the early seeds of creating information literate children who were:

- listening and looking at information in verbal and pictorial format and being asked and answering critical questions demonstrating their knowledge and understanding of what they are hearing
- working as pairs or as small groups to select information for a research activity
- evaluating selected information and evaluating a finished piece of work.

These exemplars reinforced the belief that information literacy should begin at a young age and begin at the beginning.   (Irving, 2010)

The role of the school librarian, school library and library services: engagement, opportunities and issues

LIS professionals are engaged in supporting learning in their roles as school librarians, learning resource co-ordinators, school library services, public library services and children library services, yet their role is often not explicitly recognized. However, advocacy can change this, as demonstrated by the change from no mention in the early drafts of CfE documents (University of Glasgow, 2008), to the contribution of the school library noted within the final documents, specifically the CfE principle and practice paper:

> It is expected that the literacy experiences and outcomes and this accompanying paper [principles and practice] will be read by a range of practitioners, including those who work in school library resource centres, who make an enormous contribution to the literacy skills of children and young people.
>
> (CfE, 2009b, 3)

This was an important achievement for school librarians and information literacy, as a field. However, school librarians need to continue to demonstrate their knowledge, engagement with and contribution to the curriculum. To ascertain whether this was happening, in 2009, the SILP carried out a survey of school librarians and school library services and found that respondents did have knowledge and understanding of the CfE and had identified ways in which IL could be used to achieve or assist achievement of the necessary experiences and outcomes. They had been involved in piloting activities, creating new activities or updating existing activities, based upon the appropriate experiences and outcomes. They were either working on their own, with particular subject teachers, school-wide or with other school librarians. More importantly, they suggested ways in which efforts could be optimized, so as to support IL and the CfE experiences and outcomes guidelines, both locally and nationally. These included:

- advocacy
- becoming involved in school activities through school committees, such as literacy teams
- getting the support of the head teacher
- demonstrating an understanding of the aims of CfE
- supporting cross-curricular activities
- developing links with primary schools
- being involved in all discussions, training and in-service opportunities
- liaising closely with subject departments
- working with other school library colleagues
- working with teachers to standardize terminology
- promoting a whole-school approach (in other words, a school-wide initiative, rather than one that was library or subject centric)
- involving educational NGOs. (SILP, 2009b)

The CfE purports to be a curriculum not just for teachers, but for all those engaged in supporting learning, thus placing a responsibility on all practitioners. It is, therefore, an excellent opportunity and advocacy tool, which must be understood and used by all LIS professionals engaged in learning and teaching. However, engagement and implementation raises several important issues, including that fact that too many intra-school links are informal, and direct curriculum involvement is varied and frequently unstructured. Two factors are crucial: the support of the head teacher and school management team (SMT) and the direct involvement in curriculum planning.

In addition to the support of the head teacher and SMT lies the wider question of the role and status of the school librarian (Irving, 2010, 143), reported elsewhere, most notably, by Ritchie (2008, 2009a, 2009b). It is important that the head teacher recognizes the school librarians' valuable contributions and emphasizes this to the rest of the school. The following comments are from school librarians who took part in the SILP (2009b) survey:

We need to be taken seriously by the School Management Team . . .
  I've found the Literacy Experience and Outcomes paper most useful because so much of it fits with library and information skills. I am line managed by the Head who has agreed to make me a key member of the Literacy Strategy Working

Group and will support efforts to take library skills to even hard to reach departments.

Becoming involved in school activities through school committees has been the best way for me to optimize my efforts in information literacy and ACFE. In particular, involvement in cross-curricular projects raises the librarian's profile, often freeing the librarian's role from the restrictions normally in place when working as a support to straightforward departmental teaching.

We need to be seen as the key person who has a perspective of school wide coverage of topics and try to maximize our role as facilitators within the school. The Learning Resource Centre should be seen as the central information bank for research and helping promote generic research skills to be used across the curriculum.

As regards direct involvement in curriculum planning, school librarians must be members of literacy planning groups, or CfE groups, in order to ensure that IL is built into curriculum planning. As one SILP survey respondent stated, school librarians should always be involved in in-service training days, so as to 'learn' and to 'raise awareness of the role they can play in curriculum development' (Irving, 2010, 144). Other issues identified by the SILP survey included the advantages of working with other school librarians and primary schools in order to raise the transitional agenda.

Another issue which surfaced from the SILP survey, and which seems to be common to all aspects of information literacy promotion, is the question of the lack of a common vocabulary. Teachers and librarians use different terms for the same thing, and for collaboration to work effectively the LIS profession needs to have a knowledge and understanding of educational and pedagogic terminology (Irving, 2010).

Conclusion

Whilst there are issues, there are also opportunities for the LIS profession to be recognized within education and learning and teaching multi-professional teams. However, we need to believe in ourselves and the work that we do. We need to use advocacy, work in collaborative partnerships and networks and use evidence from research and official reports to help develop strategies. It is important to reflect on the positive steer provided by Bandura (2010, 1534): 'Whatever other factors may serve as guides and motivators, they are rooted in the core belief that one can make a difference by one's actions.' I hope this case study discussion about the positive outcomes of the SILP has given you the inspiration and the tools to engage and influence policy at whatever level.

References

Andretta, S. (2009) The Multifaceted Nature of Information Literacy: solving the Rubik cube puzzle, *Journal of Information Literacy*, **3** (2), 1-5.

Bandura, A. (2010) Self-Efficacy: abstract. In Weiner, I. B. and Craighead, W. E. (eds), *Corsini Encyclopedia of Psychology*, 4th edn, John Wiley, http://onlinelibrary.wiley.com/doi/10.1002/9780470479216.corpsy0836/abstract.

BERR and DCMS (2009) *Digital Britain: the interim report*, Department of Business, Enterprise and Regulatory Reform and Department for Culture, Media and Sport, http://webarchive.nationalarchives.gov.uk/+/http://www.culture.gov.uk/images/publications/digital_britain_interimreportjan09.pdf.

Bruce, C., Edwards, S. and Lupton, M. (2006) Six Frames for Information Literacy Education: a conceptual framework for interpreting the relationships between theory and practice, *ITALICS*, **5** (1), www.ics.heacademy.ac.uk/italics/vol5-1/pdf/sixframes_final%20_1_.pdf.

CfE (2009a) *Curriculum for Excellence: literacy across learning*, Education Scotland, www.educationscotland.gov.uk/learningteachingandassessment/learningacrossthecurriculum/responsibilityofall/literacy/.

CfE (2009b) *Literacy across Learning: principles and practice*, Curriculum for Excellence, www.educationscotland.gov.uk/learningteachingandassessment/learningacrossthecurriculum/responsibilityofall/literacy/principlesandpractice/index.asp.

CfE (2009c) *Literacy across Learning: Experience and Outcomes*, Curriculum for Excellence www.educationscotland.gov.uk/learningteachingandassessment/learningacrossthecurriculum/responsibilityofall/literacy/experience and outcomes/.

CIBER (2008) *Information Behaviour of the Researcher of the Future: a CIBER briefing paper*, UCL, Center for Information Behaviour and the Evaluation of Research, www.jisc.ac.uk/media/documents/programmes/reppres/gg_final_keynote_11012008.pdf.

CILIP (2004a) *Information Literacy: definition*, Chartered Institute for Library and Information Professionals, www.cilip.org.uk/get-involved/advocacy/information-literacy/pages/definition.aspx.

CILIP (2004b) *An Introduction to Information Literacy*, Chartered Institute for Library and Information Professionals, www.cilip.org.uk/get-involved/advocacy/information-literacy/pages/introduction.aspx.

Crawford, J. (2011) Introduction, Information Literacy Beyond the Academy, Part I: Towards Formulation, *Library Trends*, **60** (2), 257-61.

Garner, S. D. (2006) *High-level Colloquium on Information Literacy and Lifelong Learning*, http://archive.ifla.org/III/wsis/High-Level-Colloquium.pdf.

Her Majesty's Inspectors of Education (2005) *The Integration of Information and Communication Technology in Scottish Schools*, www.educationscotland.gov.uk/inspectionandreview/Images/ EvICTFinal18Oct_tcm4-712716.pdf.

Information Literacy Website (2010) *IL Definitions*, www.informationliteracy.org.uk/information-literacy-definitions/.

Irving, C. (2010) The Curriculum for Excellence: knowledge engagement and contribution by Scottish school librarians, *School Librarian*, **58** (3), 142-4.

Irving, C. and Crawford, J. (2006) Begin at School, *Library and Information Update*, **5** (1-2), 38-9.

Irving, C. and Crawford, J. (2008) *National Information Literacy Framework Scotland (working draft)*, www.therightinformation.org/storage/documents/ DRAFTINFORMATIONLITERACYFRAMEWORK1h.pdf.

Macintosh, A., Malina, A. and Whyte, A. (2008) Designing E-Democracy in Scotland, *Communications*, **27** (2), 261-78.

Milne, C. (2007) CILIPS Information Literacy Toolkit: securing change through advocacy tools, *Information Scotland*, **5** (3), www.slainte.org.uk/publications/serials/infoscot/vol5(3)/vol5(3)article2.htm.

Ritchie, C. S. (2008) *The Self-Perceived Status of School Librarians*, MSc thesis, Department of Computing and Information Science, University of Strathclyde.

Ritchie, C. S. (2009a) How Much is a School Librarian Worth?, *Library and Information Update*, May, 48-9.

Ritchie, C. S. (2009b) Filling a Gap: would evidence-based librarianship work in the UK?, *Library and Information Research*, **33** (104), 26-35.

SILP (2009a) *Real and Relevant – information and critical literacy skills for the 21st century learners (early and first level)*, Scottish Information Literacy Project, www.therightinformation.org/il21stcenturyskills/.

SILP (2009b) *Survey of Scottish School Librarians and their Knowledge and Use of Curriculum for Excellence*, Scottish Information Literacy Project, www.therightinformation.org/silp-blog/2009/12/10/survey-of-scottish-school- librarians-and-their-knowledge-and.html.

SILP (2010) *Early and First Level CfE Experiences and Outcomes Linked to Information Literacy*, Scottish Information Literacy Project, http://curriculumforexcellence.pbworks.com/w/page/24176354/Early-and-First- Level-CfE-Experiences-and-Outcomes-linked-to-information-literacy.

Scottish Parliament (2005) *Public Petitions Committee Minutes of Proceedings*, http://archive.scottish.parliament.uk/business/committees/petitions/mop-05/ pumop05-1221.htm.

Scottish Parliament (2006) *Public Petitions Committee Official Report*, Information Literacy (PE902),

http://archive.scottish.parliament.uk/business/committees/petitions/or-06/
pu06-1802.htm#Col2899.

UNESCO (2003) Prague Declaration: 'towards an information literate society',
UNESCO,
http://portal.unesco.org/ci/en/files/19636/11228863531PragueDeclaration.pdf/
PragueDeclaration.pdf.

University of Glasgow (2008) *Curriculum for Excellence: draft experiences and outcomes
final report*, Scottish Government,
www.educationscotland.gov.uk/publications/c/
publication_tcm4539668.asp?strReferringChannel=curriculumforexcellence.

Williams, D. A. and Wavell, C. (2006) *Teachers' Conceptions of Information Literacy in
Relation to their Classroom Practice*,
www4.rgu.ac.uk/abs/research/page.cfm?pge=13088.

PART 2

Connecting and engaging – reaching your audience and catching the latest wave

5 Libraries, literacy and popular culture – let's get reading!

Avril Brock and Carolynn Rankin

Introduction

This chapter will help to provide the evidence as to why libraries are successful at reaching and engaging their communities in reading activities. It presents underpinning theory and research about effective provision and draws on the rich practice occurring in both school and public libraries in the UK and internationally. Perspectives and commentary from library practitioners are included, as they are actively involved in planning and delivering services and resources. Viewpoints from children and young people are also included, as their needs and desires need to be recognized by adults. This provides authentic, rich evidence about the benefits of partnership.

The chapter will discuss popular culture and will examine issues surrounding age and gender, reflecting on the attitudes and specific needs of boys and girls, both at home and at school. The valuing of cultural and linguistic diversity will also permeate the discussions, as libraries need to provide a welcoming ethos and specifically target groups, in order to connect and engage different audiences. As a result of reading this chapter, the reader should be aware of the rights of children to have access to information and resources to support their personal interests, educational attainment and enhanced family lives.

Reading, learning and a life-long love of books

Competence in literacy is essential for a successful life in contemporary society, and it dramatically contributes to people's emotional well-being, mental health and economic success. This section demonstrates how a range of particular skills, a breadth of reading materials, a depth of understanding and positive attitudes are important for children and young people becoming capable competent and active readers. The responsibility involved in achieving this not only lies with the children and young people themselves, but also with parents, teachers, librarians and politicians. Books and other literacy materials, public libraries, schools and school libraries all have roles to play in the successful achievement of developing youngsters who will read for pleasure, for information and knowledge acquisition and for educational attainment. How they engage in the reading process, the materials they access and their developing attitudes to reading are all key elements in achieving competence in literacy.

Research with children has shown that reading for pleasure is positively linked with a number of literacy-related benefits – reading attainment and writing ability for reading that is done both in school and out of school, text comprehension, knowledge of grammar and breadth of vocabulary. Positive reading attitudes are closely linked to achievement in reading, greater self-confidence as a reader and pleasure reading in later life (Clark and Rumbold, 2006).

The importance of the public library service for children and young people

Forays into the dimensions of access, reading materials, genres, attitudes and comprehension all point to the importance of actively engaging children and young people in the reading process. It is important to continually develop and enhance their literacy and critical thinking skills, as well as their attitudes to reading. Encouraging young children and their families to access a library with all its resources can provide a great foundation for developing early literacy, communication and language skills. Public libraries offer a cradle-to-the-grave service, and a library card is one of the first pieces of identification that a child receives and is, thus, part of their individual citizenship in society. Public libraries, therefore, have a unique role to play in children and young people's lives, family relationships, community involvement, nationality and public life:

> Family engagement is well understood as a key element in supporting educational achievement, and it seems that the public library use, as well as being associated with similar positive child outcomes to school library use, has in addition a particularly specialised correlation with family support for reading.
>
> (Clark and Hawkins, 2010, 17)

Community libraries are no longer regarded as quiet places, and librarians are working hard to break down the stereotypes and barriers that are often associated with using such institutions. Librarians want children to have access to books, and they do not worry that some books might not be returned by children or that they may be damaged by younger siblings in the home environment:

> We don't want people not to borrow books because some might go missing.
> The library service factors this in.
>
> (Atif, Children's Librarian)

Librarians use the term 'reader development', which means active intervention, in order to:

- increase people's confidence and enjoyment of reading
- open up reading choices
- offer opportunities for people to share their reading experience
- raise the status of reading as a creative activity.

(Opening the Book, n.d.)

Reader development sells the reading experience and what it can do for the reader, helping them to develop the confidence to try something new, rather than promoting individual books or writers:

> The idea of expecting everyone to come to us has gone now. We very much
> take the service out there, and outreach does form quite a large part of my job.
> It is not split in this way, but the librarians do a lot of work in the library, and
> learning sessions for school classes that come in, and I tend to go out more to
> different groups to try and promote the library to places where they don't hear
> about it so much.
>
> (Katherine, community librarian)

Effective public libraries will endeavour to provide inclusive services and resources for all sections of the local community. There are particular challenges in catering for the wide range of interests of children, teenagers and young people. Having community partners expands the reach of the library to connect with new audiences, and partnerships create new and improved services (Feinberg et al., 2007). Partnership working brings benefits for both the individual practitioner and the organizations for which they work:

> The public library service works closely with the school library service. Most
> local authorities have a school library service, and this is an effective way for
> schools to access and borrow really good resources, including books, artefacts,
> DVD, resources boxes, etc. In Leeds, a large ethnically diverse city in the North
> of England, all the schools – infant, primary and secondary – are 'paid in' to the

city library service and have a basic entitlement to borrow books at a basic rate of one book per pupil for a year. This can enable a school to have 150 books in a small infant school to 1500 books in a large secondary school. Each class gets its own library ticket and can borrow two boxes per term, which can be ordered through the library service website. These 'Bookworm' boxes may focus on fiction; author boxes; themed fiction; fantasy fiction; audio group reading books. The library service has a huge range of fiction and includes picture books for all ages. There are resource packs for varied genres – ancient Greece; Horrid Henry; Gruffalo. There is a 'Family Matters' collection that can help schools when they need to explore sensitive themes, such as bereavement. If schools want to promote 'Family reader groups', both the public and school library service can help with resources.

(Kirsty, school library service librarian)

Leeds library services are obviously very committed to developing strong partnerships with families, children and young people, aiming to catch them young and then continuing to support their clientele's individual needs throughout life. Libraries are key partners alongside children's centres in encouraging family reading, and children's librarians provide many collaborative activities, such as storytelling events, toy libraries, family literacy activities, craft activities and puppet shows. Librarians who specialize in providing services to young children are often actively involved in taking their provisions and resources out to the local community and much of their time can be spent on outreach work and building partnerships.

Birmingham City Council's library services are promoting a breadth of initiatives to inspire children and young people to visit libraries, participate in activities and enjoy reading. Their Young Libraries website provides enticing information about past and future events. Highlights of 'Gigglefest' (2012) include two brilliant animation workshops, the wonderful Shoofly Theatre, a mysterious magician and favourite kids' comedians. The 'Great Kindle Relay Project' uses new technology to promote digital storytelling and e-book reading for children and young people. Birmingham's seventh Young Poet Laureate 14-year-old Damani is writing and performing poems throughout the year and at the 'Book Bash' at the Young Readers' Festival, and 75 free audiobooks for children and young people are available 24/7, using the new Netlibrary service.

CASE STUDY: 'Bringing the Books to Life': booktalking services offered by Library Services for Education, Leicestershire County Council

We are both librarians working for a traded schools library service – Library Services for Education (LSE) at Leicestershire County Council – which offers high quality resources and other services, for all schools across Leicestershire and its neighbouring authorities. One of these services is 'booktalking' – an effective means of promoting reading for pleasure. LSE initially offered this to a specific unnamed school in 1996, in order to help Year 10 students broaden their reading horizons and explore more literary books, but after a rapid growth of interest, the sessions were adapted for use with Years 4–13. Booktalking does not just benefit the students, but also gives staff an insight into the range and quality of current children's literature and, in some cases, inspires them to do some booktalking themselves. It can also serve as a marketing opportunity for LSE, making us visible to different staff in various schools and demonstrates one of the unique benefits of subscribing to our services.

An initial contact with the school sets the tone for the sessions, with the school providing a variety of information, including the reading ability of the students. Sessions are geared towards more or less able students on request, but typically include books of many genres, which appeal to a wide range of ability levels. An agreement is reached with each school, in order to ensure that the sessions meet their particular needs. An LSE librarian then visits the school and speaks to a group of students, promoting a selection of fiction books and reading out extracts, where appropriate. If there is time, the students are asked to recommend some books themselves. Booktalking does not usually directly support the curriculum, though following requests from history teachers, we have trialled a few sessions using books based around the Second World War, which have helped to introduce students to stories that will deepen their understanding of this period. Following the sessions, we ask school library staff to keep track of the popularity of the different books, following the session(s), and to feed that back to us.

Booktalking gives LSE librarians an opportunity to engage directly with the students and enables us to get some direct feedback about what they enjoy reading. We have been told by many schools that, after booktalking sessions, 'those who had never been to the library wanted to know how to get a library card', and 'the kids were definitely enthusiastic, and the next time we visited the library, they were asking for the featured books'. A 'buzz' about reading is often created through booktalking, amongst those who have attended. Many schools invite us back, year after year, for further sessions and some incorporate us into important initiatives, like library inductions and World Book Day. Booktalking can, thus, often become an important part of a wider campaign to increase reading for pleasure in schools.

Alex Kingsbury and Nicole Jordan

The Reading Agency produced the following statements, following commissioned research (2004) into the question 'what should young people expect library services to offer?'

Empowerment by:

- participation in shaping the future design and delivery of library services
- volunteering opportunities with younger or older library users
- a place to develop citizenship skills and community engagement, through volunteering and sharing ideas.

Access to:

- free, safe and welcoming spaces in the local community, where they can have their personal space, to meet together and widen their horizons and have free access to the digital world
- formal and informal learning support for educational attainment, delivered by experienced staff, in partnership with school library services, teachers and schools.

Quality through:

- relevant and inspiring collections of books, magazines and other materials, supported by positive and creative activities
- reliable, up-to-date information on education, training and careers opportunities, as well as high quality information and services.

These statements express what young people themselves have said that they value, need and expect from their libraries and has been created to show the relevance of libraries' work to national policies, including Youth Matters and Every Child Matters, and to local authority priorities and targets, such as Public Service Agreements (PSA) and Local Area Agreements. Local authorities need to ensure that library services integrate youth provision.

Social capital, social mobility, social policy and the link to literacy

As discussed in Chapter 1, public libraries were originally established to produce social change, and the evidence shows that many library services and outreach work have a real and valuable role to play in community development (Matarasso, 1998). Public libraries are complex institutions that offer a place where people and families can become part of the community and connect effectively with local services. Obviously, successful partnerships are key, as working with different professionals, across the variety services for children and young people, is necessary, in order for provision, and the dissemination of provision, to be effective in reaching the targeted groups (Brock and Rankin, 2011). Researchers and policy-makers have documented the complex and powerful influences that home and community have on young children's educational and social achievement. There is, therefore, an increasing expectation that library professionals will work in partnership with parents. Parents, after all, are in the best possible position to introduce their children to the world of words, through regular reading together, sharing and talking about books. We know that fluent readers are more likely to do well in school, and reading and literacy skills will stand them in good stead for life in the 21st century. The benefits of sharing books last longer than a lifetime, since children who are brought up to value reading are far more likely to pass their love of reading (and their good literacy skills) on to the next generation (Rankin, 2011, 185).

The National Literacy Trust (NLT) - a UK-based charity - believes a strong library service is essential for building a reading culture and a literate nation. The OECD Programme for International Student Assessment (PISA) was set up to measure how effectively young people near the end of compulsory schooling are prepared to meet the challenges of today's knowledge societies, and whether they are able to reflect on and apply their knowledge and skills to meet the challenges of adult life. PISA is conducted once every three years, and is organized around three domains: mathematical literacy, reading literacy and scientific literacy. In 2000, when the first PISA data collection occurred, reading literacy was the major domain focus and was seen as a necessary foundation for young people's performance in other education subjects and as a prerequisite for successful adulthood, through being able to handle the variety of printed and written information that they will encounter throughout their lives. In the OECD (2002) thematic report, *Reading for Change: performance and engagement across countries*, reading engagement refers specifically to children and young people's motivation and interest in reading. The report examines the time that they spend in reading for pleasure and in reading diverse materials and found that these aspects are closely associated with performance in reading literacy. The PISA results suggest that changing and improving children and young people's reading proficiency could have a strong impact on their opportunities in later life.

The NLT has initiated a number of research projects, in order to gain a full picture of literacy in the UK. The NLT advocacy resource *Literacy Changes Lives* (Dugdale and Clark, 2008, 4) places literacy firmly at the heart of social policy: 'The National Literacy Trust passionately believes that low literacy levels are a barrier to social justice. They produce social, economic and cultural exclusion that scars communities and undermines social cohesion.' Literacy is strongly connected with a person's happiness, well-being and success, and it has a key role to play in improving lives and future economic success, creating safer and stronger communities and national workforce. *Literacy Changes Lives* indicates the complexity behind the reasons why people, from all ages, struggle with their literacy, in ways that range from severe educational needs to disaffection from learning and low aspirations. The NLT provides an interesting profile of a literate family, a literate community and a literate nation:

Profile of a literate family:
- A literate family is less likely to experience divorce, as divorce rates among those with high literacy are low, and significantly lower than those with poor literacy.
- Families with high literacy levels are far more likely to live in working households, with only 2% of families with good literacy living in workless households.
- Families with high literacy are more likely to own their own houses and not live in overcrowded conditions.

Profile of a literate community:
- Individuals with good literacy are far more likely to be involved in the community. Among those with Entry Level 2 literacy 21% of men and 29% of women actively participate in community activities.
- Scottish data show that individuals with good literacy are significantly more likely to trust people in their community, with only 2% of men and 1% of women saying they did not trust people at all.
- Literate residents also consider their communities to be much safer compared with those with low literacy. Only 1% of men and women with high literacy levels reported never leaving their houses.

Profile of a literate nation:
- Highly literate individuals are more likely to vote and have an interest politics, therefore participating in the democratic process and holding an interest in the governance of the nation.
- High literacy levels are associated with lower drinking and smoking, as well as higher levels of mental health. This takes pressure off the health service and public funds, and contributes to a healthier nation.
- A literate workforce is advantageous to both employees and employers. Good literacy skills provide an opportunity for flexibility in the workforce across all sectors, as data collected by the CBI show.

(Dugdale and Clark, 2008, 50)

According to Jama and Dugdale's (2010, 2) research on attitudes towards reading and writing:

- 22.2% of young people aged eight to sixteen say they enjoy reading very much and 28.4% say they enjoy it quite a lot. 39.2% say they like it a bit and 10.2% say they do not enjoy reading at all.
- 66% of adults believe that the ability to read, write and communicate is a fundamental right in modern society.
- 92% of the British public say literacy is vital to the economy, and essential for getting a good job.
- A quarter of children and young people do not recognise a link between reading and success.
- Children and young people who engage in technology based texts, such as blogs, enjoy writing more and have more positive attitudes towards writing - 57% express a general enjoyment of writing vs 40% who don't have a blog.
- There is a consistent gender difference in attitudes towards writing. Boys do not enjoy writing as much as girls (38% vs 52%), either for family/friends or for schoolwork, and are more likely to rate themselves as 'not very good writers' (48% vs 42%).

Technology-based materials are the most frequently read, with nearly two-thirds of children and young people reading websites every week, and half of children and young people reading e-mails, blogs or networking websites (such as Bebo, MySpace) every week. (Jama and Dugdale, 2010, 10). If a child, young person or adult has poor literacy skills, then they are more likely to be in a non-working household. Literacy is seen as a social justice priority, and social mobility and reading go hand in hand. The NLT Reading Connects (Clark, Torsi and Strong, 2006) research, with 1600 Key Stage 2, 3 and 4 pupils, found that 29% of these said 'I am not a reader', and some really negative responses were recorded. The non-readers did actually read; it was their perceptions about reading and what constitutes reading that led to the negativity. They believed that reading was about books of fiction, factual information and poetry, and that school is the sole provider of reading, and they did not believe their own choices of reading materials were relevant. Interestingly, they did not consider that reading e-mails, magazines, websites and blogs were reading. However, the research showed that they were reading a range of texts and that these were valid reading materials, which are part of a natural diet for successful readers. The Rowntree Research (Raffo et al., 2007) on socioeconomic status, social mobility and achievement demonstrates how enjoying reading is related to self-identity and that attitudes to reading are based on issues of gender, socio-economic status and appropriate role models.

The challenge, therefore, is to redefine reading, for those audiences who do not respond to the cultural voices that they see in reading (Cremin et al., 2008). A research project by the United Kingdom Literacy Association (UKLA) has provided insight into the children's fiction that is currently used by primary school teachers and how they choose and find out about trends in children's literature. The research raises issues of relevance to librarians working in education and children's services, which deserve serious consideration. Cremin et al. (2008) discovered that boys did access a range of reading materials, that they liked to read about heroes and challenges, yet they personally did not want to stand out from their peers and that friendship and belonging through peer approval was of paramount importance to them. It is really important to get librarians to understand this key message about provision, and, consequently, they need to provide accessible and enticing reading materials and boy-friendly access. There are definitely creative challenges ahead for the modern professional librarian.

The following interview with two boys of primary school age demonstrates how librarians should listen to the voices of children and take on board their perspectives in order to provide boy-friendly environments and reading materials. Joe (ten) and Tom (eight) live in a small town, with a central library that is ten minutes' walk away. They are avid readers, reading every day, and they ask for books, both fiction and non-fiction, for presents. Here are their opinions on the quality of public and school libraries:

Joe	I haven't been to the school library this year; my teacher doesn't even know there is a library at the school.
Tom	I go every week and get a book to read. There's not lots of choice. There are Dr Who books, but they aren't very interesting.
Joe	We don't go to the public library very often; it's a bit boring. They should make the children's section bigger – the adults' section is humungous. There's not enough for us kids. They need to think about kids more than adults for once! They need age sections on the book shelves, with different types of books. For the 9–11 year olds, they need more science, history, adventure and decent poetry books. They need to buy some decent books – more choice, more popular readers. I'd make it different, with a place for older children to sit, away from the younger children and their toys. It's very annoying; you can't read in there. Yet, in the adult section, you're always told shush and, yet, downstairs, it's manic. There's no place to read and think.

These two brothers are quite critical and feel confident to voice their opinions about libraries, library services and books – about what they like and what they feel is lacking and could be improved. How can librarians ensure that their libraries are not only child friendly, but inspiring, challenging, purposeful and exciting? They need to become not only places to access books, but also places to go with, and to meet, friends. Later in this chapter, peer group influence will be discussed, in relation to its significance in influencing how children and young people read, access books and enter libraries. Listening to the voices of children and young people is, therefore, important, and their needs and opinions should be incorporated into design, resources and activities. As stated earlier in this chapter, children's right to literacy is key to educational attainment, social and financial achievement and emotional well-being.

Children's right to information

Library practitioners are at the forefront of promoting children's rights, and they play a key role in disseminating information about the importance of early literacy to parents, children's advocates and political decision-makers. Koren (2011, 154) reminds us that the United Nations Convention on the Rights of the Child (CRC) offers support to library policy and practice, related to children and young people. She believes that children should be able to rely on libraries for their rights to information and education. Children have a basic need to find out, and the information that they gain is essential for individual development. They can use the information they obtain to change their circumstances, function better in society and be informed individuals, who can contribute to social change. This is further discussed in Chapter 15 of this volume. Article 17 of the Convention on the Rights of the Child relates to the important function of mass media - children require access to information and material from a diverse range of national and international sources, especially those aimed at the promotion of social, spiritual and moral well-being. Article 17 also encourages the production and dissemination of children's books. In order to gain access to literacy, information and an enjoyment of reading, children and young people require competency in the skills of reading through comprehension and inference, an understanding of semiotics and knowledge of how books work and how to retrieve and understand information. The next section explores these skills and explains why it is important for librarians to have an understanding of what is involved in the reading process.

What are the skills involved in the reading process?

We have only to observe a committed young reader - on the floor, in a chair, up a tree - to know that here is a child who is gone from us for a while, but will return revitalised.

(Butler, 1992, 33)

Competence in literacy is essential for life in contemporary society, and it dramatically contributes to people's emotional well-being, mental health and economic success. This section demonstrates how a range of particular skills, a breadth of reading materials, a depth of knowledge and understanding, and positive attitudes are important for children and young people if they are to become capable, competent and active readers. The achievement of these skills lies not only with the children and young people, themselves, but also with parents, teachers, librarians and politicians. Books and other literacy materials, public libraries, schools and school libraries all have roles to play in the successful development of youngsters who will read for pleasure, information, knowledge acquisition and educational attainment. How they engage in the reading process, the materials they access and their developing attitudes to reading are all key elements in achieving competence in literacy. There is much more to reading than just decoding symbols and stringing words together to make sense. Children and young people need to become critical readers and thinkers, and both schools and public librarians can play key roles in ensuring that they do so. It is, therefore, important for librarians to gain an understanding of the reading process and what are the skills of reading in the 21st century.

The reading process

Children try to make sense of their world and the learning process by using all strategies available to them, and this is the same for reading, as for everything else they learn. Children need to be interested and motivated, and they learn to achieve through building on early successes. Competence in literacy results from success in speaking, listening, reading and writing. Adults – parents, teachers and librarians – should encourage children's reading through a range of experiences – listening to stories, singing songs, creating rhymes, relating anecdotes and playing word games. Children and young people need to access a range of literary/literacy materials – fiction and non-fiction books, computer programmes, internet communications, notices, comics and magazines, to name a few. In this way, children's reading repertoires are developed and can be broadened, by enabling them to relate these varied activities to their previous and diverse experiences. Therefore, adults have important roles in supporting and scaffolding children's reading, through introducing a range of reading activities and facilitating their selection, using a wide range of reading materials, giving children time to think, look and choose for themselves and encouraging them to use a variety of clues in the reading process.

Brock and Rankin (2008) demonstrate how reading with children is a shared process, and adults should read with, and talk to, developing readers about stories, books and reading, as well as ensuring that they value the knowledge and the culture that children bring to the process. Modelling the reading of books can apprenticeship children into reading and so guide them to understanding and success. Adults can encourage children to:

- make sense of the whole text
- make connections to familiar experiences
- talk about and understand what they are reading
- ask questions about the reading process
- see patterns in words and letters
- gain visual images of words
- use illustrations to help meaning.

A holistic view of the range of skills that are required for successful reading processes includes the development and promotion of the following ten key dimensions of knowledge and experience:

1 Previous experience - personal knowledge, cultural experiences and early language development, through opportunities for speaking, listening, story, rhyme and singing experiences.
2 Practice - repetition and practice of words, phrases and structures, throughout the reading experience.
3 Knowledge of how language works - all that children have intuitively acquired, through hearing and using language.
4 Grapho-phonemic cues - letter/sound correspondence, through sounding out words or parts of words using phonics.
5 Semantics - gaining the meanings of words from the context and revising guesses, as more of the meaning is revealed, as a text develops.
6 Syntax and grammatical knowledge - using knowledge of word order in sentences, in order to determine the grammatical function of words.
7 Social learning - seeking confirmation from others and discussing what the text means.
8 Comprehension and inference - making sense of a text, understanding obvious and hidden meanings, creating opinions and drawing conclusions.
9 Positive attitudes - gender, ethnicity, a family's socio-economic status and role models all influence reading success.
10 Reading materials - a diversity of genres in texts and a range of reading materials, including books, computers and magazines.

The next sections in this chapter pursue key aspects of some of these ten dimensions that are particularly relevant for developing readers in primary and secondary schools who have acquired basic and burgeoning early reading skills and are now moving towards competence.

What is reading comprehension?

It may be obvious to state that understanding or comprehension is key to children becoming fluent readers. They need to make sense of a text, through developing a literal interpretation and then moving on to explore complex meanings that are embedded in texts, through using the processes of inference and deduction. They can begin to learn these strategies from the earliest stages of learning to read. Research on reading comprehension used to be based on the identification of the sub skill of comprehension, which were taught to children in a progressive, hierarchical order (DfES, 2005). The Primary National Strategy (DfES, 2005, 3) indicated how more recent research promotes:

- active engagement with the text to create meaning
- the acquisition of strategies gained through authentic reading, rather than as a separate set of skills
- the application of cognitive, interpretive and problem-solving strategies
- the recognition of children's individual needs, interests and personal experiences, gained through their personal, individual socio-cultural context.

Children need to engage purposefully with texts in order to gain understanding and effective comprehension of their meaning. This is best acquired when combined with direct instruction or guidance from a teacher, librarian, or other adult. Good reading needs to be modelled for children to achieve independence and autonomy. Comprehension is an active process, which involves all of these strategies and behaviours:

- understanding the text
- engaging with the text
- critically evaluating the text
- monitoring own understanding
- reflecting upon responses
- making connections with existing knowledge
- making decisions about which strategies will help.

(DfES, 2005, 2)

The most effective way to develop comprehension and improve reading is, therefore, through encouraging extensive reading. Reading varied books and literacy texts should not only promote an increased acquisition and understanding of new vocabulary, but should also develop knowledge and generate questions. Most readers construct mental images during reading and, as they are able to understand and reflect on these, this enables them to develop their metacognitive awareness. Metacognition has an important role in the reading process – an ability to reflect on one's understanding and learning will produce a 'self-awareness' of being an active reader.

What is inference and deduction?

A key finding of Kispal's (2008) NFER review, which was contracted by the Department for Children, Schools and Families, was that the ability to draw inferences predetermines reading skills and that poor inference skills causes poor comprehension. This study synthesises varied research findings conducted on the act of inferencing in the UK and the USA over the last 20 years. Skills of inference are needed, not just to be able to read between the lines, but also to detect the hidden meanings that enrich overall understandings of a text or in order to draw one's own personal conclusions about a text. The ability to make inferences and deductions involves using two or more pieces of information from a text, in order to arrive at a third piece of information that is implicit. Inference can be both simple and complex – conveyed through the choice of particular vocabulary by the writer and/or through drawing on the reader's own background knowledge. Inferencing skills are extremely important for reading comprehension and are required for coherence, making connections in a text to gain an understanding of the main point or theme of a text and developing mental representations to fully understand and enrich the meaning of the text at hand. Kispal's review of the research evidence found that, in order to be good at inferencing, children need to be active readers who want to make sense of the text, and that having a wide background knowledge and shared cultural background, assumed by the text, also facilitates inference.

Erin, a school librarian, gave much thought to promoting pupils' access to texts that would develop their skills and interests and challenge their reading and thinking:

A lot of school libraries separate the junior and senior fiction, but I didn't do that, as this could limit children's choices, so we compromised, by tagging and colour coding the books– the children have different interests and understanding and knowledge levels – one 13 year old can be very different from another.

(Erin, school librarian)

It can be easily established, here, how this school librarian has reflected on her library's provision, developed her knowledge base of pupils' skills and the development of their reading abilities and choice in materials, and factored this into her acquisition of texts and her development around pupil access of resources.

Environments for reading – promotion and partnerships

We know that certain factors promote a love of reading; these include freedom to choose reading materials, a print-rich environment, access to a variety of texts, time for reading in school, encouragement for readers, and quiet, comfortable places to read (Clark and Rumbold, 2006). Reading as an activity can take place anywhere, as long at the child or young person has access to the written word, and this can be via either books or digital media. Baumann and Duffy (1997) highlighted the following five factors that help children become readers:

1   A print-rich environment, where they are read to and given opportunities to read, where they see their caregivers read, where they have opportunities to engage in pretend play, where they are encouraged to interact with environmental print and visit the public library.
2   A language-rich environment, where they are encouraged to have discussions with their caregivers.
3   A knowledge-rich environment, where they learn about the world, through such media as television and computers, and where they interact with the outside world, by taking trips and talking with people about topics of interest to them.
4   A nurturing environment, where they interact with a variety of people, who believe that one purpose of literacy is to entertain.
5   A home environment, where they make connections with their schools.

The early interactions that occur between children and their parents and carers are crucially important for young children's personal, social, cultural, emotional and linguistic development. McKechnie (2006, 75) notes that the feature of the enabling adult turns up time and time again in studies of early reading acquisition. In discussing the work of those who bring children and books together, Butler reminds us that 'we cannot produce child readers without adults' (1992, 8).

For more than a century, researchers, teachers and librarians have been interested in what children choose to read. Despite studying children's reading interests and preferences, using methods such as surveys and interviews, there still is no definitive understanding of what children prefer to read and when these preferences develop (Clark and Rumbold, 2006). However, what studies do show is that children and young people read a diverse range of materials. For example, the Reading Connects survey (Clark and Foster, 2005) showed that when pupils were asked what types of materials they were reading outside the classroom, magazines, websites, text messages, jokes and books/magazines about TV programmes emerged as the most popular reading choices. Over half of the pupils also said they read e-mails, fiction and comics, while newspapers were also popular choices. Generally speaking, however, these materials are not traditionally regarded by schools as acceptable reading matter.

Reading in the school library

> Every Wednesday we go to the library in the morning – just our class. We have to scan our own books in and out. Our library is very big – there are a lot of books to choose from. Mrs O'Malley has people read, while we get our books. We have half an hour in the library. When we get our library books, we are not allowed to have them for more than two weeks or they will be overdue. My favourite book is probably Harry Potter.
>
> (Melissa, aged 8)

Lockwood's (2008) research into reading for enjoyment in primary schools showed that schools in which staff had managed to overcome the negative perception of the school or classroom library had used a variety of imaginative ideas to encourage use of the library. Clark's (2010) research examined young people's reading habits and attitudes to their school library and explored whether they used them. This report has shown that most young people use the school library. They use it because it gives them easy access to books, because it is a friendly space and because they believe that the school library and, by default, reading will help them do better at school. The research also shows a link between school library use and increased reading enjoyment, higher self-assessments of reading ability, as well as more positive attitudes towards reading. The research suggests that school libraries have a vital role to play in the reading patterns of those pupils who have higher literacy levels. The findings include the following key information:

1   There was a very strong relationship between reading attainment and school library use, with young people who read below the expected level for their age being almost twice as likely to say that they are not a school library user.
2   Girls use the school library more than boys.
3   School library use declines rapidly with age, with more primary pupils

saying that they use the school library than their older counterparts in secondary schools.

4 Young people from Asian backgrounds use the school library more than young people from white, mixed or black backgrounds.

5 Socio-economic background, as assessed by free school meal uptake, was not an important correlate of school library use in this study, indicating that school libraries are not disproportionately attracting pupils from more affluent backgrounds.

6 Most of the 28% of young people who do not use the school library avoid it because it does not have books that interest them, because their friends do not go and because they do not think it will make them do better at school.

7 Of those who do not have a school library (3.2%), over half said that they would use it if they had one. In particular, they would use one if it had books that interested them, if it had computers and if their friends went too.

The findings showed that school library usage differs, according to background demographics and reading attainment, and established how it relates to a wider enjoyment of reading, attitudes towards reading and reading frequency.

Reading in the public library

Public libraries, with their welcoming presence in communities, are well placed to help address the literacy challenge by designing family friendly spaces where the reading experience and book sharing is encouraged, and the personal touch that children's librarians bring to their communities sets the stage for lifelong reading (Higgins, 2007). When people talk about how public libraries have changed their lives, they always emphasize the importance of library staff, who are seen to be helpful, knowledgeable and trusted (CILIP, 2010). A visit to the library can be one of the 'learning destinations' for the Children's University, which is a national organization, offering children aged from seven to 14 an exciting and innovative programme of high quality learning opportunities, outside school hours, at weekends and in the holidays. The focus is on rewarding participation, raising aspirations and encouraging engagement with learning.

The library can also provide educational support, through the provision of homework clubs and one-to-one help. Careers advice and help with writing CVs is on offer for older teenagers in some locations. Teenagers are a particularly challenging group to engage, but there are examples of successful partnership approaches. The Book Pushers is a group of young reading advocates (aged 12 to 15) from Derbyshire, who talk about, and read extracts from, the books that they enjoy. As with any group, they enjoy a wide range of books and talk about them in different, but persuasive, ways. The concept is simple, as it was felt that the best way to promote books to teenagers was to get other teenagers to talk to them about books, in other words, using the effect of direct personal recommendation. The Book Pushers project has influenced peers, families, publishers, teachers, librarians and the Book Pushers themselves. Librarians have created Book Pushers' displays in libraries, in order to promote teenage books, and they have used comments from the Book Pushers to help with stock selection (East Midlands Public Library Authorities, 2004).

Another national project that is showing positive outcomes is HeadSpace. This is run by The Reading Agency, working with 20 community libraries. It meets the urgent need for free, local, safe spaces, where young people can take part in positive activities, and it gives a clear message that young people are welcomed in libraries, and their participation is valued. HeadSpace aims to develop active partnerships between young people, libraries and the youth sector (The Reading Agency, n.d.)

Reading campaigns

Children's librarians have a solid knowledge of their client groups, based on local demographics, and the evidence shows they are also effective at engaging hard-to-reach groups, successfully building partnerships based on reading and family learning. The Family Reading Campaign (www.familyreading.org.uk) is a partnership campaign, which is working to ensure that the importance of encouraging reading in the home is integrated into the planning and activity of all the key organizations that are concerned with education, health, libraries and parenting.

The National Reading Campaign (2010) runs two school-based initiatives that encourage young people to take up reading – Reading Connects and Reading Champions. The Reading Connects initiative promotes the building of a school community that reads for pleasure across the whole school, both in primary and secondary schools. They advise that schools undertake an audit, so as to help work out achievable action points to assist in the development of a school culture. It provides booklets and a website for information, resources and funding advice, as well as case studies on engaging families in the literacy life of a school, transforming a classroom into a library, reading buddy schemes and ways of boosting school library use. Two very successful readers and library users are Alex (ten) and Jack (eight), whose conversation we followed earlier in the chapter. In the following interview, they have all their Reading Challenge resources laid out in front of them, and they are showing them off:

Alex: We enjoy the library. There's a computer, so if you don't have one, you can go use the library one. There are maths games, and you can go onto the internet – it's very helpful, and the staff are very friendly. We've done the Reading Challenge twice before. They give you this chart thing – that's very cool – and you have to read two books, and you get a prize, like a bookmark or stamp. Over to you, Jack . . .

Jack: When you join Space Hop, you get two cards. You scan your card, go home and read six books, then you get an achievement, wrist band, spinning yoyos, certificates for school. I've got two certificates. This last one was Dragon's Quest, and I got a gold medal. I've got a book bag, and I put this medal onto it – it's really glittery and shiny. You've got to fill in all the stickers, and, when you're doing it, you get space hops and colouring books. It's really good. Over to Alex . . .

Alex: As Jack says, we all get stickers – everyone who goes to the library and completes a Space Hop. Jacks got his medal here – I don't know where mine is. Reading Challenge is probably every year, isn't it? Chris Ryan, Jack Higgins, Charles Higgins – books like that are also my favourites. Jack Higgins is my favourite book. I read it all the way through. It's about secret agents and saving the president from a nuclear bomb. Over to you, Jack . . .

Jack: This is a book about how to make stuff. I like this one for Halloween – ghosts, bats, slush drink, sweet, lemonade with lime, chocolate mousse. I like cooking books, really. You can do baking for Christmas with chocolate and mix these ingredients, using icing sugar for snow. You can make vegetable paste into a mould. Over to Alex . . .

Alex: I got the recipe for the dessert I made tonight from a magazine. I've also made this – it's a semifreddo. I used blueberry sauce. I bake lots of things. We read every day. I go on the computer every day too.

The Reading Champions programme encourages schools to develop and celebrate a male reading culture, by using the motivational power of reading role models, who model reading and reward boys for their enthusiasm for reading, rather than for their ability. There is a framework of increasingly proactive ideas that boys work through, so as to become bronze, silver or gold champions in reading.

In the USA, summer reading programmes first emerged as public library services for children during the latter part of the 19th century; now they act to bring children from different parts of the community together (Fiore, 2005). The national Summer Reading Challenge in the UK, co-ordinated by The Reading Agency, is run in 97% of UK public libraries and focuses on reading for pleasure. It is organized locally by public library services, working closely with schools and other partners in the area. Children aged four to 11 are invited to read six books over the course of the summer holiday. They join at their local library, and there are stickers and rewards to collect along the way, with an added certificate if they read the designated six books.

Conclusion

Research and policy have documented the complex and powerful influences that both home and community have on young children's educational and social achievements. Libraries need to provide a welcoming ethos and specifically selected reading resources, in order to help connect and engage different audiences. Children and young people have a right to information and resources to support their personal interests, education attainment and enhanced family life. In contemporary society we are faced with increasing opportunities to embrace enabling technology, requiring ever more effective and flexible reading skills. The fundamental skills of wide, effective reading and early literacy acquisition will remain paramount (Elkin, 2011). However the key factor in all this is the consumer – the child is at the heart of the reading process, and, whilst adults know how important reading is, it requires children themselves to be willing participants, not only in acquiring the skills, but also in developing positive attitudes, interests and desires to engage in reading, from the wealth of materials on offer.

References

Baumann, J. F. and Duffy, A. M. (1997) *Engaged Reading for Learning and Pleasure: a report from the National Reading Research Centre*, University of Georgia, http://eric.ed.gov/PDFS/ED413579.pdf.

Brock, A. and Rankin, C. (2008) *Communication, Language and Literacy from Birth to Five*, Sage Publications.

Brock, A. and Rankin, C. (eds) (2011) *Professionalism in the Interdisciplinary Early Years Team: supporting young children and their families*, Continuum Publishing.

Butler, D. (1992) *Telling Tales: the 1992 Margaret Mahy Award lecture*, New Zealand Children's Book Foundation, www.storylines.org.nz/site/storylines/files/downloads/Awards/Storylines_Dorothy_Butler_lecture_Telling_Tales.pdf.

CILIP (2010) *Libraries and Librarians: making a unique contribution to our society,*

Chartered Institute of Library and Information Professionals, www.cilip.org.uk/get-involved/uniquecontribution/Documents/ Libraries%20and%20librarians%20making%20a%20unique%20contribution %20to%20society%20Jan%202011.pdf.

Clark, C. (2010) *Linking School Libraries and Literacy: young people's reading habits and attitudes to their school library, and an exploration of the relationship between school library use and school attainment,* National Literacy Trust.

Clark, C. and Foster, A. (2005) *Children's and Young People's Reading Habits and Preferences: the who, what, why, where and when,* National Literacy Trust.

Clark, C. and Hawkins, L. (2010) *Young People's Reading: the importance of the home environment and family support,* National Literacy Trust.

Clark, C. and Rumbold, K. (2006) *Reading for Pleasure – a research overview,* National Literacy Trust.

Clark, C., Torsi, S. and Strong, J. (2006) *Young People and Reading,* National Literacy Trust.

Cremin, T., Bearne, E., Goodwin, P. and Mottram, M. (2008) Primary Teachers as Readers, *English in Education,* **42** (1), 1–16.

Dugdale, G. and Clark C. (2008) *Literacy Changes Lives: an advocacy resource,* National Literacy Trust.

East Midlands Public Library Authorities (2004) *Case Studies in Good Practice, the Book Pushers Project in Derbyshire: East Midland Public Library Authorities working together to support books and reading.*

Elkin, J. (2011) The User of Tomorrow: young people and the future of library provision. In Baker, D. and Evans, W. (eds), *Libraries and Society: role, responsibility and future in an age of change,* Chandos.

Feinberg, S., Deerr, K., Jordan, B., Byrne, M. and Kropp, L. (2007) *The Family-Centered Library Handbook,* Neal-Schumann Publishers.

Fiore, C. D. (2005) *Fiore's Summer Library Reading Program Handbook,* Neal-Schuman Publishers Inc.

Higgins, S. (2007) *Youth Services and Public Libraries,* Chandos Publishing.

Jama, D. and Dugdale, G. (2010) *Literacy: state of the nation – a picture of literacy in the UK today,* National Literacy Trust.

Kispal, A. (2008) *Effective Teaching of Inference Skills for Reading Literature Review,* Research Report DCSF-RR031, National Foundation for Educational Research.

Koren, M. (2011) School Libraries and Human Rights. In Marquardt, L. and Oberg, D. (eds), *Global Perspectives on School Libraries Projects and Practices,* De Gruyter Saur.

Lockwood, M. (2008) *Promoting Reading for Pleasure in the Primary School,* Sage Publications.

Matarasso, F. (1998) *Learning Development: valuing the social impact of public libraries,* British Library Research and Innovation Report, The British Library Board.

McKechnie, L. (2006) Becoming a Reader: childhood years. In Ross, C. S., McKechnie, L. and Rothbauer, P. M. (eds), *Reading Matters: what the research reveals about reading, libraries and community*, Libraries Unlimited.

National Reading Campaign (2010) *Reading Connects*, National Literacy Trust, www.literacytrust.org.uk/resources/practical_resources_info/728_national_ reading_campaign_1999-2009.

OECD (2002) *Reading for Change: performance and engagement across countries*, Organisation for Economic Co-operation and Development.

Opening the Book (n.d.) *Definition of Reader Development*, www.openingthebook.com/about/reader-centred-approach/definition/default.aspx.

Raffo, C., Dyson, A., Gunter, H., Hall, D., Jones, L. and Kalambouka, A. (2007) *Education and Poverty: a critical review of theory, policy and practice*, Joseph Rowntree Foundation.

Rankin, C. (2011) The Librarian – a key partner in promoting early language and literacy. In Brock, A. and Rankin, C. (eds), *Professionalism in the Interdisciplinary Early Years Team: supporting young children and their families*, Continuum Publishing.

The Reading Agency (n.d.) *HeadSpace*, http://readingagency.org.uk/young/headspace/.

The Reading Agency (2004) *What do Young People Want From Libraries? A review of the existing evidence base*, www.readingagency.org.uk/young/EvidenceFromYoungPeople.pdf.

Websites

Children's University, www.childrensuniversity.co.uk/.
Family Reading Campaign, www.familyreading.org.uk.

6 Libraries, literacy and popular culture – what's cool to read?

Avril Brock and Alix Coughlin

Introduction

In this chapter we explore how children can be encouraged to develop a varied diet of reading, through reference to strategies, research findings and the perspectives of children, themselves, on what they think is cool to read. The first half of the chapter looks at the value of diverse texts and discusses what benefits emerge from reading a range of genres. The second half of the chapter looks closely at strategies and factors that influence a child's reading choices.

Why is a range of genres important?

Reading a variety of categories, compositions or styles of writing, in different kinds of literary texts, is important for readers to gain a balanced diet of reading materials. The child's introduction to a range of genres is important, in order to help develop knowledge and wider life experiences through fiction and non-fiction texts, as well as building upon personal, individual interests and experiences. A snapshot of the range of genres available involve stories, books and information texts that include adventure and mystery, science fact and science fiction, historical fact and fiction, contemporary crime fiction, dilemma stories, romance and gothic tales, plays and dialogues, poetry and rhyme, myths, legends, fairy tales, fables and traditional tales, and the media, news and popular culture. Teachers and librarians should provide children with reading experiences by encouraging them to access as many of the genres listed above as possible. For example, if children read and explore traditional tales it encourages them to think about dealing with the big issues in life, such as: Who are we? Where do we come from? How do we deal with life's troubles and difficulties? How should we behave? What is the truth? What is our place in the big picture of things? Cultural beliefs, values or messages can be underlying themes of a traditional tale. Young readers can explore life themes and inner conflicts through literature and, in this way, critical thinking, philosophical discussion and moral decision-making can be developed.

Favourite books, classic tales and historical experiencing

Literature is a powerful medium for communicating ideas, transmitting emotions and finding out about other people's culture, language, religion and life experiences. Meek's (2001) work explores these issues, in her classic text *Children's Literature and National Identity*. Folk legends and historical narratives may vary as they get passed down from generation to generation, and through the storytelling social groups delineate their cultural mores, ideologies and ambitions. Good quality TV adaptations of classic tales have helped to keep many of these stories alive for children. As Meek (2001) observes, the growth of children's publishing, the quality of production, the quality of traditional and contemporary authors writing stories for children, the advances in printing and technology and the growth of paperback publishing have all played important parts in children gaining access to a huge variety of genres. Libraries have also played an important role, through the free distribution of texts, making them readily available to children.

The child alone – a constant theme in children's literature

Children's literature and the genres within it were first established, in publishing, in the 17th and 18th centuries (Grenby, 2008). Grenby identifies seven broad genres: fables, poetry, moral and instructive tales, the school story, the family story, fantasy and the adventure story. Within these genres, there are overarching, similar themes and re-occurring ideas, such as good versus evil, love, sacrifice, death, friendship, humour, spirituality and the search for meaning. The theme of the child alone is a common thread across most of these genres and can be found in many examples of children's literature. From Mary Lennox in *The Secret Garden*, through to Peter Pan and the Lost Boys, Barney in *Stig of the Dump*, Anne Shirley, Sara Crewe, Carrie, Alice, Max, Bernard, Matilda, the *Railway Children*, Sophie in *The BFG*, to Harry Potter, Lyra and Alex Rider – the characters that last and still have something to say are all children who have no parents or lack a sufficient parental figure. So what is the draw of the child alone?

> She had no mother or father which was actually quite nice, because it meant that no one could tell her that she had to go to bed just when she was having most fun. And no one could make her take cod liver oil when she would rather eat sweets.
>
> (Lindgren, 1945, 7)

To be accepted as a Puffin book, stories had to have the attributes of 'integrity, quality of writing and an ability to communicate with the young' stated Kaye Webb, Puffin editor between 1961 and 1979 (Grove, 2010, 147). In 2010, on the 70th birthday of Puffin books, an online vote was conducted, in order to choose the 'Puffin of Puffins' from a selection of seven classics – one from each decade of the company. This title was won by Eoin Colfer's *Artemis Fowl* – a story of a child genius and a criminal mastermind, who fights the supernatural forces in the world and holds a fairy to ransom. He is an only child, with, apparently, no parents to speak of; he orders around the only adult in his life and initiates adventures entirely on his own. Of the seven books in the Puffin list, three are focused on a child who is alone in the world and does not rely on a parent or parental figure to guide their actions. The action is seen from the child's point of view, and the child thus remains child-like in their wishes, but is almost adult-like in their independence of thought and decision-making.

More than most types of books, children's books are seen as good for a purpose, rather than just good for their own sake (Hunt, 2005). The representation of families in fiction can represent the social and cultural influences of the society in which they were written and, in some cases, how the stories are used to promote the ideas of a particular time in history, but they can also be used to challenge values (Tucker and Gamble, 2001). The paradox of the genre is that it 'includes more accounts of family disordering than family coherence' (Grenby, 2008, 118). It is interesting to trace the changing nature of the concept of the child and its place in the family, through the tradition of the family as portrayed in literature.

One of the most popular authors of all time, Roald Dahl, wrote of children who were alone, 'isolated kids – loners who don't feel quite right in the world' (Walliams, 2010, 3). James, in *James and the Giant Peach*, is an orphan, yet survived abusive relatives and a transatlantic trip; Sophie, in *The BFG*, is found in a children's home, but was strong enough to help save other children and speak to the Queen. In *The Witches*, Luke's parents are killed, and he is turned into a mouse by the witches. Sendak said of his writing that he only ever asks one question: 'How do children survive?' (Appleyard, 2009, 13). But all these children detailed above, and many more throughout the long history of children's literature, do survive and show a remarkable resilience that enables them to thrive, despite the loss, trauma and challenges that are regularly thrown at them. Benard (1990) states that resilient children demonstrate some, or all, of the following: social competence, problem-solving skills, autonomy and a sense of purpose and future. These are all characteristics that could be attributed to these characters mentioned above. They use their social skills to acquire friends and companions who help them; they see a way through the challenges that they face; they have autonomy, because the decisions that they make are their own and, thus, their strong sense of purpose could be seen to be their survival. Kraemer (1999) discusses the concept of resilience through power and how children are still relatively powerless in their lives). He asks how children are able to develop the necessary levels of resilience if they are not free to venture outside and explore the local environment by themselves for fear of traffic, bullying or strangers. Is this the pull of the literary depiction of childhood – the recognition that these characters are free from the adults who smother them and, thus, stop their adventures from happening? Do readers enact their own wish to have autonomy and power through these characters, who are alone?

Many writers have commented on the power of the story in explaining the world to children and, similarly, in explaining the world of children, thus enabling them to reflect on life's problems. We receive an 'explanation of life from stories', and although we may revel in the images and events that they describe, we do not necessarily reflect on the messages that they present (Stibbs, 1991). As Meek, Warlow and Barton (1977) observe, stories are important for children, as they offer a template of their past culture and enable children to make their own story. Lessons can be learned through stories about encounters or people who children will never meet, enabling them to ask: 'What would I do, if I found myself in that situation?' (Meek, 1988, 29). Anne Fine observes that the novel is 'the very best instrument we have for ethical enquiry' (quoted in Anderson and Styles, 2000, 96). Similarly, Lurie argues that the best way of finding out what is going on in the world of children is to read children's books (Lurie, 1990) and, as Gaiman (in Bilson, 2010) observes, fiction can teach kids how to survive in the world.

Diversity and intercultural and international themes

It is also important that children can get access to a range of books, which enable them to explore a diversity of cultures and languages. The first multicultural guide to children's books was in 1985, and it has continued to be published, revised and updated over the last two decades (Elkin and Triggs, 1985). One of the most helpful guides is *A Multicultural Guide to Children's Books 0–12*, edited by Rosemary Stones, which provides a critical evaluation of books, materials and dual-language texts (Stones, 1994). In recent years, there have been moves to encourage ethnic minority writers living in Britain, as was also the central purpose of the 2006 conference, Diverse Matters: Changing Cultural Perspectives in Children's Publishing. France Lincoln Publishers has long included stories about children from widely different backgrounds and experiences in their publishing list (Mallett, 2009). The Frances Lincoln Diverse Voices Children's Book Award in 2009 was awarded to Cristy Burne, for her new book *Takeshita Demons* - a fast-paced adventure story concerning a Japanese schoolgirl who confronts the demons from her grandmother's tales. Kate Edwards, Chief Executive of Seven Stories - the centre for children's books in Newcastle - stated: 'The overwhelming response and the diversity of storytelling have shown there's a very real place for this award in the world of children's books. We believe the publication of Takeshita Demons will help to improve the range and richness of stories available for children to read' (Scholastic Education, 2009).

Children should be able to have a diet of books that will feed them stories and factual information about immigration, asylum seekers, Gypsies, Romanies and Travellers, different cultures and ethnicities, and contemporary issues, both in the UK and worldwide, in order to develop a burgeoning understanding of global perspectives on life and life experiences. Cotton (2000) demonstrates how literature in translation can enrich our lives, by providing sensitive glimpses into the lives and actions of young people located in other parts of the world. Translated books become windows, by allowing readers to gain insights into the reality of their own lives, through the actions of characters from other cultures, who are like themselves in many ways. Cotton argues that one of the reasons why publishers are so reluctant to include books in translation on their lists is because of the complex nature of translation and the difficulties in finding qualified people. Cotton's (2000) book, titled *Picture Books Sans Frontiéres*, is a European picture book collection, intended to widen children's horizons by bringing together picture books from all of the European member states. It describes each of the books selected, discussing the signs and messages contained in the illustrations and the text, and it details how the books can help children recognize the similarities in children's experiences throughout Europe. The 19 books in the collection have a common universal theme of friendship, which enables children to engage with the books and empathize with the various characters - witches, animals and people of all ages. The books have the potential for children to become more discerning Europeans, as well as to learn about textuality in the representation of pictures, maps, graphics and photos (Cotton, 2000). The Institut èuropeen pour le développement des potentialités de tous les enfants (IEDPE) - a collaborative network of teachers, researchers, scholars, writers, publishers and translators - focuses on the importance of national identity, through its forum discussions. Participants explore how the books that children read contribute to their growing knowledge of who they are, in terms of social sameness and difference.

Literature is a valuable way to introduce and celebrate diversity and difference to children. Children and young people may benefit from a blend of fiction and non-fiction books, which helps them deal with key life experiences, such as bereavement, parental imprisonment, physical health, obesity and family conflict, to name a few. The librarian has a key role in establishing collections for children and young people, through critically evaluating appropriate texts, which can help the readers understand these issues. Frank Roger's US website (http://frankrogers. home.mindspring.com/general.html) has a large listing of books for children, teenagers and young people, all of which deal, in some fashion, with important issues such as feminism, adoption, disability and sexuality. Johnson (2010, 225) observes how many authors are able to integrate these sorts of issues, in a way that both enhances the story and benefits the reader: 'As young readers learn about the issues and struggles faced by children with mental and physical disabilities, they will begin to sympathize with others who are different from their peers'.

Inspiring children and young people to read rich and varied texts

Chambers (1991) argues that a community of readers enables a common exploration and shared understanding of texts, and Barrs and Cork (2001) observe that reading aloud enables communication of the full range of a story's force and meaning. How often do librarians hold story sessions to read to primary-age children? And, likewise, do teachers still make enough time for reading aloud to children in primary school, as part of their busy timetables? Collins (2005) explores the place of the class novel within the current primary school curriculum and the importance of reading aloud to older primary-age children. Her research with primary postgraduate student teachers investigates the students' and children's experiences. She inspired students to read aloud to their classes of children, so as to bring the texts alive, making reading and listening a shared, enjoyable experience for all involved, and this encouragement consequently elicited some incredible comments from children: 'You're just a cliff-hanger woman' and 'She's sort of dragging me into the story!' As Michael Morpurgo stated in a recent radio interview, 'We simply have to have time to simply let children listen to stories.'

One of the most effective ways of introducing children to a range of genres is through inviting authors into schools, so that they can read aloud and share their particular style of writing with the young audience:

We do transition sessions from primary to secondary school. The children's author Joe Crai, came to talk to the children in the junior school. He writes Jimmy Coates books about a boy designed to be a weapon, who was fighting against his programming. Joe Craig was quite young and also does song writing – both the boys and girls liked him.

(Erin, School Librarian)

Peter Murray, the author, came to our school to visit us. He writes scary books for children, and he had a poster with scary books on. We watched a video of one of his stories – it was really amazing. It took a whole morning to listen to Peter Murray. We were at the front, because we were the youngest, and we got more view. We were the first to get his books. I got *10 O'clock Caller* and *Mokee Joe*. All his books are meant to be scary. *10 O'clock Caller* is quite scary, but I like it.

(Melissa, aged 8)

There are many websites that enable libraries and schools to locate and contact suitable authors to visit and talk to both primary and secondary age ranges, for example, Contact an Author (www.contactanauthor.co.uk/).

World Book Day is the biggest worldwide celebration of authors, illustrators, books and reading, marked in over 100 countries all over the world. The idea for the Day came from Catalonia, where roses and books are traditionally given as presents on 23 April. The United Nations Educational, Scientific and Cultural Organisation (UNESCO) developed this festival into World Book Day, and it is held on the first Thursday in March. A large number of events and activities are organized across the country to celebrate World Book Day: 'The main aim of World Book Day in the UK and Ireland is to encourage children to explore the pleasures of books and reading by providing them with the opportunity to have a book of their own' (www.worldbookday.com). World Book Day resources can be downloaded free for use at home, in the library or classroom, from the official website. In the UK, every child in full-time education, up to the age of 18 years, can receive a £1 book token, which they can use to buy one of eight books by selected popular authors.

The National Literacy Trust (NLT) study of 20,950 children aged eight to 17, published on World Book Day 2012, showed that children and young people who read books, magazines and newspapers, as well as reading on PCs, gaming consoles, tablets and mobiles, are more likely to be reading at the expected level or above the expected level for their age, compared with children and young people who only read using technology (Clark, 2012). Librarians need to be very aware of genre, as well as what children enjoy, and so provide a breadth of genres and texts to enable children and young people not only to follow their own reading interests, but also to be successful in acquiring a breadth of literacy skills..

What factors influence children's reading?

A children's best book – what they cannot resist – is *Captain Underpants*. It's about Mr Krupp – who's like a head teacher – grumpy dude – he doesn't like any fun so when people click he turns into Captain Underpants and he fights all villains like the Turbo Toilet 2000. We like it cos it's really funny and it's a good read.

(Alex, aged ten)

Alex is an avid reader, who is very knowledgeable about books and can discuss his favourite books and stories with ease. He is a walking book reviewer and provides interesting résumés about his favourite story book, information book or computer programme of each month. His interests have developed through his home life, school and the local public library, but films, such as *War Horse*, and television programmes, such as *Just William*, also direct Alex towards reading the accompanying books. At the age of eight, Melissa is an avid watcher of the Harry Potter, Narnia and Roald Dahl DVDs. Familiarity with characters and stories seen on the screen can encourage children's reading preferences. Of course, significant adults in their lives influence children's choices, too – Melissa is keen to be an author when she grows up, having been influenced by her grandmother's authorship of educational textbooks, in which Melissa has featured, by going to book launches and by listening to visiting authors at school. An introduction to literature comes in varied forms and through a variety of people. As Opening the Book states on its website: 'The best book in the world is quite simply the one you like best and that is something you can discover for yourself, but we are here to help you find it!'

Joe (aged ten) and Tom (aged eight) are knowledgeable about their favourite books and their preferred authors:

Joe	There are some really cool books around.
Tom	Adventure books – an example is Jungle Books. I like Harry Potter, but the words are too big; I watch it on DVD.
Joe	He would like to read Harry Potter when you're older, wouldn't you, Tom? I like reading adventure books, like Narnia books. I also like Roald Dahl books – my favourite is *George's Marvellous Medicine*. It's got a weird old granny in it. I like weird grannies.
Tom	I liked *James' Giant Peach*, with all the insects and bugs in.
Joe	I do like history books – fact books – so I can remember all the facts, and I can tell everyone at school. We have a library at school. It's interesting, but the school are hoping to make the library more interesting and get more books to read. The Jack Stalwart books are about a boy who works for the World Environment Protection Agency, and he goes on different

	adventures. They're a set of books, so they're good for bedtime stories, as there's lots to read.
Tom	Harriet the Horrible is a girl who is horrible, and she's got some itching powder that she puts in this boy's PE shorts.
Joe	So they're like Horrid Henry books?
Tom	Sort of, but they're not that perfect.
Joe	Our teacher's reading a book about an Egyptian cat that comes alive – it's historical. She's great at reading a story – when she gets to an exciting part, she jumps off the chair.

These boys are critical and reflective; they are quite discerning and have strong opinions about what they consider to be 'cool' books and stories. Readers are stimulated to read through a range of activities - watching film adaptations, such as *War Horse* and *The Borrowers*; watching television programmes, such as *Horrible Histories* and *Silent Planet*; teachers serializing *The Weirdstone of Brisingamen* and *Call of the Wild*; grandparents buying book collections from popular authors, such as Jacqueline Wilson's Best Friends series, Anne Fine's novels and Michael Morpurgo's classics; forming a reading affiliation with personal heroes, such as Francesa Simon's Horrid Henry, Max Chase's Star Fighter and Anthony Horowitz's Alex Rider; and accessing a range of computer games and internet sites, such as Club Penguin.

Comics and magazines can really help with children who struggle with reading. There's a brilliant weekly magazine for Key Stage 2 children that I found for my daughter, who really got engaged in reading through comics. It's called *The Phoenix* and is really well written and interesting and has made a real difference in her interest in text, as she's a very visual learner. I've just found another one for my younger daughter, too, called *StoryBox*, which is aimed at children 3–6. Unfortunately, schools don't seem to value books other than reading schemes, so we keep it quiet that at home Charlie reads Tintin and Asterix! The library, though, has been brilliant and have always found extra Tintin books for her. We love the library.

(Syd, parent and lecturer)

The power of comics and magazines has been extensively explored and many research projects relating to this have been undertaken; the subject is further explored by Mel Gibson in Chapter 8.

Attitudes as readers are important

What parts do children's and young people's attitudes play in being a successful reader? Clark and Osbourne (2008) explored the connection between age and pupils' attitudes to reading – how do they see themselves as readers? And does this differ, according to age, in secondary or primary schools? They drew on a study by Scholastic, which demonstrated that while 30% of five to eight year olds were classified as high frequency readers (i.e., they read a book every day), only 17% read as frequently by the time that they were 15. Clark and Osbourne's (2008) findings showed that young people of all ages read some kind of material and text outside school, according to their individual interests. Secondary pupils were more likely to read materials that require technology, such as websites, e-mails and blogs/networking websites, whereas primary school pupils enjoyed reading print books and, generally, read more than secondary pupils. Clark and Osbourne (2008, 10) propose that the 'reader self-concept, and its associated views and attitudes, becomes cemented with age'. Here are the observations of Erin - a school librarian:

> It was unusual in the school, that the boys were reading better than the girls, which seems to go against research – the girls borrowed books, but the boys read them in the library and were more willing to talk about the books. It was more difficult to get the girls to read in the library. The girls would read series of books – such as Princess Diaries, Twilight series, vampire fiction – they were quite narrow in their focus. You could get the boys to read pretty much anything, and they read so much more than the girls. Even sometimes things that were more girly – one boy at GCSE level read girls' books, such as Twilight, as he believed this would help him to understand and to 'pull' girls. The boys were more reluctant to borrow things, but they would come in on a lunchtime and read a chapter at a time, getting quite cross if someone had borrowed their book. Boys liked fantasy and horror. They quite liked the Carnegie books, Frank Cotterill. Stories with animals in were popular with younger children. We'd tried to get the older children to read more complex books and make the transition into young adult books. I would select from suggestions by the School Library Association.
>
> (Erin, school librarian)

Clark and Akerman's (2008) survey, *Being a Reader: the relationship with gender*, correlates with existing evidence that girls are more likely to describe themselves as readers and are more likely to read outside school than boys and that this was true, even for the girls who do not call themselves readers. They argue that work needs to continue into targeting boys to support their enjoyment of reading and to engage them through interesting relevant materials. Clark and Akerman (2008) also argue for similar initiatives, in order to target the self-defined non-reading girl, who is likely to say that reading is boring and is for 'clever' people, who are also, apparently, boring! Their findings show that almost all young people are already reading some kinds of texts outside school, and their reading is influenced by age, gender, culture, ethnicity and personal attitude. Newspapers and comics/graphic novels seem to appeal particularly to boys; magazines, blogs/networking websites and e-mails appeal particularly to girls.

That children and young people who use the library are twice as likely to be above average readers was confirmed by research published by the NLT (2011). Clark and Hawkins' (2010) UK research, based on uncovering young people's use of their public libraries, through an online survey of 17,089 pupils, aged from eight to 16, from 112 schools, was conducted over November and December 2009. This study finds that nearly half of the eight to 16 year olds who were surveyed use their public library, and are more likely to read outside class on an every day basis; and that seven to 11 year olds are nearly three times more likely to use the library than 14 to 16 year olds. Over a third of the pupils who use the library stated that they believed it would help them to do better at school. The most common reasons that children cited for not going to the library were that their family or friends do not go. Jonathan Douglas, Director of the NLT, says: 'Our research shows just how important a role libraries play in supporting literacy. In the UK today one in six people struggles to read, write and communicate, which can affect their health, confidence and employability' (Clark, 2012).

Popular culture and childhood literacy

Popular cultural forms among a population continually undergo change and adaption and, thus, are influenced by time, age, economics, technological invention and e-learning innovation. They are also influenced according to the local, national and even global socio-cultural contexts in which people live. In fact, the ways in which children's global narratives are engendered are rarely acknowledged, and there needs to be an exploration of how popular culture, e-learning and digital literacy are accessed, acquired and adapted (Marsh, 2004). The government commissioned the Byron Review (2008) – an independent research report for the UK government on the effects of violent media on children. Professor Tanya Byron reviewed the needs and rights of children and young people, making recommendations to further support their digital safety. She believes an inherent part of their development involves them being able to play and take 'safe' risks through playing video games and surfing the net. The remit of the Byron Review was to examine children and young people's experiences across a range of technologies, acknowledging that technology provides a range of opportunities that was unheard of in previous generations – opportunities for learning, for play, for communication, for skill development, for creativity and for having fun:

> The internet is a massive resource of information, although it is notoriously unreliable. . . . It is a fantastic place to meet people and find support, friendship and happiness as well as a wealth of information as long as reliable sources are used. It is recently being used as a way to let people read rare books that they normally wouldn't find in the local library or bookshop. It's also a place to learn a massive amount about hobbies that you would normally have not much information about. . . . I play video games for the same reason I watch a film or TV, escapism, the chance to be immersed in an intriguing or exciting story.
>
> (Byron, 2008, 20)

The Byron Review addresses the increasingly accessibility of the internet at school, in public libraries or at home, for children and young people, and the ease, immediacy and speed of the access to online information. The UK Literacy Association (UKLA) responded to the Byron Review (2008), stating that its research evidence from a range of sources indicates children's and young people's increase in motivation and engagement with digital technology. Wolstencroft's (2007) research, with 240 children aged between five and 11, illustrated the cognitive and social benefits of video and online games. The young participants' enjoyment and interest in overcoming challenges and problems, in order to find creative solutions, were strong features in the interviews. The opportunity to interact with a wider online community was deemed valuable by a small number of the older children, and this promoted their self-esteem, through the shared understanding, and demonstrated their skills. The social advantages of video games played at home, included the collaborative play and the teamwork with family and friends, as well as the social advantage, in becoming part of an online community. Wolstencroft (2007) believes that the playing of video games can offer a strong, potential future advantage, in terms of life skills and flexible thinking, to society and the economy. UKLA (2008, 2) argues that children's knowledge of computer game structures of different kinds supports their understanding of text structures and can develop their ability to 'write the kinds of increasingly complex texts required by the 21st century economy'. Similarly, 'the experience of inference and deduction prompted and fostered by video gaming offers opportunities for the development of reading – both on-screen and off' (UKLA, 2008, 2).

Marsh (2011) proposes that virtual worlds have become increasingly popular with primary-aged children, and these include, to name a handful, 'Webkinz',

'Neopets', 'Club Penguin' and 'Barbie Girls'. The latter two worlds enable children to create and dress-up an avatar, decorate their avatar's home, buy and look after pets and play games, in order to earn money to purchase items for their avatar and avatar's home. Club Penguin has been developed through the use of Web 2.0 tools; it enables interactive playing of games and chat with others, in a virtual world that is aimed at children aged from approximately six to 14. The site is closely monitored, in order to allay parental concerns regarding internet safety. In 2009 (Marsh, 2009) there were approximately 22 million registered users (paid membership has more benefits), and, according to Marsh's (2011, 101) longitudinal research, members are drawn from a primarily white, working-class community. Marsh surveyed 175 children, in order to identify the nature and extent of their engagement and to examine their literacy and play practices in the various virtual worlds. She found that the benefits included fostering of multimodal skills, development of an understanding of the affordances of different modes, the ability to understand the salience of visual images and icons, the ability to manipulate images to achieve specific purposes, the ability to navigate within, and across, screens, and the use of gesture/sound appropriately, for both the specific purpose and audience.

The following interview with Jack (aged eight) and Alex (aged ten) demonstrates how they possess considerable 'insider knowledge', through being part of Club Penguin; they are very knowledgeable about the rules and mores. However, Alex has also worked out ways to get around the rules, in order to expedite the site for personal success, and he demonstrates the sophisticated way in which he has interpreted the situations, through playing the system. Jack evidences the advantageousness of the site, both for literacy development and for friendship.

Vignette – an interview with Jack and Alex (and their Mum) about Club Penguin

Jack and Alex – the avid readers of fiction and information texts and users of their local library are also avid members of Club Penguin.

Alex   Club Penguin is a fun multiplayer game – you can have people from all over the world. And you can personalize your penguin, by going to the gift shop and buying accessories – spacemen outfits, hats and puffle outfits. Puffles are pets on Club Penguin. You can get black, red, blue, red, yellow, green, purple puffles there. You can go to the Puffle shop – in real life – shops. You buy card codes that you enter to buy stuff. You can play games – Puffle round-up, Puffle Launch, Jet Pack Adventure, Cat Surfer.

Jack   You can go ice fishing. On Puffin Island, you can go to different

	places. If you waddle about and click on their smiley face and ask, 'would you like to add Wacker 22?', that's me. Ask Bobby12345 if he wants to be your buddy, and you click to accept. You can play games together. If you go into the coffee shop, you can go upstairs and click on the books and type – you can actually write or paint by letters.
Alex	There are celebrities on Club Penguin. Rock Hopper is coming tomorrow – he's a famous person, who brought Red Puffle to Penguin Island. If you are in the same room and meet him, you can get a new background. Antarctic brought Yellow Puffle – didn't he, Jack? Tomorrow is Earth Day party.
Jack	You can meet more friends. There are members and non-members; members can do more things than non-members.
Alex	My money-maker is kind of like a cheat. I downloaded it and can get up to 50,000 coins, by just clicking a button. I found it on YouTube as a Club Penguin money-maker. but it isn't actually Club Penguin. I can buy a new igloo and things for the home. You can get items for free at parties; there are boxes on the floor. It's good to meet people you don't know, make friends and socialize. It's good for learning how to use a keyboard.
Jack	I like everything about it. I've a friend from school, and we meet each other on Club Penguin, and we play games together. There's Ninjas and a Dojo called Karjitsou, and you can turn him into the three elements – fire, water and ice. You have different cards for different things. Dad pays £3.95 a month for me, and it's a really, really lot of money.
Alex	Dad thinks it's good, cos you have to earn the money. I don't, though!
Mum	It's good, because they can arrange to meet their friends after school at a specific time on Club Penguin, when they can't get together in person. I get a little bit worried, as it is a way of getting children used to being in chat rooms at too early an age. You don't know if there's a child or an adult as one of the penguins, but there's no harm in it.
Alex	Mum, you can choose ultimate safe chat!

These boys have become experts in their 'play' on Club Penguin - they are knowledgeable and can disseminate information to interested adults who are obviously less experienced in this area. As the boys have got older they continually explore further games and sites to develop their expertise and they have become quite discerning about what is on offer. The headline on the NLT website for the World Book Day research mentioned earlier in this chapter declares 'Old Meets New is the Best Way to Improve Reading'. The research shows:

- Electronic devices, such as iPods and Xboxs, are increasingly being used for reading for one-fifth (21%) of British youngsters.
- Most young people – 62% – say that they read paper-based materials, as well as at least one technology-based medium; only one-fifth just read paper-based books and magazines.
- 56% of youngsters actively read on a mobile or handheld device, while 64% read on their PCs.
- The enjoyment factor of reading is generated more from reading a book or magazine, than technology-based texts. 65% of book readers say that they enjoy reading, compared with just 26% of those who only read off their mobiles or laptops.
- Young book readers are twice as likely to read every day, compared with their counterparts, who rely on their gadgets. (Clark, 2012)

The National Literary Trust Director, Jonathan Douglas, said that while print or paper-based books remain vitally important, the combination of paper and technology-based texts would turn more children onto reading:

> Our research shows that while books remain important we should also embrace the fact that children are reading on everything from iPads to their gaming devices. Those who read books get more enjoyment from it than those who only read online or on their gadgets. World Book Day is a fantastic opportunity to celebrate both the pleasure of reading and the importance of literacy.
>
> (Clark, 2012)

E-books – the future of reading?

E-books are definitely having an impact on the reading habits of children and young people, and they can easily access these through a range of technologies, including personal computers, iPhones and portable e-reader devices, such as Kindle, Nintendo and iPads. These devices, obviously, provide a wider choice of reading material options for our youthful digital native population, and they are perceived to be particularly valuable for encouraging reluctant readers. As they can encourage reading through a variety of ways, including through interactive activities and kinaesthetic methods, they can be especially supportive for enticing hesitant or unenthusiastic learners.

The increase in pupils' use of e-readers in the USA worries some school librarians. Their concerns arise from two issues – one relates to the illegal download of e-books and the other regards the possible choice of fiction reading matter, as school librarians prefer to discuss this personally with pupils, and this may be a problem with an e-book. The main benefit of e-readers is the 'amazing upsurge in recreational reading in the student population. . . . What is being seen now as more and more kids get their own e-readers is that they see the pleasure and advantages of reading, both for pleasure and for information' (Leap in Kids, 2012). This is occurring across ages, genders and social classes, and US public and school libraries are now working to introduce pupils to the possibilities that e-readers offer them.

Maynard's (2010) research considered the e-book reading experiences with three families, each with two children in the 7–12 year age range, who experienced an e-reader for a two-week period. They recorded their experiences in a diary and were interviewed at both the beginning and end of the study. A key finding was that of the six children involved, four rate themselves as 'enthusiastic' readers, one as 'average' and one as 'reluctant', whilst all six of the parents state that they enjoy reading. The reluctant young reader (a boy, aged eight years) was inspired to read by the use of the Kindle. His parents were pleased with this enthusiasm, noting that he was spending time reading, rather than watching television, and they stated that he was excited by downloading and choosing his books to read, and it was the only time that they had known him ask to read voluntarily. When asked whether they prefer printed or electronic books, all of the adults chose printed books, whilst the children were more ambivalent, with half preferring electronic books.

The challenge of building e-book collections and of using e-readers in school libraries is explored at length by Doiron (2011). He raises questions concerning the place of the printed book as the chief way of motivating reading and the usefulness of e-reading resources. His study found that school librarians are finding ways to connect their traditional reading promotions with the online world, whether it is to provide access to e-reading materials for inquiry and information literacy, downloading an e-book for personal reading or establishing online book clubs and e-reading blogs, where so many pupils already spend so much of their time. It is apparent, from Doiron's research, that librarians, teachers and parents need to be very aware of the value of e-books and how to promote them, in conjunction with more standard reading materials, namely, the printed book.

Conclusion

This chapter has demonstrated the importance of providing a combination of paper and technological based texts to encourage children and young people's love and involvement in reading. It has drawn on many varied sources to justify this premise – not only through accessing research by respected academics, professional organizations and government, but also through presenting the voices of librarians, teachers, parents, children and young people. The chapter has outlined the ways in which many children develop a varied diet of reading, and has demonstrated strategies to acknowledge and encourage their proficiency in literacy through reading a range of diverse texts and genres. As we have continued to stress, throughout this chapter and the book as a whole, there are definitely challenges ahead for both the public and school librarian, in meeting the demands of children and young people, along with those of policy-makers, in a climate of austerity and cutbacks. However, there is a cornucopia of positives out there – the invention of accessible electronic resources should empower children and young people; there is a wealth of goodwill from librarians, teachers, authors and parents, through getting involved in reading campaigns; and last, but not least, children really want to listen to and read really cool books.

References

Anderson, H. and Styles, M. (eds) (2000) *Teaching Through Texts*, Routledge.

Appleyard, B. (2009) Nightmarish Power of Sendak's Classic, *The Times*, 22 November, 13.

Barrs, M. and Cork, V. (2001) *The Reader in the Writer: the link between the study of literature and writing development at Key Stage 2*, Centre for Literacy in Primary Education.

Benard, B. (1991) *Fostering Resiliency in Kids: protective factors in the family, school and community*, Montana Board of Crime Control and Montana Office of Instruction.

Bilson, A. (2010) Fairy Tales or Twilight, Horror and Macabre Fascinate Children, *Telegraph*, 2 April, www.telegraph.co.uk/culture/books/books-life/7545250/Fairy-tales-or-Twilight-horror-and-macabre-fascinate-children.html.

Byron, T. (2008) *Safer Children in a Digital World*, The Byron Review.

Chambers, A. (1991) *The Reading Environment*, Thimble Press.

Clark, C. (2012) *Young People and Reading in 2011: findings from the National Literacy Trust's annual literacy survey*, National Literacy Trust, www.literacytrust.org.uk/media/4616_world_book_day_research_shows_old_meets_new_is_the_best_way_to_improve_reading.

Clark, C. and Akerman, R. (2008) *Being a Reader: the relationship with gender*, National Literacy Trust.

Clark, C. and Hawkins, L. (2010) *Young People's Reading: the importance of the home environment and family support*, National Literacy Trust.

Clark, C. and Osbourne, S. (2008) How does Age Relate to Pupils' Perceptions of Themselves as Readers?, National Literacy Trust.

Collins, F. M. (2005) 'She's Sort of Dragging Me into the Story'! Student teachers' experiences of reading aloud in Key Stage 2 classes, *Literacy*, **39** (1), 10-17.

Cotton, P. (2000) *Picture Books Sans Frontières*, Trentham.

Doiron, R. (2011) Using E-Books and E-Readers to Promote Reading in School Libraries: lessons from the field, *World Library and Information Congress: 77th IFLA General Conference and Assembly, 13-18 August 2011, San Juan, Puerto Rico,* http://conference.ifla.org/ifla77.

Elkin, J. and Triggs, P. (1985) *The Books for Keeps Guide to Children's Books for a Multi-Cultural Society*, Books for Keeps.

Grenby, M. (2008) *Children's Literature*, Edinburgh University Press.

Grove, V. (2010) *So Much to Tell*, Viking.

Hunt, P. (2005) *Understanding Children's Literature: key essays from the second edition of The International Companion Encyclopedia of Children's Literature*, 2nd edn, Routledge.

Johnson, J. (2010) Addressing Physical and Emotional Issues in Children's Literature, *Community & Junior College Libraries*, **16** (4), 225-8.

Kraemer, S. (1999) Promoting Resilience: changing concepts of parenting and child care, *International Journal of Child and Family Welfare*, **3**, 273-87.

Leap in Kids (2012) blog posted by 'Tony' on 30 January, www.ebookanoid.com/2012/01/30/leap-in-kids-with-ereaders-school-librarians-see-both-good-and-less-good-in-this-situation/.

Lindgren, A. (1945) *The Adventures of Pippi Longstocking*, Oxford University Press.

Lurie, A. (1990) *Don't Tell the Grown-ups: subversive children's literature*, Little Brown & Company.

Mallett, M. (2009) *Choosing and Using Fiction and Non-Fiction 3-11: a comprehensive guide for teachers and student teachers*, David Fulton.

Marsh, J. (2004) *Popular Culture, Media and Digital Literacies in Early Childhood*, Routledge Falmer.

Marsh, J. (2009) *Play and Literacy in Virtual Worlds*, presentation at the TACTYC (Association for the Professional Development of Early Years Educators) Conference, Milton Keynes, November.

Marsh, J. (2011) Young Children's Literacy Practices in a Virtual World: establishing an online interaction order, *Reading Research Quarterly*, **46** (2), 101-18.

Maynard, S. (2010) The Impact of e-Books on Young Children's Reading Habits, *Publishing Research Quarterly*, **26** (4), 236-48.

Meek, M. (1988) *How Texts Teach What Readers Learn*, The Thimble Press.

Meek, M. (2001) *Children's Literature and National Identity*, Trentham Books.

Meek, M., Warlow, A. and Barton, G. (1977) *The Cool Web: the pattern of children's reading*, The Bodley Head.

National Literacy Trust (2011) Save Our Libraries Day to take place on 5 February, www.literacytrust.org.uk/talk_to_your_baby/news/2962_save_our_libraries_day_to_take_place_on_5_february.

Scholastic Education (2009) Japanese Adventure Wins New Book Award, http://education.scholastic.co.uk/content/7423.

Stibbs, A. (1991) *Reading Narrative as Literature: signs of life*, Oxford University Press.

Stones, R. (1994) (ed.) *A Multicultural Guide to Children's Books 0–12*, Books For Keeps and The Reading and Language Information Centre.

Tucker, N. and Gamble, N. (2001) *Family Fictions (Contemporary Classics in Children's Literature)*, Continuum.

Walliams, D. (2010) Why I love Roald . . . and of course Quentin!, *The Times*, 4 September, 3.

Wolstencroft, H. (2007) *How Can Children's Understandings of Current Game Literacy be Reflected in, and Develop, Primary Pupils' Literacy Experiences in the Classroom?* M. Ed. thesis, University of Cambridge, Faculty of Education, unpublished.

UKLA (2008) *The United Kingdom Literacy Association Response to the Byron Review*, UK Literacy Association, www.ukla.org.

Websites

Contact an Author, www.contactanauthor.co.uk/.

Opening the Book, www.openingthebook.com/library-resources/reader-centered/definition/default.aspx.

World Book Day, www.worldbookday.com.

7 Creative integration of information technology in the school library

Carol Webb

Introduction

Teaching and learning are in an era of rapid change, driven by political policy-makers and fuelled by the impact of information and communication technologies (ICTs), both in the home and at school. The potential to empower learning and track student and school progress has never been greater. If the school library is to support effective learning and teaching, then exploring the communication abilities of new technologies is certainly part of the librarian's raison d'être. This chapter will emphasize a strategic approach to integrating technologies, in order to give the school library a strong educational identity, and will look at what this means for student learning.

In the UK, education is populated by a diverse number of institutions, ranging from those that are state run or independent, to those that have academy status and those that are secular or centred on a faith, to name a few. In some areas, students move from a primary to a secondary school, while in others, they experience a middle school system. Some schools offer continuity of environment from the age of three until 18. All are unique. Equally, the level of information technology available, and the way that it is integrated into the life of a school, is varied. Competition between institutions lends a strong impetus in the drive to develop these assets. Critical within this drive is the role of the library staff to think strategically and operate educationally. The challenge is to use our professional expertise within a specific school culture, in order to create the library service that delivers the particular school's needs.

A strategic approach

It is very easy to say that the core business of any school is learning, teaching and attainment. The reality is a complex network of priorities. How we respond to these, in our leadership of reader development, information literacy, staff development and school management, is crucial for the future longevity of the library. Currently, in the UK, a school library exists at the discretion of the head teacher and so its relationship with this leader's vision is critical to its success. We know that one of the main sources of information, upon which head teachers base their judgements, is their own observation (Everhart 2006). The availability of technology enables us to innovate and to make visible what we do, taking this to the next level and, thus, proving its relevance. So it is essential that we use all the means at our disposal to highlight the contributions made by the library to the school's stated objectives. Events, examples of good teaching practices and other initiatives need to be profiled in displays, both real and virtual, on plasma screens, websites and through other visual media. They should be reviewed in reports and shared in newsletters and meetings to provide a continual stream of positive messages that show the library's contribution to the school's core business. On a wider level, it helps to promote the school to the surrounding community as a desirable choice.

A website can turn the library into a powerful information provider that can reach out to parents and beyond. It is important to identify the strengths that we wish to profile, and to ask which aspects you want to be associated with – and which of these you are willing to take responsibility for, in response to enquiries. The leader's vision is key, but so, too, is our own, and using our professional expertise to strategically and philosophically align the two together is vital in delivering the school's stated aim and objectives.

Projecting an image to all staff, which is at the forefront of educational ideas, is strategically important. Our own awareness of reports, such as one on the Google generation (Rowlands et al., 2008), gives us evidence from which to argue the need for information literacy teaching in school. Articles in our professional press and educational journals (Shoham and Shemer-Shalman, 2008; Valkanova, 2004) and material shared through social learning or bookmarking websites (Roche, 2010) feed our knowledge of how ICT can be used and to what effect. Thinking strategically requires this kind of professional information base, coupled with our knowledge of the particular school culture.

It also enables us to contribute to staff development, by highlighting reports, websites, Web 2.0 tools, books and articles. So using professional guidelines (Bradnock, 2007), training courses (www.cilip.org.uk and www.sla.org.uk), collaboration with others, visits to other libraries, and online groups like School Librarian Network (http://groups.yahoo.com/group/sln/), and following key thinkers (www.philb.com), RSS feeds, and so on, are all invaluable. This is an area where technology provides us with not only access to the information product, but also a whole variety of ways for communicating, as Ruth, a school librarian, demonstrates below:

> Ruth realized that digital literacies (Gillen and Barton, 2010) had several audiences in her school: persuasive material for the VLE (Virtual Learning Environment) manager, an overview on ICT's impact on learning for the senior leaders and as a current awareness tool for governors. She e-mailed copies, created a folder in the shared network for all staff, and advertised this in her electronic bulletin and on the staffroom noticeboard. Subsequently, one of the other deputy head teachers included Ruth in her teaching and learning group, knowing that she would contribute her knowledge of what happens across the curriculum and ideas and materials from outside the school.

Ruth's processes were straightforward ones, but where tasks are more complex, we need to consider the level of support from administrative and technical staff and gauge how much time is available. Choices need to be realistic, in relation to our resources, both physical and financial.

The educational identity of the library

Strategic thinking leads to operational decisions, which then lead to tasks and the choosing of tools. The following vignette is an example drawn from a library-based reading lesson in a specialist school for the performing arts. It shows the librarian in a lead teaching role:

> Aaron wanted to clearly identify library reading lessons with active learning, one of the school's current priorities, so he began to use some of the drama department's teaching strategies to get students to study why stories capture the imagination. The teacher organized the students into groups. They were asked to choose a recently read story and create a physical freeze frame to portray a key scene from it to show the class why it had captured their imagination. The students were enthusiastic and lively during the activity. Aaron was able to generate some focused group reflection, through the use of a Flip video camera. He captured their planned frame, and they were able to study it and think of ways to improve it. The result was an enthusiastic discussion of why some stories worked so well and a flurry of activity to borrow those books.

The camera was a useful tool, but the quality of the questioning between staff and students, in order to encourage them to examine the story more closely and what it meant to them, was crucial. By getting them to articulate this during the practice, they were able to develop a more meaningful discussion with the whole class. There is an optimum to be achieved between the task, the chosen tool and the energy required to manage it and the quality of the outcome.

It is difficult to imagine any library activity that does not involve technology in some form. Choices should not be driven by the availability of technology, as Brabazon (2007) has said, we should not assume benefits. When is a personal demonstration, discussion or hands-on experience vital for learning? When should these be captured or facilitated by technology? A guiding principle should be the inspiring words of Ross Todd (2001), namely, that the library is not an information place, but a knowledge-making space. Indeed, one might say that the core business of the library is more than learning, teaching and attainment, instead, that it is the drive to develop critical thinking in ourselves, students, teachers and parents. Part of the knowledge that we make should refer to the evaluation of the technology and the information that it provides. Brabazon (2007) supports the concept of teacher as subject expert and preselects good quality resources for her students, believing that it is how they *use* the resource that is key to their intellectual development, rather than whether they can find it by themselves. Underpinning integration of technology is the need to model the critical literacies, which make the difference between students who are able to take control of their own learning or students who are passive receivers of information:

> Diana wanted to establish the library area of the VLE as a must-visit place for students. Inspired by some public library ideas, she designed an 'Ask the Librarian' service for homework enquiries. Diana was clear in her policy of identifying resources and advising how to improve a piece of work, rather than simply providing the answers for the homework set. Her vision for the educational identity of the service supported her in opening a dialogue with teachers about making the work more accessible for some students. These opportunities led to collaborative work, organizing resources and tasks on the VLE. Ultimately, it has established her as a direct source of support for homework outside of curriculum time, in both student and teacher eyes.

As Diana has shown, the library is more than a physical place, when it is enabled by the librarian to reach beyond those boundaries and into the virtual space. Her choices were driven by the understanding that the quality of work that is achieved depends on the quality of the question, the task that is set and the support that is available when needed.

Students and learning

Students today are referred to as the digital generation, because they have experienced sound and visual surroundings of ever-increasing complexity since birth. Prensky (2001, 2) identified that:

> Digital Natives are used to receiving information really fast. They like to parallel process and multi-task. They prefer their graphics before their text rather than the opposite. They prefer random access (like hypertext). They function best when networked. They thrive on instant gratification and frequent rewards. They prefer games to 'serious' work.

Prensky's promotion of a computer-gaming approach in all subjects and at all levels could be criticized as an indiscriminate attempt to merge technology with learning itself (Lockard, 2009). More recently, Prensky (2009) has tempered his view, by observing that learning is successful when collaborative and self-directed, while coupled with mastering new technology, where students and teachers are peer learners together. Engineering such opportunities is what makes the library a knowledge-making space. Indeed, the vignette described earlier, where Aaron uses drama teaching strategies, enhanced by the Flip video camera, might be said to meet the experiential needs of digital natives, as described by Prensky (2001, 2009). Regardless of technology, teaching at its best encompasses experiences for all learning styles, for all of the senses.

Online learning has been criticized as reductionist and as a form of social control (Lockard, 2009). One might agree, if students were placed in front of laptops as the only source of learning available, but our students are, on the whole, extremely fortunate to have a variety of educational experiences on offer to them. Some students prefer online self-testing packages as a revision method. This brings us to the question of learning styles. Learning is personal, and this should be acknowledged. We do not all do things in the same way, and maturing as a learner means being able to make choices about what works best for the individual. The fact that different learning styles need to be accommodated in what we do means it is not effective to simply stand at the front of the classroom or learning space and talk about what to do. It is essential to model the practice, discuss the ins and outs, and demonstrate the choices available. Then there needs to be an opportunity to try different methods out, so that students can adopt those that suit their own comfort zone; for example, a dyslexic student may well steer towards a visual method for organizing his notes, rather than a linear text-based approach. He will only know about the visual method if he is introduced to a range of possible methods:

> Amir's teaching in research lessons had been made easier by using the interactive whiteboard. However, what really enhanced the learning was the smart pen and interactive software. The software allowed him to move the locus of control for the session to the students. They used the smart pen to re-sequence items during their discussions to illustrate the relationships between concepts. Usually, by the end of lessons, his hand-drawn spidergrams had been almost illegible; now, they were not only clear, but he was able to save them on to the VLE, for students to refer to during their homework session.

The task of introducing different methods need not rest with the teacher or librarian, but can be placed in the control of the students. Teaching others not only reinforces personal learning, but hones thinking and communication skills, too. Imagine a bank of YouTube-style videos made by students, demonstrating how to get the best out of Google: taking control of a text, skimming and scanning, making judgements about useful sections in relation to a question, examining an author's agenda, showing how to use evidence in writing to construct an argument and how to cite quotations. This is a resource that students could click on, when they need study guidance, or that teachers could use, in a lesson to demonstrate a technique.

There are both behaviourist and constructivist approaches to using ICT with students, and each has a place in different educational contexts. Programmed learning through a software package or online service might be characterized as behaviourist. The same product is available to everybody, and they work their way through these products individually, step by step. A more constructivist approach believes that one size does not fit all and would develop a more differentiated set of tasks, where social exchange is an important element. The process would ascertain what the students already know and begin from there. Do we assume that the whole class still needs to learn how to do a catalogue search? Or do we take the time to find out what knowledge already exists and how that can be utilized for the benefit of all? Peer-to-peer teaching can be very powerful, as demonstrated below:

> Ian organized a group of Year 8 students to act as reading mentors to Year 6 students. Once a story was chosen, and the reading was under way, he introduced the idea that they create a PowerPoint about the story that could be shown to other Year 6 students. So half-way through each session, the students would move from reading to the computers. The confidence of the Year 8 students was boosted by the experience of teaching ICT skills to the younger ones. Reading in the eyes of the Year 6 students gained a huge amount of prestige.

Ian's project was successful, because, prior to it, he ran a training session on mentoring skills. Student-teacher relationships were discussed, and boundaries were established. Ian's preparations made this a safe experience for the students.

Recent research on the brain (Curran, 2008) has shown that for learning to be effective, the emotions need to be engaged in a positive way. If the sense of risk involved is too high, the reptilian part of our brains responds with fight or flight responses. We know that students experience anxiety and confusion (Kuhlthau, 1993) during the finding and assimilating stages of a research task, which is, traditionally, the stage when students are expected to work by themselves. Evidence (Williams and Wavell, 2006) shows that meaningful interventions tailored to the student, and not a pre-defined skill, are critical, at this stage, in defusing negative emotions that block engagement and generating student confidence. All the messages are telling us that relationships are key to learning. This is no less so when technology is involved.

A constructivist approach to learning places an emphasis on the collaborative experience and the importance of discussion. Social learning tools on the web are able to offer the kind of contact that some students find comfortable and emancipatory:

> Vivienne organized a poetry performance event at lunchtimes in the library each half-term for students and staff to take the microphone and share their work. Some students who wrote poems were not always willing to perform them, and someone else would do so on their behalf. After taking part in a collaborative VoiceThread project (www.voicethread.com) with other schools, Vivienne realised this web tool would be a great way to allow students to give their poem voice without a live performance. So, now, the live Poetry Jam is interspersed with a VoiceThread on the interactive whiteboard. The ultimate result has been that the practice with a recording microphone has given some students the confidence to step up to the real microphone.

For most students, not just those with special educational needs or English as an additional language where discussion is crucial, collaboration is a catalyst for learning. A tool like VoiceThread enables a creative and collaborative experience to be engineered. Whether the learning experience is real or virtual, we believe its success lies in the quality of the dialogue and the degree to which it is tailored to the students involved.

These vignettes give snapshots of practice, but are not able to really demonstrate the complexity involved, the detail of the interactions and the holistic long-term benefits of good quality library experiences. Even mundane tasks, like the issue of laptops to students to use in the library space, can provide an opportunity for modelling values, as the following shows:

> Sue decided to label the laptops and ask students to sign them in and out, so that she could monitor their use. She gave them names, instead of numbers, and decided to refer to them as babies, so as to engender a caring attitude. Sue wanted the process to be more personal and for students to realise that the equipment should be valued. In practice, it generated a lot of humour, as students were told 'your baby's name is Edina. Take good care of her, because then she will work well for you'; 'if you have to leave the library, make sure your friend looks after your baby or ask one of us to mind it for you'; and 'how was she today?' Gradually, students began to ask for particular names: 'I need Tony, he and I really get on'. At the end of the year, the ICT technician reported that the library trolley had required only one repair, a much lower figure than any other trolley in the school.

Sue has engineered an opportunity where both the rewarding and onerous aspects of caring can be acknowledged in an authentic situation, which is relevant to the emotional and affective school curriculum. This is the library service operating educationally.

Evidence-based practice

The most effective negotiators and salespeople are those with the best listening skills (Shepherd, Castleberry and Ridnour, 1997). As they listen, they tailor their product knowledge to the needs and interests of the customer and so develop a rapport with them. On a micro level, this is what we do when talking with a student, in order to help find just the right story. On a macro level, it is what we do when evaluating a range of feedback about what is needed from the library service. Developing quantitative and qualitative data for evaluation purposes has been effectively covered elsewhere (Markless and Streatfield, 2006; Markless, 2009). There is little point in publicizing library data, such as borrowing statistics. Borrowing tells us nothing about the student's use of that item. We need evidence that speaks to teachers.

Technology has made available detailed student and school assessment data. Using this to design lessons or activities for specific target groups shows a school leadership that we are targeting their priorities, be it white, free-school-meal boys in Year 4 or Year 9 high-performing science students. Final outcomes for students are important, but equally so is our professional judgement about their changing confidence levels, the types of questions that they ask and their use of language.

Contributing this knowledge to school conversations and, thus, participating in formal assessment systems makes us part of the school circle and closes the evidence-base loop.

Conclusion

School library leadership of learning and teaching involves many challenges, and the integration of technology expands the channels that are open to us and enhances what we are able to achieve. Our professional judgement of when, where and how to integrate, so as to maximize benefits, is essential, in order to deliver the school's stated aim and objectives, as opposed to simply being driven by its presence. Technology should be chosen where it enhances what we do, because it suits the task and the audience, and offers sufficient advantage to warrant investment of our time, energy and resources. Its use opens many channels of communication within the school and beyond, and one needs to be prepared to engage in the dialogue that follows. We must use communication technologies to innovate and inspire learning and then make this visible to others. This will create the community-engaged school library and will provide the best means for its survival.

References

Brabazon, T. (2007) Won't Get Googled Again. In Lockard, J. and Pegrum, M. (eds), *Brave New Classrooms: democratic education and the internet*, Peter Lang.

Bradnock, M. (2007) *SLA Guidelines: blogs and bytes: ICT and the secondary school library*, School Library Association.

Curran, A. (2008) *The Little Book of Big Stuff about the Brain*, Crown House Publishing.

Everhart, N. (2006) Principals' Evaluation of School Librarians: a study of strategy and nonstrategy evidence-based approaches, *School Libraries Worldwide*, **12** (2), 38–51.

Gillen, J. and Barton, D. (2010) *Digital Literacies: a research briefing by the technology enhanced learning phase of the Teaching and Learning Research Programme*, Economic, Social and Research Council, www.tlrp.org/docs/DigitalLiteracies.pdf.

Kulhthau, C. C. (1993) *Seeking Meaning: a process approach to library and information services*, Ablex Publishing.

Lockard, J. (2009) Manifesto for Democratic Education and the Internet. In Lockard, J. and Pegrum, M. (eds), *Brave New Classrooms: democratic education and the internet*, Peter Lang.

Markless, S. (ed.) (2009) *The Innovative School Librarian: thinking outside of the box*, Facet Publishing.

Markless, S. and Streatfield, D. (2012) *Evaluating the Impact of your Library*, 2nd edn, Facet Publishing.

Prensky, M. (2001) *Digital Natives, Digital Immigrants*, www.marcprensky.com/writing/Prensky%20-%20Digital%20Natives, %20Digital%20Immigrants%20-%20Part1.pdf.

Prensky, M. (2009) *What I Learned Recently in New York City Classrooms: how to keep all kids busily engaged at all times*, www.marcprensky.com/writing/Prensky-What_I_Learned_in_NYC_ Classrooms-final.pdf.

Roche, C. (2010) *Using Technology to Excite Learners – free Web 2.0 tools*, www.slideshare.net/carolineroche/using-technology-to-excite-learners-older-3040032.

Rowlands, I., Nicholas, D., Williams, P., Huntington, P., Fieldhouse, M., Gunter, B., Withey, R., Jamali, H. R., Dobrowolski, T. and Tenopir, C. (2008) The Google Generation: the information behaviour of the researcher of the future, *Aslib Proceedings: new information perspectives*, **60** (4), 290–310.

Shepherd, C. D., Castleberry, S. B. and Ridnour, R. E. (1997) Linking Effective Listening and Salesperson Performance: an exploratory investigation, *Journal of Business and Industrial Marketing*, **12** (5), 315–22.

Shoham, S. and Shemer-Shalman, Z. (2008) Web Sites and Digital Services in Israeli School Libraries: how is the digital environment changing how school libraries work?, *School Libraries Worldwide*, **14** (1), 86–98.

Todd, R. J. (2001) Transitions for Preferred Futures of School Libraries: knowledge space, not information place; connections, not collections; actions, not positions; evidence, not advocacy, *IASL Conference Proceedings, held on 9–12 July 2001, organized by International Association of School Librarianship , Auckland, New Zealand*, www.iasl-online.org/events/conf/virtualpaper2001.html.

Valkanova, Y. (2004) Enhancing Self-Reflection in Children: the use of digital video in the primary science classroom, *Journal of eLiteracy*, **1**, 42–55.

Williams, D. and Wavell, C. (2006) *Untangling Spaghetti? The Complexity of Developing Information Literacy in Secondary School Students*, Robert Gordon University of Technology, www.scotland.gov.uk/Resource/Doc/924/0093122.pdf.

8 Comics, manga and graphic novels – developing, selecting and promoting a core collection for teenagers and young people

Mel Gibson

Introduction

Comics, manga (Japanese comics) and graphic novels are all different kinds of what has been called 'sequential art'. They can be created for any age group and in any genre. This body of work is best thought of as existing within a structure parallel to that of text fiction, which is equally flexible, being capable of creating very basic and simple material, right the way through to extremely complex and challenging texts. Comics, manga and graphic novels, in addition, may be non-fiction, despite the label 'graphic novel', and there are a range of texts, often autobiographical, but not limited to that genre, which may well form part of a core collection. You may also wish a collection to include, for instance, books about comics, such as histories of national schools or genres, 'how to draw' guides, academic analysis of the medium or material about specific creators.

Given the way that this is such a complex area, one needs to be aware of the potential of the medium, before building a collection, which is why I have begun with a loose definition (although definitions of this medium are widely debated, as Stegall-Armour (2010) discusses). Not knowing about the scope of the medium can result, for instance, in collections for younger readers, containing material written for older adults. This can occur because of the way that national stereotypes of the medium can dominate one's perception of it. For instance, in Britain, the stereotype dictates humour comics for very young readers, whilst in the USA, it is the superhero genre. Developing your knowledge, then, is the first stage in developing a collection and avoiding common pitfalls, which are created by assumptions about the medium. This chapter will talk about some of the resources you can draw on, in order to develop both your knowledge and a collection.

Where to start

It is possible to build a manga and graphic novel collection in any kind of library, which challenges a skilled reader of any age. It is also true, as with the traditional text-based book, that some work will be useful to support emerging readers, but, as the reader needs to become skilled in multiple literacies, both visual and traditional, it is important to remember that these are not simple texts. Being clear about the nature of the collection you wish to develop is key, as is thinking through location and display. Collections in Britain have been developed to broaden current leisure reading material in children's, young adult and adult libraries. They can also be located by film and music collections, and, given that some of these books are non-fiction, they might be placed in, for instance, a section of text-based biography or autobiography, as is the case with the classic, by Art Spiegelman (1987), *Maus I: a survivors tale* and (1992), *Maus II: and here my troubles began*. Another approach is to develop a touring collection, which visits a number of branch libraries; if well publicized this can be a good way of judging possible uptake across a number of sites. Robert G. Weiner's (2010) collection of essays on libraries and comics, reflecting current views and data from the USA and Canada, offers examples from across North America of a range of settings, including academic libraries. Several of the essays focus on collections for young people.

Where to place your collection

In most libraries, the typical approach to creating a collection has been to place all graphic novels, irrespective of subject or genre, in one or more age-related sections. In relation to manga, this has been made easier by some publishers' practice of detailing suggested age ranges on the back covers. Manga publishing differentiates some genres by age and gender, which can help in focusing collections. Original English-language manga is also appearing, although it may not offer the same kind of explicit guidance. In other collections, all the books have been grouped together in the non-fiction section on art and allocated a Dewey number accordingly. In contrast, yet other libraries have all of their collection as reference and so count footfall, rather than issues. I have seen all of these approaches used successfully in developing collections specifically for teenagers and young people. Some interfile graphic novels with text-based fiction, but that can result in titles being swamped or lost, so most opt for a separate collection.

In addition to this, once a collection is more established, you may find that manga and graphic novels need to be shelved separately, as the readership for these two kinds of sequential art can be very different. This can also encompass issues concerning format, given that, currently, most manga published in English will fit on a paperback spinner, whilst the diverse range of sizes of graphic novels means that they are best shelved with their covers facing outward, on magazine racks, for instance, thus making the most of their display potential. Displays specifically focusing on graphic novels or manga are an obvious way to promote them, but, given the range of subjects and genres they can encompass, including a few relevant titles in other kinds of displays, with a note to readers to check the relevant section, can also be useful, making potential readers aware that this is a graphic novel friendly space.

Manga?

This chapter emphasizes manga, because it continues to grow in popularity among young adult readers in Britain, to the extent that it could now, arguably, be seen as a mainstream cultural interest. Developing a collection in this area makes the library more relevant to that age group, but, in addition to this, the growth of the area means that this is not a swiftly passing fad, but, quite possibly, a lasting phenomenon. Material for younger readers comprises around 57% of the market, as Paul Gravett (2004) noted. There have already been major initiatives tapping into the enthusiasm of younger readers for Japanese culture in Britain, one of the first being Manga Mania, run by The Reading Agency in 2004. The passion for wider Japanese culture in Britain is also explored in magazines like *Neo*, which reviews some manga amongst a range of other material. Such publications may be useful primers for staff, as well as making good additions to a collection.

There are, as I've already suggested, differences between the readership of manga and other comics and graphic novels. Whilst, for example, American superhero titles tend to have readerships which are predominantly male, and some collections are developed with the notion of attracting young male readers, precisely because of this bias in readership, most manga have a readership which is, typically, around 60% female. This is, in part, because of the genre of shojo manga - titles published specifically for girls (independent comics, too, often have a different readership, but that usually operates at the level of individual titles, rather than at the level of genre).

The appeal of some contemporary shojo manga titles will be familiar to some older British women. Many of the stories include romance, adventures with magical companions, lonely girls, who have to battle with injustice, either in school or at home, or narratives about groups of friends - all of which are common tropes in the British girls' comics that used to exist and thrive. The manga narratives, however, may be up to 22 volumes long (with some even longer), asking for a big commitment from the reader. Although the narratives unfold across a number of volumes, the nature of serial publication, and the tendency to finish each book on, in effect, a cliff-hanger, will also be familiar to those brought up on narratives that typically unfolded – in *Bunty*, for instance – over 14 weeks. A similar structure applies to titles for boys, with a genre known as shonen manga, although in this genre the emphasis is more upon what happens than about the people that these things happen to. Narratives focus on adventure, but also contain themes about growing up and the responsibilities that are thrust upon younger people by their parents, in genres ranging from sports to science fiction. The gendered appeal of these titles will form part of staff considerations in building a collection.

As a result of cultural perceptions of the medium and a general lack of confidence among library professionals about working with comics, manga and graphic novels, it can feel quite a challenge to build a collection for young people. However, looking through what already exists on library shelves will probably reveal familiar series, like The Simpsons, Futurama and other media tie-ins, classic *bandes dessinées* (BD) albums, like Asterix and Tintin, along with some of Raymond Briggs' titles, many of which could be transferred into a graphic novel collection for young people, depending on the age and gender of the target audience.

Who can help?
Staff

In order to develop a collection, I would advise any librarian to put out a 'call for people', amongst staff in their setting. This is useful, because most of those who engage with the medium are passionate and informed advocates, typically about a specific genre, but often about broader aspects of the medium. When I did this in one school library I worked in, it turned out that one of the technicians was also knowledgeable and specialized in material that I was less familiar with. Pooling knowledge is invaluable. No single individual can be expected to know everything about this medium. It would be like asking someone to be an expert in every genre of the novel, from every country and every era. Given the scale of the task, getting to grips with a huge area like graphic novels, comics and manga means that partnership working at all levels is the best way to move forward.

Library users and non-users

On a similar note, the second group of individuals to be involved are library users or non-users. The school librarian, for instance, will be able to note if any students using the library are drawing using a recognisable manga style (this is often staff's first clue that there may be students who are interested in helping to develop collections), and they can simply approach them. Advertising for interested parties to meet with you can also be successful. These individuals can support what you are doing in a number of ways, but one of the most useful, as outreach, partnership working and promotion, is to form a reading group. These can be created with a gender and age specific group in mind or for a general readership, as is the case with Newcastle group (predominantly consisting of adult readers), Readers of the Lost Art. You may find it appropriate to begin separate groups for manga and graphic novel readers, as those who read one form of comic do not necessarily read others.

Obviously, these groups may review books, as well as discuss them, but they sometimes move into creating manga and comics, too, allowing different members to take on roles as artist, author or editor. They may also engage with other related activities, such as cosplay (making costumes based on manga, anime and game characters) or visiting comic festivals, such as Thought Bubble, which is held in Leeds. Participants are usually happy to act as advisors, so see them as partners in a comic reading community. Members can often be involved in book selection and buying visits. I've worked with teenagers, as well as older readers, on such visits, and the sense of ownership involved in collection development – for younger readers, in particular – is very significant. You will also find that they are enthusiastic partners in promoting collections. When you launch a collection, these powerful advocates will disseminate for the library service through word-of-mouth publicity, and they may also help with promotional events, possibly through 'book-talking' their favourite titles.

Specialists

If there is a specialist comic shop in your area, you will probably want to involve the staff as your third group of people to work in partnership with. They will be able to guide you to appropriate material, for, as yet, many library suppliers are not experts, with regards to this medium. I would strongly advise working with a specialist supplier. Even just visiting a comic shop will give you an idea of both the scope of material and the range of readers (whilst many mainstream book shops now stock manga and graphic novels, they do not often have the level of expertise of the specialists).

Read, read, read!

Along with all of these other forms of assistance, I would advise that you look at actual books when selecting, so as to develop your familiarity with the medium and help you identify what will be suitable for the age group that you are selecting for. For instance, just because a title is part of the superhero genre, this does not necessarily make it suitable for younger readers. Furthermore, I have found that what is seen as appropriate for a specific age group in one library service may be seen differently in another, so remember that age classifications are only basic guidelines. In addition, as a series progresses, the content may become more challenging, as was the case with the Harry Potter novels. Finally, whilst some titles are single, self-contained volumes, like Bryan Talbot's (1996) *Tale of One Bad Rat*, others can extend into a number of volumes. Buying the first in a series and gauging responses to it before purchasing more is a useful approach. Using a specialist supplier also means that you may be able to acquire material that is out of print. Basically, out of print does not mean unavailable, which helps with filling 'gaps' in series.

Specialist suppliers will also be able to help you become aware of the rich range of British small press titles that are available, extending what you might offer. They should have good links with locally based creators, who you may wish to collaborate with. Some suppliers, for instance, the Travelling Man chain of shops, also run very active publishing activities of their own. I have sometimes advised talented younger illustrators to go along to their events and start to participate in creating work for publication. There is scope for working with these shops on cross-promotional activities. Several comic shops that I know have, for instance, offered bookshops as part of school book weeks, run events supporting new creators or held workshops. You could also contact writers and artists directly and run an author event, as you would for any other kind of book.

Sources of support: websites and print

Inevitably, there are a range of websites which you can draw on to develop your knowledge of the medium and to help you select stock. These are international in scope and include No Flying, No Tights, which is a graphic novel review site created by a librarian. The site is divided into three sections: first, the original one, which focuses on titles for teenagers; second, Sidekicks, devoted to graphic novels for younger readers; and, lastly, The Lair, featuring graphic novels for older teens and adults. Reviews include guidance on suitability levels for different age groups, and these reviews are split into genres. They also regularly review manga. My website, Dr Mel Comics, includes links in the resources sections to a number of useful sites for libraries, universities and schools, supporting research, collection development and promotional activities about the medium.

Finally, you will also find information in print form, such as Paul Gravett's (2005) *Graphic Novels: stories to change your life*, which predominantly deals with titles for adult readers, but offers a wealth of knowledge and advice. You may even find that your local library still has a copy of Keith Barker's (1993) *Graphic Account*, which was one of the first positive appraisals of the medium in Britain. Many of the titles that are flagged up in this volume are still available. In addition, Massachusetts librarian and author Stephen Weiner's books will also be useful, including his (2005) *The 101 Best Graphic Novels*, which includes age-relevant categories.

Having a go with manga and graphic novels: Japan week

The fact that consultation with a range of interested professionals and readers of the form (even if they are not library users) is central, when developing this kind of collection, shows how straightforward and satisfying it can be to develop outreach work and partnerships around graphic novels and manga. I have already suggested a number of ways that this could occur, but I will now talk through a few examples.

One event under consideration involved the whole school, and every subject, in a Japan week. This type of activity could focus on promoting a newly developed collection and could be translated into other kinds of setting. Here, there were book talks about the manga and graphic novels in the library, whose staff had been central to developing the event for students in every year, in a tightly themed version of a school book week. The wide range of other activities meant that those who did not enjoy manga were also catered for.

During this week, there were many opportunities for working across the school. The event offered opportunities to develop classroom work focusing on, for instance, cultural difference and globalization. Art and English worked together, analysing and then creating manga, drawing on developing student knowledge. This was stimulated by use of a wide range of titles, including the Manga Shakespeare version of *Romeo and Juliet*, which was contrasted with other comic and filmic versions of the play. Further, given that Japanese was an increasingly popular A level subject (Advanced Qualification in Further Education in England, Wales and Northern Ireland), the students from that course offered lunchtime sessions in basic Japanese. There were screenings of Studio Ghibli films, such as *My Neighbour Totoro* and *Spirited Away*, which generated discussion around animation in the field of media studies. There were also explorations of other aspects of Japanese culture, including food. A display of cookery books, for instance, incorporated manga on that theme. In this case, the cross-curricular work across the school was supported with partnerships working with a range of outside organizations and individuals (including myself), both in terms of content and sponsorship.

Having a go with manga and graphic novels: creating comics

A contrasting project developed to promote a collection, which had more of a focus on younger readers, was that generated for another school group – this time, for Year 7 students. Here, again, the project incorporated reading and writing activities, but was rather more focused upon a specific genre – that of the superhero comic (although it was broadened out during some of the sessions to incorporate references to British humour comics). Here, the activities also formed part of the students' welcome entry to the school, as they took place around the fourth week of the autumn term, thus familiarizing them with the entire site, introducing them to various teachers in a less formal way and introducing them to students from older years, which helped to run activities. The core of the event concerned problem-solving and relationships. Over the course of the day, the students pooled their knowledge and used graphic novel collections and websites to research and then create their own superheroes and villains, who they then had to work into a narrative about solving a problem in the local community.

Creating comics is, itself, an example of partnerships working and, potentially, of outreach, as suggested above. The youngest group that I have met engaged with making comics were four girls aged ten, who were creating and selling their shojo manga. In relation to creating graphic novels rather than manga, an ambitious recent project is Fool's Gold (2009), by a group from Dearne High – a specialist humanities college. The project centred on the college students working with authors, teachers, museum workers, photographers, comic creators and librarians, as well as younger students from linked primary schools, to create a mixed-medium book, based on a historical theme, with a ghost story twist. This incorporated photo-stories, drawn sequences and elements in the form of text message exchanges, and featured a number of stories within the story created by different groups and individuals. The book that was published out of this cross-sectoral project could be added to collections, as inspiration for others based on the way that comics help develop reading into writing activities.

Conclusion

To conclude, the possibilities and potential for outreach and partnership working around this medium are terrific with all ages, although I have focused on teenagers and young people here. This small snapshot, suggesting some basic understandings about comic strip materials, offering some information about several types of comic and suggesting some ways of developing collections and working with the medium, can only offer a taste of what is possible, by drawing on the enthusiasm of those engaged with sequential art, working with a range of readers and professionals and developing an understanding of the medium.

References

Barker, K. (ed.) (1993) *Graphic Account*, Youth Libraries Group.

Dearne High (2009) *Fool's Gold*, Grosvenor House Publishing Limited.

Gravett, P. (2004) *Manga: sixty years of Japanese comics*, Laurence King Publishing.

Gravett, P. (2005) *Graphic Novels: stories to change your life*, Aurum Press.

Spiegelman, A. (1987) *Maus I: a survivors tale*, Penguin.

Spiegelman, A. (1992) *Maus II: and here my troubles began*, Penguin.

Stegall-Armour, A. (2010) The Only Thing Graphic Is Your Mind: reconstructing the reference librarian's view of the genre. In Weiner, R. G. (ed.), *Graphic Novels and Comics in Libraries and Archives: essays on readers, research, history and cataloging*, McFarland & Company Inc.

Talbot, B. (1996) *The Tale of One Bad Rat*, Titan Books.

Weiner, R. G. (ed.) (2010) *Graphic Novels and Comics in Libraries and Archives: essays on readers, research, history and cataloging*, McFarland & Company Inc.

Weiner, S. (2005) *The 101 Best Graphic Novels*, NBM.

Websites

Cosplay, www.cosplay.co.uk/.

Dr Mel Comics, www.dr-mel-comics.co.uk/sources/index.html#other.

Manga Shakespeare, www.mangashakespeare.com/.

Neo, www.neomag.co.uk/.

No Flying, No Tights, www.noflyingnotights.com/index2.html.

Readers of the Lost Art, https://readers-of-the-lost-art.org.uk/.

Studio Ghibli, www.onlineghibli.com/films.php.

Thought Bubble, www.thoughtbubblefestival.com/.

9 Connecting and engaging with children and young people – the Australian public library perspective on outreach and marketing

Carolyn Bourke

Introduction and background

Australia is a geographically vast country, with a relatively small population of approximately 22 million. Most of the population lives in the major cities, which are situated on the coastline. Australia is a very multicultural nation, with 25% of people born overseas, while indigenous Australians make up only 2.4% of the population (Australian Bureau of Statistics, 2010). Despite the overall aging of the population, children and young people still account for approximately one-third of the Australian population (Australian Institute of Health and Welfare, 2009, 1).The country has a three-tier government system – federal, state and local – and while models vary from state to state, in most cases, public libraries are funded by local government, with a small amount of state funding. The benefit of this system is that local programmes can be targeted specifically to local issues, but it can also make it difficult to run large-scale services, which would be an advantage to the whole population. Public library outreach and marketing is all about connecting and engaging with local communities, finding out what they want and attempting to match services and resources to those needs, as well as to the funding body's mission. The other key components involve promoting those services back to the community, physically running the event or delivering the service and then adequately evaluating it afterwards. This process is always a juggling act between community needs and expectations, budget and time constraints, the mission of the funding organizations and the skills and expertise of staff and partnering organizations. In Australia, some of the key considerations in connecting and engaging communities are geographic distance and isolation, language, socio-economic and cultural barriers, and access and equity issues.

Librarians have become increasingly aware of the important role that public libraries play in building social capital in their local communities. Libraries are a logical point of community intersection and interaction. They give people in the local community access to the increasingly technological world of information. This is particularly important for children and young people, who can be disengaged from school and the community, due to family stress, poverty, literacy and language barriers. Libraries can provide a space with resources and support in a non-judgemental environment, which gives young people the opportunity to dream and achieve (Bourke, 2005). This chapter will provide suggestions for strategies and approaches to outreach and marketing for children and young people and will look at a number of successful Australian projects as relevant case studies.

Marketing: with whom do we need to connect and engage?

One of the key issues which needs to be defined, before embarking on any marketing campaign, is the target audience. The most obvious group is, of course, the young people themselves. However, we must also consider their parents, our library staff, any community partners or other stakeholders and, importantly, the relevant funding body. These very different target audiences will require correspondingly different promotional strategies, which will be discussed in detail in this section.

Connecting and engaging six to 18 year olds

When marketing any service to the six to 18-year-old age group, it is important to carefully consider that this group covers a very wide range of interests, abilities, resources and levels of independence. For the younger cohort, especially, their parents must also be included in our target audience. Fairfield City Library Service in Sydney's multicultural south west has developed a range of strategies to connect with this age group and their parents.

Traditionally, libraries have produced flyers, bookmarks and posters to promote upcoming events, and these methods are still very useful, as long as they look professional and carry consistent branding – clip art is not appropriate for the technologically savvy market that we are targeting. The same is true for electronic marketing. Websites and promotional PowerPoint slides on flat-screen TVs and as screen savers on public access catalogues need to be well designed and branded. Social media technologies are also extremely useful ways to both give and receive information. Blogs, wikis, Twitter and Facebook allow direct contact with a large number of customers, as well as giving them an opportunity to respond, if they desire.

The local media is another great potential partner. They are always looking for good local stories, and the library should have lots to share, including some excellent photo opportunities. However, it is important to learn how to write a good media release, so that you can get your message across succinctly.

Visits to schools can be time consuming to organize, but help build good relationships between the library service and these key partners. Depending on the event or service to be publicized, the librarian may arrange to address the school assembly, a year group, the school staff at one of their professional development sessions, or even the parents at a parent and citizen meeting.

Some strategies are so simple that they can often be easily overlooked. Direct conversation with customers about upcoming events can be an extremely successful promotional tool, as well as providing good opportunities for informal feedback. A survey carried out by Fairfield City Library Service (Bourke, 2010, 89) showed that 45% of young people learned about library activities from their friends. Obviously, the more people you tell, the better this strategy will work.

Connecting and engaging library staff

Few library staff in Australia will have had specific formal training in working with children and young people. Most training in this area is informal, on-the-job training. While some library services offer specific training aimed at running effective storytime and baby rhyme time sessions, many still do not. Public library staff tend to work with children and youth almost by default, because the six to 18 age group forms one of the major customer groups for libraries. Staff may have little inclination or interest towards this important market segment, and the best programmes and activities can be shipwrecked, if staff do not or, worse still, will not promote them to customers. These are some of the successful strategies to connect and engage staff:

1   Training – ensure that staff know how the programme works, so that they can be confident and knowledgeable when answering customer enquiries. For example, online databases are a great resource for students, but staff need to be well versed in their use, in order to demonstrate them confidently to customers.
2   Event teams – comprising representatives from each library or department to run the programme. This gives each location a local champion, who can answer questions and encourage participation from other staff. For example, a representative from each branch can work with the children's and young adults librarian to plan, run and evaluate the summer reading club each year.
3   Awareness campaigns which promote the programme to staff first. For example, if a significant new programme is planned, staff really need to be

on board, in order to make it a success. An e-mail teaser or a quiz with prizes for staff can be used to engage their attention, interest and, hopefully, enthusiasm for the programme. This is particularly important for casual staff, who may tend to be a bit 'out of the loop', otherwise. Fairfield City Library Service initially used incentives to encourage staff to register young people for their first summer reading club. The staff member initials the registration, and if that child is selected in the prize draw, the staff member also receives a prize. This programme has now been running for a number of years, and the staff incentives are no longer needed.

Connecting and engaging other stakeholders

Another important group to take into consideration is colleagues within the broader organization, in other libraries and in community agencies and schools. The key strategy for connecting and engaging these other stakeholders is networking. Time spent in meetings and reading posts on e-lists can be a productive way of creating a contact network and building good relationships with them. Knowing and being known is an essential element in building effective partnerships and networks. The Children's Services Department of Fairfield City Council contacted the Fairfield Library when they wanted to produce an early literacy book. The resulting partnership also included the Council's cultural planners and leisure centres, as well as a community partner from a local school. Together, the group produced *ActiveGator's Adventure* – a bilingual early literacy book, promoting reading and healthy lifestyles, as well as Fairfield City itself (Quilty, 2011). Building relationships with other potential stakeholders and partners takes some time, but it is worthwhile in the medium and longer term.

Connecting and engaging funding bodies

Sustainable programmes need sustainable funding. Programmes need to be linked in with the parent organization's mission and vision, in order to continue to receive internal funding and ongoing support. Partnering with other agencies involves an awareness of their priorities and objectives and an understanding of how they mesh with your own. For example, a partnership between Fairfield City Library Service and a local not-for-profit agency, MTC Work Solutions, has provided funding for guest speakers and refreshments for Fairfield's version of the Finding MY Place programme, discussed below. The library provides the venue, liaison with the schools and logistical support, while MTC Work Solutions provides contacts with speakers and assists with funding for the associated costs.

This programme fits MTC Work Solutions' key objectives of helping at risk young people gain personal skills, education and employment (South West Connect, 2010; MTC Work Solutions, 2011).

There are a number of strategies that can be engaged, in order to help achieve sustainable partnerships:

1   Know the organizational vision and ensure that all programmes and projects meet the key performance outcomes of your organization, as well as any partner organizations.
2   Make connections and build partnerships with other groups who have a similar vision, as they may have access to other funding and/or expertise.
3   Learn to write good grant applications, including meaningful evaluation processes, and then ensure that you use the statistics and the evaluation results to back up progress reports to the funding body.
4   Invite key people from the relevant funding organizations and the media to launches, celebrations, etc. and ensure that they get good publicity from the event.
5   Providing positive feedback to the funding agency is very effective, when it is received from parents, teachers and the young people themselves.

Connecting and engaging with targeted sections of the community

One of the dilemmas of public library service is the need to provide an equitable service to everybody in the community - effectively, becoming all things to all people - usually with diminishing staffing and budgets. In practice, this means that decisions must be made to target specific groups with specific programmes and resources. This section outlines some of the target groups, including multicultural communities, at risk young people, indigenous children, schools and families, all of which have been successfully reached by libraries throughout Australia.

Multicultural communities

As our communities become more culturally diverse, libraries need to adjust their resources, services and events so as to better meet the changing needs of their communities. One such community is Fairfield, Sydney, and the following section gives some examples of the way that the library service is working within its diverse community.

CASE STUDY: Fairfield City Library and Museum

Fairfield City is located about 32 km south-west of Sydney's Central Business District and covers an area of approximately 104 square km. It has a population of just over 194,000, with 49% born in a non-English speaking country and 67.3% speaking a language other than English at home. Of the current population, 20.1% are between five and 17 years of age. Fairfield City is rated the most socially and economically disadvantaged local government area in Sydney, according to the SEIFA (Socio-Economic Indexes for Areas) Index of Relative Socio-Economic Disadvantage (Fairfield City Council, 2010).

For the Fairfield Library and Museum Service, connecting and engaging with children and young people in this very multicultural community has revolved around programmes and resources designed to build literacy and language skills, as well as ways to promote cultural harmony. Supporting this important skill development and cultural harmony are key elements of Fairfield City Council's city plan (2007), and therefore they sit within the funding criteria. Research by the library service and other community agencies has highlighted the need for literacy-based programmes in the Fairfield area (Bourke, 2007). The library service provides resources in 16 major community languages and provides access to other languages, through loans from the State Library of New South Wales. Specialist outreach librarians for children and young adults, the culturally and linguistically diverse (CALD) community, learning and development, and local studies all work with other staff and the local community to find out what they require and to promote library services and resources to the different parts of the community.

Some examples of these outreach activities are:

1   A joint project by the CALD and children's and young adults outreach librarians offered to the Intensive English classes of one of the local high schools. The librarians work with interpreters, so as to explain to these newly arrived teens (many of whom are refugees) the specific services that the library can offer to support them in their learning.

2   The Outreach Librarian–Local Studies organization has instituted an annual high school project, where students help create digital content relating to their school. One school principal commented that the project was exactly what the school was looking for to help them collate, digitize, archive and celebrate their history and achievements as a school. The programme culminates in an event called Achievers Day, where 100 Year 9 to Year 11 students (15 to 17 year olds) get the opportunity to hear former students talk about their lives after school and some inspiring career options that are open to them. It is also an opportunity for students to consider librarianship as a career option. This programme provides ongoing partnerships between the library and local

schools, which facilitates future projects. After Achievers Day, one school invited library staff to address their teaching staff on the services and resources that the library had to offer staff and students.

3   The Fairfield City Museum and Gallery facilitated a programme called Our Neighbourhood, which engaged ten local students to work with a photographer in a week-long photography workshop, a digital media exhibition, a blog and a printed catalogue featuring the student's images. This project aimed at engaging young people in the process of recording their own cultural history, while learning new skills and building community awareness. One of the young photographers from this project was subsequently engaged by the Council to provide community photographs for an early literacy book ActiveGator's Adventure, which is discussed later in the chapter.

4   Family literacy classes are on offer for students who are struggling with reading and writing in English, as are homework centres, staffed by qualified teachers two afternoons a week at four locations; online tutoring is available from 4pm to 8pm on weeknights, either in the library or remotely, from home internet connections using a library membership; there are subject support lectures for senior students and space for study.

These programmes aim to actively encourage local young people to participate in the community across cultural, socioeconomic and geographical boundaries and, in the process to develop skills, which will support them in their educational and career aims. The most effective promotion is achieved by directly targeting specific groups. This is often in partnership with schools, early childhood centres and other agencies that work with young people and their families in the community and use all of the promotional strategies outlined earlier.

At-risk youth

At risk young people are not a typical target audience of public libraries, who tend to appeal to the more academically minded student. The Finding MY Place programme highlights the way that public libraries can be an active part of the solution to the growing trend of disengaged youth in our communities.

CASE STUDY: Finding MY Place

Natasha Griggs, creator of the programme Finding MY Place (FMP), makes the bold statement that Finding MY Place 'has proven that librarians can have a profound positive impact on disadvantaged youth' (Griggs, 2010, 42). The programme had a small beginning in the city of Belmont, Western Australia, in 2003. Natasha was concerned that while the library service was actively working with babies, toddlers and younger school-aged children, it was not reaching some of the most disadvantaged members of the community – teenagers who were disengaging from the school system, before they had completed a reasonable level of education.

In order to meet the needs of these young people, a partnership was set up between the city of Belmont and the Department of Education and Training of Western Australia. This led to the creation of Finding MY Place – a series of workshops run in the library for young people, many of whom are indigenous and who are considered at risk of disengaging from the school system. One of the key aims is to help young people to find their 'place', both in the school system and in the community. Students are chosen by the school and are given the choice to attend the workshops in the library once a week, instead of coming to school. While many of them come from disadvantaged backgrounds and have poor literacy and numeracy skills, the library is still seen as a friendly community space. Specialist workshop presenters are sourced through community agencies, on the basis of their ability to connect with young people and allow them an opportunity for growth. The workshops include topics such as self-defence, healthy relationships, and job and study skills, as well as opportunities to consider different career paths and future options. The presenters engage students and get them involved in activities to build self-confidence and problem-solving skills, and also deal with behavioural issues. The students have the opportunity to look at alternative options for education, employment and personal life in a non-threatening environment (Adeline, 2010).

The success of the initial pilot programme in the city of Belmont led to the expansion of this programme to 49 public libraries and 75 schools across Western Australia. The programme has also been successful in Victoria and South Australia and is currently in the process of being set up in New South Wales. The individual programmes are based on the original Western Australian Finding MY Place model, although they may take a slightly different form, in order to suit local conditions. Finding MY Place has also diversified into offering a programme for children in their final year of primary school, as an early intervention strategy, with those at risk of disengagement (Griggs, 2010).

Indigenous children

The overall size of indigenous community in Australia is very small, approximately 2.4% of the population. However, indigenous communities tend to be strongly represented in some parts of the country, particularly Queensland and the Northern Territory. Several libraries have set up programmes specifically for indigenous children, and two of these are discussed in detail below.

CASE STUDY: Culture Love – art and culture school holiday programme for indigenous young people

In Queensland, specialized library services, called indigenous knowledge centres (IKCs), are run by a trained local community member and provide traditional library resources and services to indigenous communities, as well as safe places, where the community can share and learn in a culturally appropriate setting. The State Library of Queensland, in partnership with indigenous shire councils through their local IKCs, has set up a unique school holiday programme called Culture Love. The programme is run by the IKC co-ordinator, using local artists and volunteers to provide an opportunity for young people to develop skills in arts-based activities. It is intergenerational and gives children and young people access to learning from elders in their community. Wujal Wujal Aboriginal Shire Council in far North Queensland has a population of 356, with 28 as the median age (University of Queensland, 2010). In this community, nearly 100% of the children and young people attended a Culture Love session in 2010. Using the theme 'Our Community, Our People', children worked with a singer-songwriter to create a song in both English and their local language about what their community means to them (FNQ Independent, 2010).

CASE STUDY: Kids Activity Time (KAT) Tales in the Park – indigenous storytelling project case study, City of Palmerston Library, Northern Territory

KAT Tales is a storytelling programme, which uses indigenous storytellers and stories to connect with, and engage, the local community. While targeted to six to 12 year olds in the indigenous community, the sessions are open to the whole community, as a way of promoting and sharing cultures. Palmerston population includes 14% indigenous people and more than half of these are under 18. Despite this, there are few culturally specific services that are currently available for young people in the area. In this programme, indigenous elders are able to share their stories with the younger generations. It is also a way of increasing the number of indigenous adults and young people who regularly use the library service (Howarth, 2008).

The funding for the programme came from the Australian Government Department of Communications, Information Technology and the Arts and allowed the indigenous storyteller to be a paid position. While the library service found that sourcing the storytellers and encouraging the indigenous community to attend the sessions was a challenge, overall, the programme has been able to open broader communication and cultural understanding in the community.

School support

CASE STUDY: Tutoring Australasia/University of Western Sydney/ Council partnership

In order to provide the services which are needed in local communities, regardless of restricted budgets, it is necessary for library services to look beyond their own walls to the corporate world and academic institutions. Several innovative partnerships have been formed between 14 local councils, four universities and the online tutoring company, Tutoring Australasia. Separate memoranda of understanding (MOUs) are set up between the councils and the other parties involved. The MOUs allow each partnership to set the parameters and time frames of the partnership, so as to suit local needs and differences. They also allow libraries to have a guaranteed funding stream for a set number of years. An example of this is the first such partnership between the University of Western Sydney, Tutoring Australasia and Fairfield City Council.

The partnership provides high quality, real time, online educational assistance by experienced tutors to primary and high school students in a wide range of subjects, including mathematics, English, science, essay writing and research. This is accessed in a number of ways, through the library's website, through public access PCs, in one of the libraries or remotely from home. The students log in, using their library barcode to provide access to the service. The day-to-day running of the service, including recruiting and training the tutors, as well as monthly educational reporting, is carried out by Tutoring Australasia. The University of Western Sydney matches Fairfield City Council's funding dollar for dollar, which enables this very crucial service to be offered to a much larger target group of students.

This programme adds great value to the students' lives, and their feedback comments show this. An example of a favourite student feedback comment on the programme was this short missive from a Year 9 (15-year-old) student, who wrote: 'thnx so much, you helped me finish my assignment, thnx again. Mwa, mwa, mwa (represent sms text kisses) XOXOXO' (personal communication).

By connecting and engaging with businesses and universities, public libraries are building a more sustainable funding basis, as well as providing a better service to their customers. In this case, the library is able to offer twice as much access to the online tutoring service than it would be able to provide without the financial support of the university. The university benefits, by having a larger pool of young people completing their school studies successfully and being in a position to attend university, thus building increased sustainability of tertiary participation. These partnerships are directly promoted to students through school visits, to parents through school newsletters and parents and citizens groups, through local media, as well as through the marketing arms of Tutoring Australasia, the universities and the councils that are involved.

Family support

CASE STUDY: Pizza and Pages after school club case study, Kyogle, NSW

Kyogle is a town of approximately 9500 people, set in the beautiful hinterland of the far north coast of New South Wales; it is called the 'Gateway to the Rainforests'. Kyogle Library is a small branch library of the Richmond–Upper Clarence Regional Library Service. One of the issues associated with regional living is that young people often live a long way from their schools and can, therefore, be required to wait in the closest town for parents to pick them up after school. Therefore, the library service offers a place where young people can wait, while also offering the benefits of homework and social support.

Pizza and Pages youth book clubs have been running in the USA and Australia for many years. The Kyogle club was modelled on other existing clubs, but was modified to meet the specific needs of the local community. The main changes are that the club is a youth-directed programme, which is run by the young people themselves, with minimal input from library staff, and it also includes peer-taught craft sessions. The young people themselves decide what activity they are interested in, and one of their number demonstrates the skills and knowledge to the rest.

This programme can easily run on a modest budget and requires minimal supervision and guidance from staff on the day. The library service promotes the programme, through flyers and the local council's website. This is a value-added service, which allows the local young people the opportunity to practise leadership and organizational skills, as well as encouraging positive use of the library service (Kyogle Council, 2011; Hughes, 2010).

Conclusion - sustainability

How can we ensure that programmes, activities and even libraries are sustainable? In 2009, the State Library of NSW commissioned a study into the future of public libraries in NSW. Known as the Bookends Scenarios (State Library of NSW, 2009), some of the possible futures portray a rather bleak image for libraries. While all the scenarios provide a place for libraries, their role differs dramatically, from a no-tech community space to an almost entirely virtual existence. The importance of libraries taking a proactive stance, by connecting and engaging with their communities now, has become very clear:

> The 'Shush!' days are over! Making connections with users, stakeholders and the broader community and engaging them in the work of the library will become increasingly important to counter scenarios where society becomes highly fragmented along socioeconomic and/or technology lines.
>
> (State Library of NSW, 2009, 53)

To be sustainable, we need to make best use of the current technologies. Libraries can get young people on board as content creators, not just as consumers. For example, the Our Neighbourhood programme, which gave young people the opportunity to participate in building the cultural record of their community, is one effective, encompassing way to achieve this aim.

Libraries also need to look at ways of providing a sustainable service, which goes beyond reliance on technology. The only given related to technology is that it will continue to change and evolve and will require ongoing flexibility in our organizations. However, the partnerships and networks that we develop in our communities will help provide a stronger basis for our programmes and activities. Library funding is far from guaranteed, and staff expertise can be limited in some areas, but partners can provide extra funding, expertise and, most importantly, other avenues of promotion. Partners and networks enable information about services and programmes to be spread much more widely than through the normal library promotional channels. This allows us to reach audiences who might not otherwise get to hear about the services and resources that the local library has to offer.

To connect and engage with our communities, librarians need to consider all the major target audiences – the babies and young children, the six to 18 year olds, their families, the aging population, our staff, other stakeholders and funding bodies. Key strategies to reach these audiences will need to be planned and executed. The examples given in this chapter show that public libraries can be involved in innovative programmes and partnerships, which not only raise the profile of the library service, but bring increased social capital to their communities. The Finding MY Place programme illustrates that an idea by one librarian can make significant changes to individual young people's lives, reach a previously unreached segment of the community, build positive relationships with schools, government departments and non-government agencies and, ultimately, start something positive that spreads across a whole nation.

Each local community differs in many ways, but the need for partnerships and networks, as well as adaptability to current technologies, remains a constant.

Public libraries are well placed to build these kinds of partnerships and, consequently, make a significant difference to their communities, if librarians are willing to step outside their comfort zones. A proactive approach to programming, resources and marketing is the key to connecting and engaging target audiences and, ultimately, to securing the public library's position as a valuable and viable community asset.

References

Adeline, D. (2010) *Finding MY Place Term 2 2010*, unpublished report.

Australian Bureau of Statistics (2010),
      www.ausstats.abs.gov.au.

Australian Institute of Health and Welfare (2009) Australia's Population: children and young people. In Australian Institute of Health and Welfare (eds), *Australia's Welfare 2009*, Australian Government,
      www.aihw.gov.au/WorkArea/DownloadAsset.aspx?id=6442455453.

Bourke, C. (2005) *Building Social Capital through Networking: how public libraries can be more than repositories of information*, State Library of New South Wales,
      www.sl.nsw.gov.au/about/awards/docs/building_social_capital.pdf.

Bourke, C. (2007) Working with Schools, Parents and Other Community Groups. In Bundy, A. (ed.), *Learning Futures: public libraries for the new generations in Australia and New Zealand: proceedings of a conference held on 9-10 March 2007, Adelaide, Victoria*, Auslib Press.

Bourke, C. (2010) Library Youth Spaces vs Youth Friendly Libraries: how to make the most of what you have. In Bundy, A. (ed.), *12 to 24s@ Your Public Library in Australia and New Zealand: proceedings of a conference held on 11-12 June 2010, Beenleigh*, Auslib Press.

Fairfield City Council (2007) *Fairfield City Plan, Broad Aim 2: a healthy, skilled and resourceful population; Broad Aim 6: cultural harmony*.

Fairfield City Council (2010) *Community Profile*, www.fairfieldcity.nsw.gov.au.

FNQ Independent (2010) Wujal Wujal Artists Join Holiday Program, *Far North Queensland Independent*, 21 January.

Griggs, N. (2010) Finding My Place: a Western Australian public library program for at risk youth, with national potential. In Bundy, A. (ed.) *12 to 24s@ Your Public Library in Australia and New Zealand: proceedings of a conference held on 11-12 June 2010, Beenleigh*, Auslib Press.

Howarth, S. (2008) *Indigenous Storytelling Project*, unpublished report.

Hughes, C. (2010) E-mail correspondence with author.

Kyogle Council (2011) *Kyogle Library FAQ*, Auslib.
      Press,www.kyogle.nsw.gov.au/library/faqs/1286.html.

MTC Work Solutions (2011) *Youth Connections*,
    www.mtcwork.com.au/youth.php?file=youth04.htm.
Quilty, P. (2011) *ActiveGator's Adventure: Fairfield City's multilingual literacy initiative*,
    Local Government Cultural Awards,
    http://culturalawards2011.lgsa.org.au/projects/10-activegators-adventure-fairfield-
    citys-multilingual-literacy-initiative.
South West Connect (2010) Finding MY Place, *The Link Newsletter*, **15** (4), 2,
    www.swconnect.org.au/Portals/swconnect/docs/newsletters/.
State Library of NSW (2009) *The Bookends Scenarios: alternative futures for the public
    library network in NSW in 2030*, State Library of NSW in association with Neville
    Freeman Agency,
    www.sl.nsw.gov.au/services/public_libraries/publications/docs/
    bookendsscenarios.pdf.
University of Queensland (2010) *Queensland Places: Wujal Wujal Aboriginal Shire*,
    http://queenslandplaces.com.au/wujal-wujal-aboriginal-shire-council.

Websites

Australian Bureau of Statistics, www.ausstats.abs.gov.au.
Finding My Place, www.kojonup.wa.gov.au/shire_services/library/finding_my_place.

10 Case study. Partnerships and library outreach in the National Year of Reading 2008

Carolynn Rankin

Introduction

This chapter will discuss the Government-sponsored National Year of Reading (NYR), held in the UK in 2008. The NYR was designed as a social marketing campaign, and the chapter will provide a description of the planning, promotion and delivery of the NYR, so as to show the attempt to reach specific target groups. The discussion will focus on the role of public libraries as key partners in delivering the campaign. During the NYR, a number of reviews and evaluations were undertaken, and the chapter will comment on findings from a case study in Yorkshire, which used the generic social outcomes framework to look at the impact of NYR in two public library authorities. Views and observations from the library staff involved in the NYR, in the Yorkshire case study, are used to highlight the challenges and successes that were involved in the 2008 campaign. The practitioner voice is important – and this chapter reflects the librarians' view of their experience in planning and delivering the NYR, as part of outreach work with children and young people.

NYR 2008 – celebrating and encouraging reading

The aim of the first Year of Reading in 1998 was to promote a culture of reading. Ten years on, the aim of the second NYR was to promote reading in the family and beyond and to help build a nation of readers (Thomson, 2009). The government-sponsored NYR campaign was about celebrating and encouraging reading in all its forms, aiming to promote reading in the family and to help to build a nation of readers. Plans for a second NYR were announced in February 2007, and the campaign ran from January to December 2008, with organizations and local authorities asked to pledge and plan their support between January and March. The Department for Children, Schools and Families (DCSF) commissioned the National Literacy Trust (NLT), with lead partner The Reading Agency, to run the NYR campaign, supported by a consortium of organizations committed to promoting reading. The consortium included Arts Council England, Booktrust, Campaign for Learning, Centre for Literacy in Primary Education, ContinYou, Museums Libraries and Archives Council, The National Youth Agency, NIACE and Volunteer Reading Help.

To create a national public relations campaign and provide advocacy, the NLT recruited a central NYR team, who also represented the NYR at national level to various stakeholders and government departments. The central team provided support for the local NYR co-ordinators, who were nominated in upper-tier local authorities in England. In recognition of the particular role of libraries in supporting reading, library authorities also nominated a lead contact to work directly with the Central NYR Team Library Advisor.

The NYR as a social marketing campaign

The NYR campaign wanted to engage all schools, libraries, community and voluntary organizations, as well as the business sector, in reading activities and celebrations. These activities started in April 2008 to support ongoing work to achieve national literacy targets, engage parents and families in reading with their children, and develop adult literacy. The NYR was promoted as a social marketing campaign. Social marketing is one of many marketing activities undertaken by the non-profit sector, aiming to influence social behaviours, to benefit not the marketer, but the target audience and society in general. It relies on the principles and techniques developed by commercial marketing, especially the marketing mix strategies, conventionally called the 4Ps – product, price, place and promotion. Kotler and Lee (2008) emphasize that social marketing is about influencing behaviours and trying to influence the target audience towards four voluntary behavioural changes – accepting a new behaviour, rejecting potential undesirable behaviour, modifying a current behaviour or abandoning an old, undesirable behaviour. The NYR campaign focused on community mobilization related behaviour, associated with literacy. The key values that were identified for the year-long social marketing campaign were:

- impact – both personal and social
- celebration – positive, enjoyable experiences
- diversity – of reading experiences and communities
- participation – co-production of the year, with communities and partners
- creativity – in development and delivery

- legacy – to create a lasting change in lives and systems.

The NYR campaign strategy was to create a network of partnerships to provide engagement and to stimulate community-based reading activities. There was a desire to encourage reading for pleasure, but also as a means of learning, achievement and individual prospects.

Low literacy levels are seen as a barrier to social justice, producing social, economic and cultural exclusion that can scar communities and undermine necessary social cohesion (Dugdale and Clark, 2008). Competence in literacy is essential for life in contemporary society, as it dramatically contributes to people's emotional well-being, mental health and economic success. The NYR campaign addressed specific audiences, who had low levels of literacy, where there was evidence that these were associated with low perceptions of the value of literacy. Whilst the NYR included a universal offer, the DCSF also identified the following priority underachieving audiences:

- early years
- National Curriculum Key Stage 3 (ages 11 to 14), especially boys
- white, working-class boys on free school meals
- blind and partially sighted children
- children with dyslexia
- looked after children (this term is generally used to mean those looked after by the state)
- Bangladeshi and Pakistani children
- Eastern European children
- Skills for Life adults (a Government strategy developed to improve the basic skills of adult literacy, numeracy and English for Speakers of Other Languages (ESOL)).

A number of secondary target audiences were also identified, including the extended family, the childcare workforce, adult learners, the primary and secondary school workforce and the children's workforce.

The campaign planning acknowledged that for some target groups reading has an image problem. This challenge was confirmed, by research undertaken by the NLT into young people's self-perception as readers (Clark and Osbourne, 2008). Self-professed 'non-readers' find reading boring, and they do not see its relevance to their lives outside school. Clarke and Douglas (2011) investigated young people's attitudes to reading and writing and suggest that the promotion of reading to children and young people reached a peak in 2008, with the NYR campaign. The focus of much of this activity has been on the 'narrowing the gap' target audiences – in other words, those pupils who had been identified as being less likely to reach the expected levels in reading and writing. Engaging these complex target audiences is particularly challenging, and aspects of literacy and reading support are discussed further in Chapter 3 by Birdi, Chapter 5 by Brock and Rankin, and Chapter 6 by Brock and Coughlin.

The public library contribution to NYR partnerships

Public libraries were identified as central to the NYR campaign, and there was a 100% sign-up rate from the 149 public library authorities (Thomson, 2009, 10). Public libraries in the UK are at the heart of their local communities, providing universal services that are open to everyone, reflecting the diversity of the population that they serve (Goulding, 2006; McMenemy, 2008). In order to meet key legal requirements, a local library service must provide services for both adults and children and offer value for money, working in partnership with other authorities and agencies. Guidelines from the Chartered Institute of Library and Information Professions (CILIP) state that a good library service should provide a positive experience for local people. Libraries meet key policy objectives by providing a positive future for children and young people; strong, safe and sustainable communities; equality, community cohesion and social justice; and health improvements and general well-being (CILIP, 2010, 3). The contribution that public libraries make to their communities is discussed further in Chapter 1. The enjoyment and promotion of reading is at the heart of public library provision, and for many decades librarians have been actively promoting reading campaigns, targeting children and young people (Freeman, 2009).

The inclusion of public libraries as key partners is built on three themes, first identified as priorities in the 1998 campaign, held a decade earlier. These themes were changing attitudes to reading among different audiences, the role of libraries in developing readers, and working in partnership (NLT, 1999; Streatfield et al., 1999). The first NYR, in 1998, provided many opportunities, not only for the emergence of numerous reading promotion and literacy development schemes, but also for existing schemes to raise their profile (Ghelani, 1999; Hall, 2000; Attenborough, 2000). Dolan and Khan (2011, 85) note that the 2008 NYR campaign involved many partners, and 'it gave libraries a bigger stage on which to perform'. Librarians were involved in local authority NYR steering groups, which brought together many different services and agencies, and early on there was a realization that the NYR provided an opportunity for creative connections. A librarian, describing his involvement in the local steering group, stated:

> We suddenly got access to everyone else's knowledge and could piggy back on other people's events. The NYR was a way of reaching other staff. People don't always respond to e-mails – meeting people makes such a difference.

There was an impetus and a specific focus for the local steering groups to work together on joint projects, as the NYR provided a banner head to help promote outreach work. As one interviewee pointed out:

> When it is NYR, you can say to people, 'come along for NYR, and let's plan to do this', but, whereas, if you say, 'come along and talk about literacy in the community', then it is a little bit vague . . .

The inclusion of public libraries as key partners effectively acknowledged that public libraries make a measurable and substantial contribution to local economies and help to bridge social divides. This observation from a Yorkshire librarian, actively involved in the NYR, acknowledged the importance of the library as a place:

> In terms of redevelopment, a place becomes a hub, if it becomes a place where the community gets used to expecting exciting and valuable reading events, workshops, festivals on a regular basis. I hope that will emerge from the NYR.

The NYR media campaign and library membership

The NYR campaign needed to focus on ways of attracting people to start reading or to develop their existing literacy skills. A national headline media campaign promoted several targeted key messages:

- Everything begins with reading.
- Join your library – everything you could wish to read, for free.
- Reading anything, anytime, anywhere is good.

The year launched with the library campaign to promote the accessibility of reading to all citizens, beginning with a four-page supplement in the *Daily Mirror* newspaper on the joys of libraries. This was mailed to one million homes of target families and subsequently circulated to 600,000 individuals, via the *Sunday People* newspaper. A key measure of the success of this approach was the drive to increase library membership. The initial new membership target, which was agreed with the Society of Chief Librarians, to be achieved between April and

December 2008, was a total of 300,000. According to the evaluation report published by the NLT, by the end of the year, the total was 2.3 million new members, far exceeding all initial target expectations. (Thomson, 2009, 55).

The NYR also had exposure on UK television. The 'Consequences' TV filler advertisement featured comedians and other celebrities, who created a short filler film, promoting the key messages for the year – that we all read in a range of media for a range of purposes. The examples included everything from domestic DIY and cookery to reading for pleasure and entertainment. The filler was made available via YouTube and for partners to broadcast locally – it is worth a watch.

Monthly themes and the Wikireadia good practice guide

The NYR coordinators received regular newsletters, and, to help with planning for the year, the NYR central team suggested monthly themes, as a focus for promotional activities. Many libraries used this as a basis for enhancing existing programmes or introducing new ideas; Table 10.1 lists the suggested themes.

Table 10.1 *Monthly themes in the National Year of Reading, 2008*

Month (2008)	Theme
April	Read all about it! Links to newspapers and magazines. The library membership campaign.
May	Mind and Body. Reading and learning at work. The knock-on benefits of reading.
June	Reading escapes. Holiday and summer reads.
July	Rhythm and Rhyme. Poems, poetry and lyrics.
August	Read the Game. The influence of sport, and how this can help promote reading.
September	You are what you read. Cultural, personal and local identity.
October	Word of Mouth. Storytellings, reading out loud, reading together, reading aloud, live literature.
November	Screen reads. Exploring the diversity of reading and writing; scripts, TV and films.
December	Write the future. Writing, texting, blogging, etc.

Library practitioners were encouraged to share ideas and good practice about reading and literacy events, using the newly created Wikireadia. A wiki is an online collaborative space, which allows a group of people to pool their knowledge, in order to create the best possible resource. Anyone can add to or edit pages in a wiki – the website can be developed with no prior knowledge of HTML or other any other mark-up languages. The Wikireadia that was developed as part of the NYR was promoted as a searchable and editable encyclopedia of good practice in reading, writing, listening and speaking. It provides an interesting record of all sorts of library-related activities and events that took place during the NYR, and it is still available, as a shared resource and reference point.

The evaluation of the NYR campaign

In the informative *Reading: The Future* report, Thomson (2009) provides a detailed account of the experience of running a national communications campaign and offers an evaluation of the NYR. The campaign reached nearly 13 million individuals in the target social groups C2DE. (The national readership survey (NRS) social grades are a UK system of demographic classification based on occupation. C2DE refers to the lowest three social and economic groups in society.)

The headline results of the report *Reading: the future* include the following encouraging changes in behaviour:

1 There was an increase in library membership nationally, with 2.3 million new library members recruited between April and December 2008, far exceeding expectations.
2 There was a significant increase, from 58% to 70%, in library membership among C2DE parents and their children.
3 The proportion of C2DE parents reading to their children every day increased from 5% to 20%.
4 Over a quarter of C2DE fathers who read to their children said that they now read every day – this was a significant increase, compared with 19% at the baseline survey.
5 There was a significant increase in children saying that they read with their mothers every day – 32%, up from 17%.

The report commentary includes case study descriptions of many of the organizations that were involved and the events that took place. Thomson (2009) also provides information on the NYR work plan and the messaging activity that was aimed at different target groups.

Review of cross-authority partnership working by ERS

In October 2008, ERS (consultants in economic research) were commissioned to review the NYR. They looked at the implementation of cross-authority partnerships working at local levels, in order to help inform the development of legacy. The framework for this review was not agreed with DCSF until the autumn of 2008 and so was not part of the original briefing to local authorities at the start of NYR. The ERS report highlights issues raised in consultation with stakeholders across the 35 local authorities and feedback from 85 NYR co-ordinators. One common concern was that the restricted planning time led to many areas focusing on the delivery of activities, rather than adopting a more strategic approach. A positive outcome of NYR involvement, for some, was the adoption of a stronger performance culture, driven by senior managers within the library service. This recognized the value of clearly showing the contribution that reading and literacy (and library service projects) can provide to the achievement of local targets and partner's strategic objectives. The ERS report provides a thorough background for those interested in a more detailed overview of the implementation and delivery of the campaign (ERS, 2009).

NYR in Yorkshire case study – the librarians' perspective

The next section will provide an overview of the NYR campaign in the Yorkshire case study. Yorkshire had a regional co-ordinator, who was interested in mapping the impact of the project and, therefore, built an evaluation project into the work of the steering group. Researchers from Leeds Metropolitan University were contracted by Museums, Libraries and Archives, Yorkshire (MLA, Yorkshire) to carry out a longitudinal evaluation of the social impact of the NYR in Yorkshire. The Generic Social Outcomes (GSO) framework was used to help show evidence of the public library offerings in two contrasting public library authorities, Calderdale and North Lincolnshire. For those interested in the methodology that was utilised, a more detailed commentary on the evaluation project has been published by Rankin (2012) and Rankin, Brock and Matthews (2009), and a case study was published on the MLA website (Rankin and Brock, 2009). This was primarily a qualitative study, involving the gathering, analysis and interpretation of information from semi-structured interviews with librarians and group discussions with NYR steering groups. The interviews formed the basis of the case study conducted in 2008 and 2010, and included questions concerning the target beneficiaries of NYR, what was happening with partnerships and experiences of cross departmental working. Supplementary information was provided by readily available material produced for general promotional purposes, such as leaflets, brochures, advertisements, photographs and website links.

The GSO framework was developed and piloted by the Burns Owen Partnership (BOP) in 2005. It was devised using a bottom-up process of developing the framework with practitioners and a top-down process of aligning the sector's potential social contribution with key drivers of government policy. The result was the creation of three broad thematic areas, referred to as first-tier outcomes. The first tier in the GSO framework is stronger and safer communities, strengthening public life, and health and well-being. These are then sub-divided into more detailed areas (MLA, 2008). The GSO framework can be used by practitioners to help provide evidence for how public libraries contribute to diverse agendas and demonstrate their value to the community. Public library authorities can use this evidence for planning and advocacy, with a range of audiences, including local and central government.

Outreach and engagement – what happened in Yorkshire

The NYR promoted a year of engagement with reading and literacy for a diverse range of children and young people. Library services have many activities and services on offer all year round for these target groups, but in this year events could be 'badged' as part of the NYR, providing extra publicity and awareness. The evidence showed that many new events and activities were held, using the NYR as an opportunity to try out partnerships and to entice the public to get involved. These activities included new literary festivals, reading volunteer schemes, manga events in the public library and even a bear hunt in a country park. Many librarians stepped up to the challenge afforded by the NYR:

> The NYR has pushed towards a service located outside the library. Were it not for the NYR, we would have contented ourselves with providing stock within the library, and the outreach might not have happened.

Another benefit for the library practitioners was an increased knowledge of different genres and types of events that were possible. A librarian in North Lincolnshire organized the physical space for a brand new event to take place and quickly recognized the value in connecting with a wider community of potential users:

> The Manga event brought all sorts of people into the library, who have never been before. I want to go one step further and consult those people about using our services.

Information on NYR-related events was regularly posted to Wikireadia, promoted via library websites and also offered via photo opportunities for local newspapers, which were keen to record the community involvement. Although many partnerships existed before the campaign, the public library profile was undoubtedly raised through NYR. This encouraged partners to approach the library to be involved in new initiatives and enabled libraries to show their impact in helping children and young people to enjoy life and make a positive contribution to their communities. The library interviewees, who recorded their views during year, felt extremely strongly that partnerships were a key aspect of the NYR activities:

> There will be people in early years teams or education departments who have the same outlook on life as children's librarians, who are there to encourage children to want to have that experience of reading, and reading for pleasure . . . so, you know, there are good partnerships there already, but the NYR has given us an opportunity to provide extra focus.

It is interesting to review the comments from library interviewees in phase two of the evaluation project, 18 months after the NYR campaign had finished. There is evidence that effective connections were made at the practitioner level:

> We do a lot of partnership work – we are heavily involved, now, in Every Child a Talker – our profile was raised in NYR and that means that the people we work with come to us now, without us having to push it.

The steering groups in both of the Yorkshire case studies had some success in their joint endeavours, but there were challenges in working in NYR partnership activities. The NYR steering groups brought together people with different organizational agendas and expectations of the campaign. For the library staff, the opportunity to get involved in NYR activity had a clear purpose, as the promotion of reading and reader development is core business. For other partner organizations, the NYR engagement may have been less clear. Maintaining contacts requires dedication, and keeping track of new initiatives is demanding. Keeping the momentum going in such partnerships is challenging, particularly at a time of shrinking budgets and making decisions about who will pay for activities involving people and resources. There were positive outcomes in the two locations, driven by highly motivated practitioners, who were using the NYR as a focal point for showcasing new projects and refreshing ideas about existing provision. The NYR proved to be an opportunity for stimulation, and it was hugely effective in further developing both existing and new partnerships.

The interviewees reflected positively upon the challenges offered by the NYR. These included the initial problems around NYR promotion and publicity and the difficulties of getting the year under way, with minimal time to plan and implement. The absence of any additional funding was an issue – this was in direct contrast with those who had experience of the first NYR in 1998, when bids for funding provided additional local resources.

Some observations on the NYR Yorkshire case study

The NYR objectives were dedicated to a specific point in time, making it easy for a wide range of organizations to get involved. In the Yorkshire case study the campaign provided the impetus for joint events and initiatives; some were built on existing relationships, some relationships were consolidated and others planted seeds for the future.

Using the NYR activities, the GSO framework helped to show how libraries can contribute to diverse agendas and thus demonstrate their value in the community. The Yorkshire evaluation showed that there is a wealth of goodwill and professionalism evident among the library staff who participated in the interviews. It is clear that there is a keenness not only to improve services, but also to contribute to the betterment of the lives of local people. As indicated throughout the chapter, NYR provided a strong focus to the year and helped to raise the profile of library services in both the local authorities under discussion. The NYR has certainly had an impact on the visibility of reading in local communities, and the analysis of the evidence gives an indication of the enthusiasm and professionalism that was involved in delivering the campaign. This is an example of adventurous and successful outreach planning shared during an interview focused on the bear hunt event:

> Do you know the children's book *We're going on a Bear Hunt?* We are going to recreate that as part of an 'Art in the Park' weekend. We are going to tell the story as we walk through the long grass, and I'm planning to be dressed in a bear costume. When we were first thinking of hiring a bear costume, they were all booked, because it is the same weekend as the 'Book Start' day, but we have located one now. I have been out planning my route – I think the event will have a real impact and be something different and capture families who are not coming through a library or a reading event, but are coming to an art and craft event.

This event took place in Normanby Hall Country Park, near Scunthorpe, and is a great example of the energy and enterprise of library staff during the NYR. It attracted hundreds of children and their families. As the librarian with experience of dressing in a bear suit expressed it: 'Doing library promotion in a country park was an unexpected outcome of NYR.' As well as running the bear hunt, the library staff created a children's library on the grass, providing lots of books for families to share. The bear hunt also showed how, with the support of the children's library service, a day out in the park could offer a safe, inclusive environment. This intergenerational experience provided the opportunity to read books and engage in interactive stories in an unusual setting.

The feeling of achievement and accomplishment might be best summed up in the very positive comment made by one librarian: 'Why can't every year be a National Year of Reading?'

What comes next . . . Reading for Life

The NYR was designed as a social marketing campaign and this chapter has discussed the key role of public libraries in delivering the campaign aims and objectives. It has drawn on evidence from published research evaluations and the voices of library practitioners in a Yorkshire case study. It can be seen that the NYR enhanced the partnership opportunities for those involved, encouraging them to provide innovative activities for the target groups. The responses and involvement from children and young people demonstrate the wealth of literary experiences during the NYR. To build on the success of the NYR, the Reading for Life campaign was launched in 2009, with the aim of improving the life opportunities of people in need through reading. Online resources and support materials developed in the NYR are available, via the Reading for Life website, including support for local authorities to develop cross-cutting reading strategies. Children's librarians and young people's librarians are continuing to encourage reading for pleasure and as a means of learning, achievement and individual prospects. Reading anything, anytime, anywhere is a positive experience.

References

Attenborough, L. (2000) The National Year of Reading in the United Kingdom, *New Review of Children's Literature and Librarianship*, **6** (1), 103–13.

CILIP (2010) *What Makes a Good Library Service? Guidelines on public library provision in England for portfolio holders in local councils*, Chartered Institute of Library and Information Professionals,
www.cilip.org.uk/get-involved/advocacy/public-libraries/Documents/What_makes_a_good_library_service_CILIP_guidelines.

Clark, C. and Douglas, J. (2011) *Young People's Reading and Writing: an in-depth study focusing on enjoyment, behaviour, attitudes and attainment*, National Literacy Trust.

Clark, C. and Osbourne, S. (2008) *How Does Age Relate to Pupils' Perception of Themselves as Readers*, National Literacy Trust.

Dolan, J. and Khan, A. (2011) The More they Change, the More they Stay the Same:

public libraries and social inclusion. In Baker, D. and Evans, W. (eds), *Libraries in Society: role, responsibility and future in an age of change*, Chandos.

Dugdale, G. and Clark C. (2008) *Literacy Changes Lives: an advocacy resource*, National Literacy Trust.

ERS (2009) *Local Authorities in the National Year of Reading: a review of cross-authority partnership working*,
www.literacytrust.org.uk/assets/0000/3233/NYR_Final_Report.pdf.

Freeman, M. (2009) Reader Development in Practice: bringing literature to readers, *New Library World*, **110** (7/8), 392-3.

Ghelani, T. (1999) Reading is Fundamental: value of a national book promotion initiative, *New Review of Children's Literature and Librarianship*, **5** (1), 105-13.

Goulding, A. (2006) *Public Libraries in the 21st Century: defining services and debating the future*, Ashgate.

Hall, C. (ed.) (2000) *Read Smarter, Not Harder: reading promotions for children's libraries*, Youth Libraries Group.

Kotler, P. and Lee, M. (2008) *Social Marketing: influencing behaviors for good*, 3rd edn, Sage Publications.

McMemeny, D. (2008) *The Public Library*, Facet Publishing.

MLA (2008) *Inspiring Learning: generic social outcomes*, Museums Libraries and Archives Council,
http://www.inspiringlearningforall.gov.uk/toolstemplates/genericsocial/.

NLT (1999) *Building a Nation of Readers: a review of the National Year of Reading*, Department for Education and Employment and the National Literacy Trust.

Rankin, C. (2012) The Potential of Generic Social Outcomes in Promoting the Positive Impact of the Public Library: evidence from the National Year of Reading in Yorkshire, *Evidence Based Library and Information Practice*, **7** (1), 7-21,
http://ejournals.library.ualberta.ca/index.php/EBLIP/article/view/11727.

Rankin, C. and Brock, A. (2009) *National Year of Reading Evaluation - Yorkshire, MLA case study*,
http://research.mla.gov.uk/case-studies/display-case-study.php?prnt=1&prjid=476.

Rankin, C., Brock, A. and Matthews, J. (2009) Why Can't Every Year be a National Year of Reading? An evaluation of the social impact of the National Year of Reading in Yorkshire, *Library and Information Research*, **33** (104), 11-25.

Streatfield, D. R., Tibbitts, D., Swan, R., Jefferies, G. and Downing, R. (1999) *Rediscovering Reading: an evaluation of the role of public libraries in the National Year of Reading*, Information Management Associates for the Library and Information Commission.

Thomson, A. (2009) *Reading: the future*, National Literacy Trust.

Websites

Consequences, www.youtube.com/watch?v=CuNqgEud7u8.

National Literacy Trust, www.literacytrust.org.uk.

Reading for Life, www.wordsforlife.org.uk/.

Wikireadia, www.wikireadia.org.uk/index.php?title=2008_National_Year_of_Reading.

PART 3

Buildings, design and space – libraries for children and young people

11 Library place and space transformation – designing for the digital natives

Carolynn Rankin

Introduction

Libraries today aim to attract children and young people, with a range of services and facilities appealing to the particular age groups. This includes a welcoming physical space, a rich mixture of books, computers and a range of activities and services. According to Lushington (2008, 8), successful children's library design in the 21st century will do the following:

- give children a choice when selecting their own materials to take home
- provide a comfortable place to use computers and do homework
- provide a variety of attractive programme and activities
- support the work of talented and well-trained children's librarians.

Added to this is the provision of a welcoming place to 'hang out' and socialize, particularly for teenagers and young people, who want to develop their independence. As discussed in Chapter 1, there are challenges facing public libraries in the digital age, as many other activities are competing for family time, and young people have opportunities to access knowledge and resources, without using the library. The children and young people of today represent the first generation to grow up spending their entire lives surrounded by, and using, computers, video games, digital music players, video cams, cell phones and all the other toys and tools of the digital age. Prensky (2001, 1) has designated this generation as the digital natives – all 'native speakers' of the digital language of computers, video games and the internet.

This chapter considers the design approaches that libraries have used and discusses what makes for a good design in children's libraries and library spaces designed for teenagers and young people. The challenges and opportunities relating to library space design for the five to 18 age range are discussed. The common factor relates to the use of the actual space, which brings the community under the same roof. The chapter is not attempting to be comprehensive, particularly in view of the differing needs and expectations of the wide age range, but rather is aiming to give examples of innovative practice and to suggest other sources of information. The focus will be on provision in public libraries, but it is important to also mention school library provision. Librarians have responded to the challenges brought about by the information age, and this chapter will discuss examples of innovative and successful designs from the UK and other parts of the world.

Space is a resource that needs to be well designed, in order to meet the present and future needs of those who use it, but it also is a resource that must be managed, along with stock, staff and finances. For those interested in trends in library design, Edwards (2009) provides a guide to addressing key design issues, in relation to the changing ways in which libraries are used, such as the digitization of knowledge and the impact of new technologies on reading and library practice. There are helpful books available on the topics of building and designing libraries (Sannwald, 2009; Dewe, 2006, 2008) and many sources of information on libraries for children and young people (Feinberg and Keller, 2010b; La Marca, 2010; Bolan, 2008a, 2008b; Lushington, 2008; Dubber and Lemaire, 2007; Dewe, 1995 and 2007; CILIP, 2002). American architect McCarthy (2007) gives overall guidance on creating a realistic budget for new library construction, determining the responsibilities on both sides and the importance of communication in effectively getting your case across.

Library practitioners need to negotiate with architects and designers in order to achieve a successful end product that is fit for purpose. To ensure that your library provides the best possible environment for the children and young people who use it, it is important to take the time to consider the most appropriate and user-friendly layout, structure and design of the building. A well designed building has a greater value to all involved. Planning a new or refurbished public library means considering not only facilities for collections, services, staff and users, but also examining the local context, reviewing the library image and developing relationships with other community facilities and agencies (Dewe, 2006). As Derr and Rhodes observe: 'Engaging young people with public libraries is not about changing what a public library is; it is more about expanding its stereotypical definitions and broadening or reassessing its capabilities, capacity and potential within the community' (2010, 12). The next section will discuss the role of the library building in the community.

The case for the place – the library in the community

There is a strongly held view that libraries offer a welcoming, neutral space that provides opportunities for personal, cultural and community development in appropriate circumstances (Harris and Dudley, 2005, 18). Research by Ipsos MORI (2003) demonstrates the impact of the built environment on our quality of life. Homes, schools, surgeries, streets and parks combine to form the 'physical capital' of a local area. If we are concerned about improving quality of life, then we must focus more attention on the design quality of our urban fabric. Policy-makers have been focusing on the importance of social capital, deprivation and cohesion over the last few years, and the evidence suggests that we should also be paying attention to the very structure and nature of the places we are creating (Ipsos MORI, 2003, 3).

In his book *The Great Good Place*, the urban sociologist Oldenburg writes about the importance of informal public gathering places and why these are essential to community and public life (1999). He identifies third places, or great good places, as the public domains on neutral ground, where people can gather and interact. In contrast to first places (home) and second places (work), third places allow people to put aside their concerns and simply enjoy the company and conversation around them. The library can, perhaps, be regarded as a 'third place' for children and their families, as it is a welcoming space for all. It can also be considered a 'third place' for teenagers, as it is a space where they can access needed resources and socialize and interact with their peers. As Van Riel, Fowler and Downes (2008, 78) observe: 'The public library is free, warm and safe. Friendly informality is a great strength of the UK public library tradition and it is why libraries have been safe havens for all kinds of people who are uncertain of their welcome elsewhere. Libraries should be proud of their record here.' Libraries can help to build social capital, by providing a safe place to meet, socialize and relax. In sum, they form an important part of our communities (Block, 2007).

Children's libraries – a brief look at design trends

It is only in relatively modern times that library special collections and services have been devoted specifically to the reading needs of children (Black, Pepper and Bagshaw, 2009). Early children's libraries were not for the very young, as the normal age range of the children's library was seven to 15 years old. Readers younger than seven years might be catered for at the discretion of the librarian, while the upper age limit was sometimes dropped to 14 years. At the turn of the 20th century, the need for children's libraries was by no means accepted, but after the First World War, work with children became increasing recognized as a legitimate and important aspect of librarianship. Increased demand for children's facilities came from the growth of children's literacy, following the arrival of compulsory education. Libraries responded by attempting to satisfy the growing demand for reading materials.

As a building-type, the design history of children's libraries has existed for little more than a century. Black and Rankin (2011) investigated the history of children's library design, mainly in a UK context, and identified four periods, each of which is characterized by distinct design themes. These four design themes describe the children's library: school and shelter; middle-class domesticity and constructive play; open plan and modern office; and domestic comfort zone and pop culture playground. The current trends show that the original schoolroom image has now diminished, and the early shelter function of the children's library can be seen, today, in its role as a cocooned comfort zone. The open plan of post-war modernism was in keeping with contemporary developments in office design. The domestic environment, in the 1920s and 1930s, has recently re-appeared, under the guise of the high-styled IKEA-like environments for young library users. Design for constructive play in the interwar period has re-emerged in the early 21st century, in the form of the children's library as a playground. Now, many children's libraries have space designed for puppet shows and activity areas. A current trend is for funky furniture, such as reading towers and pods, which encourage a playful engagement with the space. Innovative design incorporates multimedia experiences – is this the way of the future? This presents a professional challenge for library practitioners, forcing a, perhaps welcome, change in the stereotypical view of the children's library setting.

Although the name 'library' is still a strong brand in society, today, we have many alternative names for children's libraries, such as Ideas Stores, Discovery Centres, Book Bars and The Trove. Library provision for teenagers and young people also has a variety of 'cool' names – for example, Teen Zone or Teen Space. Later in the chapter we will discuss the diversity of services on offer. So, what's in a name – is it all about image?

Meeting their needs – demographics and the digital natives

Digital technologies and new media are now prevalent in many aspects of day-to-day public and private life. This can be seen positively, as a cause for celebration and for optimistic predictions about life, work and learning in a networked society. For children and young people, who are already growing up in a world in which digital technologies are an everyday and familiar presence, it is especially important to become informed and educated digital participants, equipped with the capacities to be active in interpreting the world around them (Hague and Williamson, 2009). There is recognition in the library profession that service providers need to embrace the world of the digital natives – the born digitals – in order to make creative connections (Fasick, 2011). Prensky (2001) suggests that today's students are the digital natives, who need to learn in ways that are meaningful to them. Ito (2009) reports on a three-year ethnographic investigation in the USA into how young people are living and learning with new media in varied settings – at home, in after school activities and in online spaces. Today's teens seem constantly plugged in to video games, social network sites and text messaging, and this research investigates the intricate dynamics of youth's social and recreational use of digital media.

Libraries are potentially well placed to take advantage of new technologies, in order to extend their activities and support the reading and learning needs of the 'digital natives'. Librarians are aware of the importance of social media, and many are now actively using social software, in an attempt to get closer to their users, and, similarly, progressive library practitioners have started building a presence on MySpace and Facebook, by creating user profiles. By keeping up to date with social media trends, youth librarians at Wellington City Library in New Zealand have successfully used a variety of methods, including a Teen Blog, for initiating and maintaining contact with young people aged from 13 to 18 (Hannan, 2010).

Boon (2003, 151) points out that the designing of library space for young people takes specialist knowledge and skills, the most important of which is a knowledge of behaviour and information needs. There is a challenge to make the space inviting, so as to suit all ages across the youth spectrum. Public libraries are important in helping a young adult make the transition from childhood to adulthood, through an effectively designed young people's library space (Vandermark, 2003, 161). Encouraging young people to visit and enjoy libraries can be a rewarding experience, and it is important in creating the next generation of library users. The findings from a review of the literature indicate that teenagers are less likely to visit libraries, but there is evidence of services and programmes currently in place in libraries, which aim to reverse this trend (Snowball, 2008). From their experience as youth librarians in Melbourne Library Service in Australia, Derr and Rhodes (2010) comment that the needs of those 16 year olds and under differs strikingly from those over 16 years of age. Their wants, desires and expectations of the library service come from their life experiences and social, educational and cultural influences. They are growing into more independent living and socializing, and the challenge is to provide welcoming space in the library to network, socialize and enjoy the reading experience. However, Edwards (2009, 143) has suggested a polarization of library usage, with a backlash by older readers, who insist upon books, whilst younger readers avidly surf the internet. The two worlds are increasingly becoming separate systems, but the use of space in the public library can facilitate freedom and access to information cyber-culture.

Good design is important

The Commission for Architecture and the Built Environment (CABE) was set up in 1999, as the UK government's design champion. Funded through central government, it aims to promote the role of quality design in new buildings and produces a range of publications on planning and design (CABE, 2006). The interior design specialist Kugler has commented: 'Libraries are the new community living room, so the emphasis should be in creating liveable environments, that appeal to all senses not just the psyche' (Kugler, 2002). Children's library design has expanded to include a wide variety of functional concepts to satisfy the needs and wants of children. Design teams now use many different methods to create effective children's libraries. It is important to create a welcoming atmosphere in the space, and the ambience, layout, design, furniture and fittings will all have a part to play. The key physical elements which help create the 'library environment' are space, light, flow, materials and collection. The first four are architectural, while the last is concerned with the collection and its interaction, via book stacks and the building itself (Edwards, 2009, 142). Producing good designs requires more than an understanding of aesthetics – looks are undeniably important, but the usefulness of the end product is what really matters. An interior design brief is a document that outlines all aspects of the project. The role of a design brief is to inspire, to give direction and to ensure the required outcome is achieved. A successful design brief should consider the following:

- context – both within the organization and within the specific community
- current technological, social and service trends
- users and flow
- stakeholders – who is driving the project and why?
- desired outcomes – quantity and quality. (Kugler, 2007, 144)

Stanley (2003, 85) suggests that to maximize the design strategy opportunities when developing a new public library, the team should bring together a team, consisting of an architect, asset manager, librarian and, also, a retail consultant. Rachel Van Riel discusses using ideas from retail markets at length in Chapter 12.

There are many aspects of library design to consider, and Table 11.1 – based on McDonald (2007) – can be used as a planning framework for determining the best qualities that are required in designing and resourcing effective library spaces for children and young people.

Table 11.1	*Planning framework for considering aspects required in designing and resourcing effective library spaces for children and young people (based on McDonald, 2007)*
Functional	space that works well, looks good and lasts well
Adaptable	flexible space, the use of which can be easily changed
Varied	with a choice of learning, research and recreational spaces and different media
Interactive	well organized space, which promotes contact between users and services
Conducive	high-quality humane space, which motivates and inspires people
Environmentally suitable	with appropriate conditions for users, books and computers
Safe and secure	for people, collections, equipment, data and the building
Efficient	economic in space, staffing and running costs
Suitable for information technology	with flexible provision for users and staff
Oomph or 'wow' factor	inspirational space, which captures the minds of users and the spirit of the institution

Why should children's (and school) librarians be concerned about architecture and design?

The premise in this chapter is that librarians *should* be concerned about architecture and design, and, therefore, they should take an active interest in the place and space in which their services are delivered to the user community. Libraries began to change dramatically in the 1980s, with the introduction of new media formats, and Latimer and Niegaard (2007) remind us that from the beginning of the 21st century, the concept of the library began to shift in focus – from collections to connections and communications and from storage to access, in order to respond to the challenges posed by an increasingly digitized and networked information-based society. Architecture and design does matter, as it communicates identity and values, and well designed spaces are more efficient to manage and better cared for by the people who use them.

Library practitioners will have expertise in what is necessary, practical and desirable in the library. There may be an opportunity to be a member of a multi-disciplinary team planning a purpose-built setting in a new school or to be involved in the refurbishment in a public library setting. Perhaps you have been appointed to a new position and have inherited an existing children's library or you need to take a fresh look at the current provision in your area. Whatever the scenario, it can be beneficial to have a regular review of the use of the spaces provided for children and their families and young people. This demonstrates the positive impact of refurbishment at a library, from the perspective of a community librarian.

We have recently had Moor Allerton Library in Leeds, where I am based, refurbished, and it is lovely. In my opinion, it has fixed everything that is wrong in a lot of children's libraries – the improved layout, the shape, the height of the shelves, the attractive furniture, the great colour scheme. There's a wobbly mirror and a pod, which you will have to come and visit, if you want to know what it is.

From my office, there is a little porthole window into the library, and I can see kids literally running to grab books and then dive on the furniture to sit there and enjoy the books. And there's a big beanbag that they can throw themselves on, and they will keep doing that. They will sit and read for ages. You will see parents in there, too. I will sometimes go down to choose a book on something I am working on and then I will go back an hour or two later, and they are still there, because it is such a comfy environment, and the parents can sit there, too, and watch the children read and play.

(Katherine, community librarian)

There is considerable practical advice and expertise available to those about to embark on a building or refurbishment project for the first time, and decision-making can be supported, by looking at what has been achieved elsewhere. Feinberg and Keller (2010a) offer practical advice on the benefits of visiting other libraries and children's facilities during busy periods, so as to gather information about what works and what does not work. Good ideas for creating space can be inspired by looking at completed projects and talking to the staff involved about what has been successful or otherwise. Looking at the floor plans of other library projects can also be extremely helpful, as, when starting a new design, it is often hard to visualize size. Comparing your library's floor plans to an actual space helps staff to prepare for proportion and size, what the new space will feel like, how it will be used and whether the space is big enough for all the resources and activities that the library hopes to offer.

When looking for ideas, it can be helpful to look outside the usual library zone, as many of the materials on display or used in other spaces, such as museums, sport facilities and childcare settings, can be replicated or adapted for the public library environment. Creative ideas can be generated in consultation with families and youth users. This also presents an opportunity for librarians to take a more innovative approach to the design of space, as Nusrat - a children's librarian - argues:

I think it [design] is something we could improve on, though. I think, in general, we tend to come up with how many books we need to fit in, and we get the shelving people to provide different plans, and we work at that.

(Nusrat, children's librarian)

One freely available internet resource is the website Designing Libraries: the gateway to better library buildings. This was established in 2004 with funding from the Museums, Libraries and Archives Council (MLA), as part of its Framework for the Future programme. Designing Libraries is a gateway to the world of libraries and a source of information on all aspects of the design and use of library spaces, including virtual, as well as physical, spaces, with examples of practice from around the world. It also acts as a guide to products and services, innovation and development in the industries that partner with libraries, in the areas of design, technology, content and consultancy. It includes:

- a buildings database, providing a permanent record of library building, refurbishment, improvement and extension projects in the UK and Ireland
- a resource for interactively sharing expertise and experience on library planning and design, through discussion forums and email lists
- links to a range of online and offline resources, useful to anyone involved in planning, designing or building libraries.

Role of the librarian as client and consultation opportunities

A well designed building is one that contributes to the business, is suitable for its intended use and is built to last. Library staff may be asked to be part of a project team, working alongside other specialists in the development of a new centre or making contributions to planning discussions. This provides the opportunity to interact with the architects and designers commissioned to develop the plans. Khan (2009) provides a useful discussion checklist for librarian and architects. The client role is very important in the design-and-build partnership. As already suggested, to be a successful client, you can look at other library building projects to get ideas and talk to people involved in similar projects about their experiences. Another important aspect is to commit to sustainability (CABE, 2003) - the architect needs to know how the building will be used, who the clients will be, its purpose and how it will complement its surroundings. Decisions involving functions, budgets and materials performance are improved when people who are knowledgeable in these areas contribute their experience and expertise to the design. Architects and contractors can be asked to provide cost estimates for alternative designs and materials.

According to Feinberg and Keller (2010a), good library design is underpinned by:

- integrating ideas about how children and teenagers learn and perceive the world
- understanding how architectural and design features can influence learning and usage patterns
- listening to, interpreting and incorporating ideas from the staff and community
- reflecting the current and future goals of the library.

Professional knowledge and expertise can provide a very positive input to the planning discussions, but it may be equally important for the library staff to consult and listen to the views of the local user community. Where possible, children and their parents, teenagers and young people should be consulted and included in the resulting discussions, so as to allow the architect to fill in the details. The importance and value in this type of consultation is a consistent message throughout the literature related to building and redesigning libraries, and this approach is discussed in detail in the next section.

Consultation with users – involving children and young people in designing their library space

Innovative practitioners will actively involve children and young people in the design of the library spaces and the type of services and activities on offer (Bolan, 2006; Parsons, 2008). The 2020 Mars Express Project in Sweden involved children and young people in the development and design of the library room of their local library (Claesson, 2008; Håkansson, Claesson and Gullstrand, 2008). Based on Howard Gardner's educational theories about multiple intelligences (Gardner, 1993), the three-year project started by focusing on what public libraries needed to do, in order to develop into more interesting, creative and welcoming libraries for children and young people – in other words, to be perceived as places that will stimulate reading.

Mattern (2007) undertook extensive research on recent developments in a number of downtown American city libraries, including the design of library space for children and teenagers. Denver Public Library considered one of its primary roles to be that of a 'children's door to learning', and, early on in the design process, staff conducted focus groups with local Denver children and their parents. They learned that the children wanted a space that accommodated a variety of activities, from solitary reading to noisy group activities. These responses mirrored children's requests from elsewhere – the older children, aged between ten and 12, wanted a space of their own, others asked for nooks and crannies, kid-scaled service counters and kids-only computers, visual stimulation and comfortable furniture (Mattern, 2007, 30).

The Phoenix Public Library: Teen Central opened in 2001. The planning stage for the teenage space in the public library involved a teenage users group, whose members had taken part in planning sessions with the architect and explained how important it was that the teenage area *not* be a themed space. The teenagers asked for the space to have food and drinks, plenty of computers, a surround-sound system, video projection capability, CDs, magazines, videos and, of course, books. All of these requirements were provided, and Teen Central also has round computer kiosks to allow for collaborative work, group study rooms and private study areas. Teenagers used the downtown library for school research projects, and the open discussion enabled them to say that they would like the library to be open longer on a Sunday. The consultation in Phoenix revealed that for teenagers, the library was a social space just as much as it was a study space, and the young people preferred to help themselves, either because they might be intimidated by interaction with adult librarians or because they are too cool to ask for assistance.

For Phoenix's Teen Central and Denver's Children's Library to work, the library planners had to take control of the design process, and they had to know how to talk about design with teenagers and with children and their parents. The key issues are, then, when, and how, to allow the comments to inform the design (Mattern, 2007, 32). This is an important message for library practitioners, as it may mean carefully balancing users expectations following consultation, against what can feasibly be provided, within the budgetary, design and planning constraints. Consideration should also be given to consulting non-users about their views.

'An aquarium, a wobbly mirror and a reading tower please' – designing for children

Esson and Tyerman (1991) suggest that one of the most visible ways of creating a child-centred library is to locate the children's area in the main library. This raises the profile of the service, by making it highly visible. A ground floor location provides easy access for parents with small children and children with disabilities. However, controversy exists as to whether the children's library should be a separate room altogether or an area in the main library, as there are advantages and disadvantages to both scenarios. Lushington (2008, 71) discusses how in older buildings different library functions are often separated by solid walls; flexible open-plan libraries use functional zones and boundaries to separate activities that can conflict with each other. Having a separate library area allows children to make noise to a high level and makes it easier to carry out activities, such as film shows, musical events and messy crafts. Library practitioners in Denmark have recognized how future library services for children can match their media and various other cultural needs, with a focus on the position of play, social inclusion, cultural formation and good reading skills (Enemark, 2008).

Choosing books together is an important activity for children and their families. As practitioners, we may take our workplace setting for granted, but it is vital to remember to make book selection an enjoyable experience. Whitehead (2007) observes that careful thought and organization must go into the environment in which children hear stories and investigate books. Although Whitehead is primarily writing about the classroom setting, her ideas are applicable to library environments for young children. She suggests that the books should be displayed on tables and low shelves, with their attractive covers showing or open at interesting illustrations (Whitehead, 2007). See also Chapter 12, where Rachel Van Riel provides practical ideas about appropriate environments for young library users. Children already have great ideas about what they would like to see in a library. Peters Bookselling Service in the UK invited children to draw and describe 'My Dream Library' in a competition, and, with over 300 entries, the suggestions ranged from waterslides, jungle libraries and cola-bottle-shaped shelves to trampoline flooring, roller coasters, igloos, discos and even a casino. The theme running through all the entries was that children wanted somewhere fun and exciting to read, and that they view the library and books as a way to exercise their imagination (see the 'My Dream Library' 2010 winner and short-listed entries at www.peters-books.co.uk/news_20101208a.htm).

Exciting examples of children's designed spaces

The design of the new Jacksonville Public Library in Florida, which opened in 2005, came about as the result of an international design competition. This included the requirement to design discrete spaces for the children's and teen areas. The new Children's Library was created to reflect the geography of the region, with the entrance spaces modelled on the swamplands of northeast Florida - children enter through a two metre high sculptural rendition of the high swamp grasses that line the many inland waterways. Inside the library, the colours of the floors and walls reflect the dappled green and blue of the environment. Round 'porthole' windows between the main space and subsidiary creative labs give the feeling of being underwater. The various designated spaces are well used and allow for programming concurrently for different groups. There are two art-and-craft rooms, with sinks, flooring, which can be easily cleaned, work spaces and child-sized furniture. The message here is that the Children's Room should be a place for exploration, whether in books, on computers, through listening to stories, making music, singing and dancing, making crafts and interacting with other children and family members. Another lovely suggestion is to have a world globe in the children's area. Jacksonville has one in its children's space, and it has been so heavily used with little fingers 'finding' Jacksonville that Florida is now completely worn away.

The Trove in White Plains Public Library, New York, was opened in October 2005. It is a children's space that has been remodelled from the old space. The director, Sandra Miranda, wanted to re-create the library for a new generation that is used to being entertained, engaged and active. She and her staff looked at museums, playgrounds and bookstores for ideas. White Plains Library has created a multisensory, multimedia space. You actually enter The Trove through a jagged brick opening in the wall on the library's second floor – a motif for the traditional library that has been literally blown apart (Kenney, 2006; Rasmussen and Jochumsen, 2009). There is further information on The Trove in the case study by Sandra Miranda in Chapter 13.

The new Hjoerring central library, in the north of Denmark, opened in 2008. This library is on the first floor of a shopping centre, with 40 shops and underground parking for 500 cars. The library's identity is reflected in the red ribbon, or thread, winding through the whole space like veins – sometimes it is on the floor and sometimes it moves up from the floor, turning into tilted shelves, bookcases, seats and tables with bar stools. Sondergaard (2009, 74) discusses how the over-riding approach was to see the whole project in terms of the 'third place' – one of 'the great good places', mentioned by Oldenburg (1999). In the children's department, the designers wanted to express, even more strongly, the idea that experience includes the whole body. As a symbol of this, there is a rollercoaster bookcase in the middle of the library. There are areas for action and activity and areas that offer more silent pursuits, like the bubble wall with reading tubes. Another top priority is play – there are toys and a room for children's own play culture. The area for picture books is built up like a park with a tree, so the whole year round, children and their families can sit or lie in the park reading. There is also a VIP (Very Important Parents) corner, where adults can have coffee and browse the book collection (Lunden, 2009; Sondergaard, 2009).

Cerritos Public Library in California has won international recognition as The Experience Library, which offers themed places. During the design process, the city staff looked outside the library world, in order to find new ways to provide cutting-edge services, including interactive learning. The Guggenheim Museum in Bilbao, Spain, designed by Frank Gehry, served as an additional inspiration for the layout and modern design of the exterior of the building. At the entrance to the library, a floor-to-ceiling salt water aquarium sends the message that this is not an ordinary library. The library is designed and divided into eras and themes. Images and exhibits on display, as well as sounds emanating from the rainforest and aquarium areas, add to the multi-sensory experience for the visitor. When children walk through the ten-foot-tall book-shaped entrance, they actually become part of the story, as their image is captured in a story, shown on the TV monitor. The children's library is designed to stimulate children to explore, and it has a theme based on the concept 'Save the Planet', including a huge dinosaur skeleton, a rainforest and a lighthouse (Kaur-Petersen and Laerke, 2009).

Teenagers are a different species! – designing cool spaces

> There is no mistaking where you are and who the space is intended for.
> (Ikin, 2010, 75, describing the new Teen Space in
> Dunedin Public Library, New Zealand)

Libraries are in the unique position where they can help foster the digital growth of young people today. Teenagers today can use the library as an outlet, away from home and school, where they can meet to socialize and safely access the internet. Libraries can focus on updating or creating a teenager-only space, by offering suitable age-specific activities, fully developing the young adult collection and providing technology for teenagers to use to create and collaborate at the library. Bolan (2008b) provides a comprehensive overview of involving teenagers in the space renovation process, along with a discussion on what other libraries have achieved in this area.

The Dunedin Public Library in New Zealand opened its new Teen Space in the city library in May 2008, developed in consultation with Dunedin City Council youth action committee. The architect's aim was to make the space as different as possible from the rest of the library, just as a teenager aims to make their bedroom as different as possible from the rest of the family home. The Teen Space floor is covered with carpet tiles organized to appear as different rooms, and it has quirky and controversial design fittings. This is a library to investigate further, as the Teen Space won a Southern Architecture Award for its interior architecture. In the Teen Space 'a chaotic interior environment uses a strong conceptual basis to appeal to youth . . . the result is raw, fun and comfortable' (Ikin, 2010, 78).

Youth librarians in Melbourne, Australia, report on how the City Library has benefited from the inclusion of the Journal Café, located at its entrance. It also has a gaming area, with PlayStation and Wii, which are installed beside the audiovisual, graphic novel and zine collections. They reinforce the message of encouraging young people to feel welcome, and thus provide a space which enables them to behave in age-appropriate ways (Derr and Rhobes, 2010).

As we have already discussed, involving young people in creating new spaces and undertaking library makeovers will involve them in shaping services. There is a role for volunteer activism in designing and planning spaces. In the UK, The Reading Agency takes a strategic approach to library innovation, working alongside national and local partners to achieve greater community impact (The Reading Agency, n.d.). Its Big Lottery funded HeadSpace project has worked with young people across 20 libraries to develop youth-centred spaces and creative positive activities. Guidance from The Reading Agency indicates that the benefits of this approach include:

- a visible statement of the importance of young people's involvement
- a practical, hands-on activity that young people are likely to enjoy
- the creation of a new area that will be appealing and accessible to young people
- increased library membership and usage by young people
- opportunities to build lasting relationships between library staff and young people
- new ideas and fresh input that can be transferred to other library redevelopments
- a creative, educational activity that is likely to appeal to teachers and youth workers, who can provide young volunteers
- an opportunity to work in partnership with schools, youth groups and arts agencies.   (The Reading Agency, 2009)

Phoebe – a young local – on seeing the library space that she had helped to design as part of a HeadSpace project, stated:

> The colours really stand out, and the way we've done the shelves for the books and magazines and comics makes it really easy to find things. The seating is really relaxed, too – we've got beanbags, so you can move them around and sit where you want to. At the opening, I looked at it, and it was so satisfying, because we have been involved with it, and it has worked!
> (Phoebe Hill, HeadSpace, Lyme Regis) (The Reading Agency, 2009, 20)

In Jacksonville Public Library, the Teens' Library is located on the ground floor of the four-storey building, entered through a covered threshold, which is separate from the rest of the library and, thus, gives it a distinct identity. It is purposefully placed immediately adjacent to the popular materials area, which has a bookstore-feel, with casual seating, music listening stations, a dropped grid of spotlights, movable book and material cases, and a youthful sense of colour and design. Director Barbara Gubbin provides practical guidance, when she says that space used for teenagers must be flexible. This Teens' Library is used for a broad range of activities – groups using the computers, individuals listening to music, reading, making crafts, drawing and painting, writing, watching movies, talking, playing games on the computers and doing homework. One lesson learnt from the Teen Library in Jacksonville, Gubbin says, is to put as much as possible on wheels, so that it is easy to move around. Anticipate that teenagers will enjoy sitting on the floor and so provide the space and furnishings to support this preference.

School libraries in primary and secondary school settings

Many of the design issues in children's libraries are also of relevance in school libraries. There is a difference in core purpose and focus, as school libraries are there to support the curriculum. The emphasis is on a learning space, rather than a 'playful' environment. School libraries are essential to learning, and good design is seen as a central consideration in creating effective learning environments (see, for more information, the Designing Libraries website). School libraries are striving to create learning-driven environments, and the environment in which students learn affects their experiences and impacts on their attitudes towards learning. La Marca (2010) looks at research and learning theories and uses these as the foundation for planning. She provides a comprehensive overview of design considerations, including the issues associated with providing reflective and collaborative learning spaces, ICT requirements, lighting and acoustics. Recognizing that school libraries need careful planning in order to maximize both use and educational values, an Australian perspective is provided by La Marca (2007), using 12 case studies of school libraries from around Victoria. These examples include primary, secondary, state, Catholic and independent schools, with a wealth of useful ideas on how to decide on signage and furniture placement.

According to the CILIP guidelines for primary schools (2002), the library, ideally, should be a whole school resource and also be a single-use area, centrally located within the school. It should be easily accessible to all classes and all children, whatever their particular needs. These guidelines also provide basic advice on size and appropriate shelving types, furniture and equipment. There are also important issues to consider concerning the siting of school libraries. Lockwood (2008) raises some concerns about the physical location of primary school libraries, which are often relegated to a corridor or an inaccessible corner, resembling more of a storage space than the heart of a reading community.

Erikson and Markuson (2007) share their experiences of working on more than 100 media centre building projects in the USA, using conceptual plans from actual school libraries. They discuss floor plans, furniture, technology, bidding for funding and evaluation. The current and future technological needs of the student population, the unique needs of the community library that combines school and public library services, and sustainability and conservation issues to help designers and planners are all covered in this comprehensive text.

Practical stuff about designing
Space/room planning – some things to consider

A collaborative process acts to encourage people to think about how they are currently doing things and how they would, ideally, like to be doing them in the future. When planning the use of new space, keep in mind that the fixed features of a building can constrain its interior design. In the planning stage, also consider electrical outlets, plumbing, floor surface, lighting and the all-important natural light from available windows. A well-chosen colour scheme can also help towards creating the right atmosphere and image.

Lighting will control how the library feels and looks. A successful library must incorporate both the best of natural light and internal lighting techniques, in order to produce a truly flexible facility (Kennedy, 2003). As a general rule, readers like to work in natural light, but different lighting levels are needed for study spaces and for creating ambience in more reflective areas. In addition to this, adding varieties of mood lighting is essential for areas designed for teenagers.

Design to create boundaries

In the children's library, boundaries increase children's security and focus, protecting their activities from traffic and other distractions, and encouraging longer-lasting, sustained play. Think about different uses in the space that is available, and design quiet corners for reading and noisy stimulating spaces for role play and group activities. Even in a small room, well defined activity areas can be created, and children will show a higher degree of exploratory behaviour and social interaction as a consequence. Display and shelving space can act as boundaries, and a carpet can be a visual boundary, when used to designate a reading corner. Space should also be provided for puppet shows and storytelling.

Flexibility is important, and there are advantages in being able to offer a variety of room layouts. This allows for seasonal changes and for catering for different groups, with differing needs. New staff members will have different preferences, and space that may be shared by a number of partner organizations needs to be flexible. You can use portable screens and dividers to create small, cosy, safe places for individual work or expand an area for a storytelling group gathering.

Furniture and equipment

Check library furniture catalogues and attend conferences and tradeshows that display children's furniture and equipment, so as to see what is on offer and keep up to date. Furniture and equipment for the library setting should be sturdy enough to withstand energetic use. It will receive much greater wear and tear than in the average home. Only invest in technology, equipment or furniture which can withstand heavy use and can be repaired easily. For teenagers, include plenty of comfortable furniture - couches, coffee tables and beanbags. Your planning should include a selection of some heavy-duty furniture, as teenagers are very hard on furniture, as they like to lean back in chairs and share seats when they are socializing around computer screens (Vandermark, 2003).

In the children's library it is important to provide an inviting space, enhanced by carpeted floors and appropriate furniture. The exposure to language and literature begins with books and reading, so you need spaces where children, and the adults who are looking after them, can spend time with books. Comfort is an important consideration. Think carefully about the seating provided for adults, as not everyone wants to relax on floor cushions, however inviting they may appear. The Family Place Libraries model in the USA focuses on providing a nurturing family experience, and Family Place design integrates comfortable adult seating into the children's area (Feinberg et al., 2007). When considering the purchase of furniture, such as tables and chairs, ask your suppliers to let you try them out before you decide to buy. You can involve parents, children and young people in helping to choose comfy, squashy sofas and contemporary and imaginative seating.

Jacksonville Public Library has custom-made furniture in the shapes of local plants and animals. A large circular bench is in the form of an alligator, another in the form of a manatee, a third like a lotus blossom. There are chairs that look like leaves, turtles and snails, and small tables that take the form of mushrooms (Gubbin and Lamis, 2009).

A number of companies produce furniture that can double for book display and be used for playful activity. For example, a reading tower, produced by The Opening the Book Company, has an upper level with back shelving for older children and a lower level with picture-book shelving for younger children. A book loft or raised area is a great place to curl up with a book and is a popular addition to a children's library, as are ever-popular reading trees.

Carpets and soft furnishings

Carpeting is the preferred library flooring material, mainly for its acoustical absorbency. The interior designer Celia Kugler uses flooring and, in particular, carpet tiles to create logical spaces and to help make busy places in libraries accessible to the public. As well as defining zones, carpet tiles can help with way-finding and framing the furniture within any given space. Carpet tiles are cost effective and are the most inexpensive and easily changeable flooring material available today. Carpets can also act as room dividers, showing where a story time or group activity area starts.

Signage and guiding

The signs in your library are an important part of the communication system with users. Signs with friendly wording (in more than one language) will make people feel more welcome. Dewe (2006, 27) discusses how to improve the appeal and signage of library buildings by adopting the ethos of the bookstore, supermarket and other retail outlets. Libraries rely on signs to help users find their way around. Library signs and guiding may be overlooked at the planning stage. Consider the impact on your users and avoid having too many signs and, equally, signs with too many words or signs which are too big or too small. Dewe (2006, 263) suggests that signs and guiding perform three main tasks:

- to inform – plans, opening-time notices, safety procedures
- to direct – arrows to destinations
- to identify – when a destination has been reached, such as toilets or the information desk.

Signage that gives children visual and textual pointers to what is available should be a strong design feature. Makaton signage (a language programme that uses signs and symbols to teach communication, language and literacy skills) can also be displayed and act to provide children and families with special educational needs full access to resources. Leeds Library and Information Services provides access to Boardmaker software, so as to enable staff and users to make simple signs (Tutin, 2011).

Noise

When designing a library, the impact of noise is an important aspect to consider, but it is often overlooked. In a shared public library building, there may be some tensions when adult and children's services share the same space. Children and adolescents need to make noise, and chatting with friends is an important part of socializing. Adult users tend to find the noise from children's library settings intrusive and undesirable, especially when sound from children's activities spills over into the adult (quiet) areas of the library. Undesirable noise can be dampened by using curtains, textured wall hangings and carpets and sound-absorbent ceiling materials.

Conclusion: future libraries, innovative libraries

This chapter has discussed the importance of architecture and design for libraries for children and young people. There are wonderful examples of innovative and exciting library designs from all around the world. Major city public libraries are more likely to have the funding and investment to create the immediate 'oomph' or 'wow' factor, as suggested by McDonald (2007). However, it is possible to create a pleasing impact on a modest budget and in a smaller space, by clever use of furniture and effective presentation of the book stock. The characteristics of the future-innovative library can, therefore, be summarized as:

- a place of change – interactive and dynamic
- excitable and adaptive
- light, spacious – easy patron flow
- educational, entertaining, busy
- multi-sensory – look, touch, listen, read, talk
- upgraded often. (Kugler, 2002)

There are examples of innovative ideas from all over the world, as librarians work with their available place and space to offer traditional book-based services, blended with the latest interactive, digital options. The library has a continued role as a valued, trusted community place that can offer learning via experience for the digital natives. In the next chapter, Rachel Van Riel will discuss the children's room as a specialized space in the public library.

References

Black, A. and Rankin, C. (2011) The History of Children's Library Design: continuities and discontinuities. In Bonn, I., Cranfield, A. and Latimer, K. (eds), *Designing Library Spaces for Children*, De Gruyter Saur.

Black, A., Pepper, S. and Bagshaw, K. (2009) *Books, Buildings and Social Engineering: early public libraries in Britain from past to present*, Ashgate.

Block, M. (2007) *The Thriving Library: successful strategies for challenging times*, Information Today.

Bolan, K. (2006) Looks Like Teen Spirit, *School Library Journal*, **52** (11), 44-8.

Bolan, K. (2008a) *The Need for Teen Spaces in Public Libraries*, American Library Association, www.ala.org/yalsa/guidelines/whitepapers/teenspaces.

Bolan, K. (2008b) *Teen Spaces: the step-by-step library makeover*, 2nd edn, ALA Editions.

Boon, L. (2003) Designing Library Space for Children and Adolescents. In McCabe, G. B. and Kennedy, J. R. (eds), *Planning the Modern Public Library Building*, Greenwood Press.

CABE (2003) *Creating Excellent Buildings: a guide for clients*, Commission for Architecture and the Built Environment.

CABE (2006) *Better Public Building*, Commission for Architecture and the Built Environment and Department for Culture, Media and Sport.

CILIP (2002) *The Primary School Guidelines*, Chartered Institute of Library and Information Professionals.

Claesson, L. (2008) The Key to Future Libraries for Children and Young People, *Scandinavian Public Library Quarterly*, **41** (3), 10-11 .

Derr, L. and Rhodes, A. (2010) The Public Library as Urban Youth Space: redefining public libraries through services and space for young people for an über experience. In Bundy, A. (ed.) *12 to 24s @ Your Public Library in Australia and New Zealand: proceedings of a conference held in June 2010, Beenleigh*, Auslib Press.

Dewe, M. (1995) *Planning and Designing Libraries for Children and Young People*, Library Association Publishing.

Dewe, M. (2006) *Planning Public Library Buildings: concepts and issues for the librarian*, Ashgate.

Dewe, M. (2007) *Ideas and Designs: creating the environment for the primary school library*, School Library Association.

Dewe, M. (2008) *Renewing Our Libraries: case studies in re-planning and refurbishment*, Ashgate.

Dubber, G. and Lemaire, K. (2007) *Visionary Spaces: designing and planning a secondary school library*, School Library Association.

Edwards, B. (2009) *Libraries and Learning Resource Centres*, 2nd edn, Architectural Press.

Enemark, A. (2008) Ten Commandments for the Future Children Library, *Scandinavian Public Library Quarterly*, **41** (3), 8-9.

Erikson, R. and Markuson, C. (2007) *Designing the School Library Media Centre for the Future*, 2nd edn, American Library Association.

Esson, K. and Tyerman, K. (1991) *Library Provision for Children*, AAL Publishing.

Fasick, A. (2011) *From Boardbook to Facebook: children's services in an interactive age*, Libraries Unlimited.

Feinberg, S. and Keller, J. R. (2010a) *Designing Space for Children and Teens*, American Libraries, http://americanlibrariesmagazine.org/features/03142010/designing-space-children-and-teens.

Feinberg, S and Keller, J. R. (2010b) Designing Space for Children and Teens in Libraries and Public Places, ALA Publications.

Feinberg, S., Deerr, K., Jordan, B., Byrne, M. and Kropp, L. (2007) *The Family-Centered Library Handbook: rethinking library spaces and services*, Neal-Schuman.

Gardner, H. (1993) *Multiple Intelligences: the theory in practice*, Basic Books.

Gubbin, B. and Lamis, A. (2009) Jacksonville Public Library Children's and Teens Libraries, *'Libraries Create Futures: building on cultural heritage': proceedings of the World Library and Information Congress: 75th IFLA General Conference and Assembly held on 23-7 August 2009, Milan*, International Federation of Library Associations and Institutions, www.ifla.org/annual-conference/ifla75/index.htm.

Hague, C. and Williamson, B. (2009) *Digital Participation, Digital Literacy and School Subjects: a review of the policies, literature and evidence*, Futurelab.

Håkansson, E., Claesson, L. and Gullstrand, A. (2008) 2020 Mars Express – towards the future children's and young adult's library, *World Library and Information Congress: proceedings of the 74th IFLA General Conference held on 10-14 August 2008, Québec*, International Federation of Library Associations and Institutions, ifla.queenslibrary.org/IV/ifla74/papers/155-Hakansson_Claesson_Gullstrand-en.pdf..

Hannan, A. (2010) Communication 101: we have made contact with teens. In Bundy, A. (ed.), *12 to 24s @ Your Public Library in Australia and New Zealand: proceedings of a conference held in June 2010, Beenleigh*, Auslib Press.

Harris, K. and Dudley, M. (2005) *Public Libraries and Community Cohesion – developing indicators*, Museums, Libraries and Archives Council.

Ikin, S. (2010) Our Library Their Space: the Dunedin City Library Teen Space. In Bundy, A. (ed.), *12 to 24s @ Your Public Library in Australia and New Zealand: proceedings of a conference held in June 2010, Beenleigh*, Auslib Press.

Ipsos MORI (2005) *Physical capital: liveability in 2005*, Ipsos MORI.

Ito, M. (2009) *Hanging Out, Messing Around, and Geeking Out: kids living and learning with New Media*, MIT Press.

Kaur-Petersen, R. and Laerke, J. (2009) Cerritos Public Library – world-famous library for experience and learning. In Niegaard, H., Lauridsen, J. and Schulz, K. (eds), *Library Space: inspiration for building and design*, Danish Library Association.

Kennedy, J. R. (2003) The Importance of Lighting. In McCabe, G. B. and Kennedy, J. R. (eds), *Planning the Modern Public Library Building*, Greenwood Press.

Kenney, B. (2006) Welcome to the Fun House: when is a children's room not a children's room? When it's The Trove, *Library Journal,* **131** (9), 58.

Khan, A. (2009) *Better by Design - an introduction to planning and designing a new library building,* Facet Publishing.

Kugler, C. (2002) Spaced out in the Digital Age: the future of library design,*The Inside Story: a library interiors forum held on 3-4 February 2002, organized by the State Library of Victoria, Melbourne.*

Kugler, C. (2007) Interior Design Considerations and Developing the Brief. In Latimer, K. and Niegaard, H. (eds), *IFLA Library Building Guidelines: developments and reflections,* K. G. Saur.

La Marca, S. (ed.) (2007) *Rethink! Ideas for inspiring school library design,* School Library Association of Victoria.

La Marca, S. (2010) *Designing the Learning Environment: learning in a changing world,* Australian Council for Educational Research Ltd and ACER Press.

Latimer, K. and Niegaard, H. (eds) (2007) *IFLA Library Building Guidelines: developments and reflections,* K. G. Saur.

Lockwood, M. (2008) *Promoting Reading for Pleasure in the Primary School,* Sage Publications.

Lunden, T. (2009) The Red Thread - new central library in Hjoerring, Denmark, *'Libraries Create Futures: building on cultural heritage': proceedings of the World Library and Information Congress: 75th IFLA General Conference and Assembly held on 23-7 August 2009, Milan,* International Federation of Library Associations and Institutions.

Lushington, N. (2008) *Libraries Designed for Kids,* Facet Publishing.

Mattern, S. (2007) *The New Downtown Library: designing with communities,* University of Minnesota Press.

McCabe, G. B. and Kennedy, J. R. (eds) (2003) *Planning the Modern Public Library Building,* Libraries Unlimited.

McCarthy, R. C. (2007) *Managing Your Library Construction Project: a step-by-step guide,* American Library Association.

McDonald, A. (2007) The Top Ten Qualities of a Good Library Space. In Latimer, K. and Niegaard, H. (eds), *IFLA Library Building Guidelines: developments and reflections,* K. G. Saur.

Oldenburg, R. (1999) *The Great Good Place: cafes, coffee shops, bookstores, bars, hair salons and other hangouts at the heart of a community,* 3rd edn, Marlowe & Co.

Parsons, S. (2008) Lancashire's Innovative Get it Loud in Libraries Initiative, *Public Library Journal,* Summer, 2-4.

Prensky, M. (2001) *Digital Natives, Digital Immigrants,* www.marcprensky.com/writing/Prensky%20-%20Digital%20Natives, %20Digital%20Immigrants%20-%20Part1.pdf.

Rasmussen, C. and Jochumsen, H. (2009) Urban Development and Libraries - the children's library as placemaker. In Niegaard, H., Lauridsen, J. and Schulz, K. (eds), *Library Space: inspiration for building and design*, Danish Library Association.

Sannwald, W. W. (2009) *Checklist of Library Design Considerations*, 5th edn, American Library Association.

Snowball, C. (2008) Enticing Teenagers into the Library, *Library Review*, **57** (1), 25-35.

Sondergaard, B. (2009) The Red Ribbon. (In Hjorring). In Niegaard, H., Lauridsen, J. and Schulz, K. (eds), *Library Space: inspiration for building and design*, Danish Library Association.

Stanley, J. (2003) Retail Technology Applications and their Role in the Modern Library. In McCabe, G. B. and Kennedy, J. R. (eds), *Planning the Modern Public Library Building*, Greenwood Press.

The Reading Agency (n.d.) *HeadSpace: the first 3 years*, The Reading Agency, www.readingagency.org.uk/young/HeadSpace%20Update%20June%202010%20 20-%20edit%5B2%5D.pdf.

The Reading Agency (2009) *Participate: involving young people; youth involvement methods*, The Reading Agency, http://readingagency.org.uk/young/Youth%20Involvement%20methods.pdf.

Tutin, J. (2011) *Across the Board: Boardmaker in Leeds Library and Information Service, Implementation Report*, Leeds Library and Information Service.

Vandermark, S. (2003) Using Teen-Patrons as a Resource in Planning Young Adult Library Space in Public Libraries. In McCabe, G. B. and Kennedy, J. R. (eds), *Planning the Modern Public Library Building*, Greenwood Press.

Van Riel, R., Fowler, O. and Downes, A. (2008) *The Reader-Friendly Library Service*, Society of Chief Librarians.

Whitehead, M. (2007) *Developing Language and Literacy for Young Children*, 3rd edn, Paul Chapman.

Websites

Boardmaker in Leeds Libraries, www.leeds.gov.uk/boardmaker.
Designing Libraries Database, www.designinglibraries.org.uk.
The Reading Agency, http://readingagency.org.uk/.

12 Making space for reading – designing library spaces for children in public and school libraries

Rachel Van Riel

Introduction

Libraries have a long and proud tradition of providing services for children. In the UK, a library card is a child's first public expression of independent participation as a citizen in a local democracy; on all other formal papers, a child is an appendage to an adult, but a library ticket carries the child's own name and can be used without adult support. Library staff were also among the first to address the child directly, not their accompanying adult, and the library was established early on as a safe space for a young child to make an independent journey to. It was quite normal, as a child in the early 1960s, for me to make a three-mile bus trip to the library by myself on a Saturday morning, from the age of eight.

When I began working in public libraries in the 1980s, I found a tradition of active intervention in working with children, which was not part of adult library work, until the influence of reader development in the 1990s. Staff saw their role as active and developmental – engaging with individuals and helping them move forward, not just providing materials and leaving customers to find their own way. This meant lots of group activities – reading aloud, craft sessions – as well as engaging with individual children about their reading choices. In many places there was an articulated understanding of an open value system; everyone knew that if a child expressed enthusiasm for a popular format, whether superheroes or pony books, this should be met with encouragement and not disapproval. The approach should always be 'and have you seen this as well?', not 'why don't you read this instead?'

With book issues on the increase and children's publishing booming, should we expect that children's libraries are safe to continue and grow, on the assumption that their place in culture and community is assured? This chapter will argue that radical shifts in thinking and practice are needed, in order to keep children's libraries as relevant and valued in the next 30 years as they have been in the last 30 years.

Making the physical space attractive

The physical presentation of the library experience is the issue that is most in need of rethinking. This is true of both public and school libraries. The contents of the library may be rich and varied, and the staff, similarly, may be wonderful and helpful, but does the first impression, looking in from the doorway, convey this reality? Children in the Western world are sophisticated consumers; they are used to commercial standards of presentation, both in real life and on television. If we want to make our services easily accessible, we need to present them as 'readable', in the same way.

It is possible to challenge the dominant commercial presentation of the 21st century and offer children an alternative experience, but you are likely to need far more money and available staff to do this successfully, rather than less. Rum för Barn, in the Kulturhuset in Stockholm, was set up on Rudolf Steiner principles in 2005. The library offers a series of specially created environments to stimulate awareness, exploration and imagination. The core area, for four to seven year-olds, is especially successful, with a magical storybook environment, built in traditional wood and full of clever details to discover. The philosophy, certainly in the early years, immediately after opening, was disciplined and consistent; children arriving on group visits were taken through stages of adjustment and focus. There is also a great arts workshop space, adjacent to the library, where an extensive complementary programme of children's art workshops is run every day. The emphasis is on developing a child's imaginative growth, using simple materials to create stories and art. Computers were not included, on principle, and all of the more commercial entertainments that are now aimed at children were excluded. The anti-commercial stance is followed through, in offering high-quality alternative experiences.

Let us return, however, to the more common experience of children's and school libraries in the UK – a large space, which may be awkward in shape, large quantities of shelving, which is inflexible, furniture acquired over the years, which does not match, and a proliferation of posters and notices on every available wall space. It is possible to use basic design principles to improve the experience, even where there is very little budget available. In the future, maybe learning such principles should be part of professional training. Library staff need to understand the basic concepts of spatial design, people flow and use of colours; these are all objective principles, which should replace the personal taste of individual staff, which is often the only criterion to fall back on.

If your space is too small, and you want to make it feel bigger, you will need to keep clean lines, remove clutter and maintain a unity of colour and finish. Make sure that not all the space can be seen at once, even the smallest space can contain another area to discover. If your space feels large and cold, you can make it friendly, by breaking it into separate areas, each with a distinct identity. Here, you can use colour to zone the space, make contrasts of busy and quiet areas and build sightlines, which pull people forward into the space and create routes through it.

Always work with your building and not against it. You may not like its proportions or materials, but trying to disguise them never works. The space will look better, the more that you reveal the original concept of the architecture, whether that is Carnegie late-Victorian, 1960s feature brickwork and wood or modern glass and concrete. You can place contemporary shelving and furniture in any building, as long as you respect the building's volumes and features. Library staff are sometimes too fond of complaining that the space is wrong, instead of looking at how to make it right. This is, partly, a lack of confidence and skill; a clear training need can be identified here. As I have already suggested, the librarian of the future will need to better understand how to manage space, so as to create enticing customer experiences.

Creating a welcoming experience

The first, and perhaps the hardest, thing to learn is to see the space through the eyes of your customers. Library staff tend to assume that everyone entering the area will know how friendly and helpful they are, but the first impression that will be made will be determined by what the environment looks like, not by an encounter with library staff. A survey of non-users in Kent Libraries in 2002 revealed greater levels of negativity towards libraries among children aged six to ten, than in any other age group (Wilkins and Jenkins, 2002). Of the children surveyed, 75% felt that libraries were uncomfortable, and only 42% of children who were surveyed thought that libraries were welcoming. The report concluded that this perception may be discouraging the use of libraries and that better furniture is needed.

Children's libraries must appeal across the age spectrum. Suffice to say that a nine year old and a three year old have very different needs and tastes. The desire to signal children quickly and to instantly differentiate them from adults means that children's spaces tend to announce somewhat young messages very strongly. Wall decorations - for example, cartoon characters, alphabets and famous storybook characters - are designed to appeal to young children. Children's furnishings are offered in strong primary colours; shelving, kinderboxes, seating and rugs all come in bright red, blue, green and yellow. All of this adds up to a message which speaks directly to under-fives and their carers. Maybe this was a very important message 20 years ago, when libraries had to convince parents, carers and other children's professionals that children could come to the library before they were of school age and before they could read. But now, this message, appealing to the very young, is making it harder to attract the older children, who tend to use libraries less.

The under-fives do not choose to come to the library; the choice is made for them by their accompanying adults. When the child is old enough to voice an opinion and to have their choices taken seriously, what, in this environment, will encourage them to ask to be taken to the library? It is not designed to appeal to a ten year old. Even a seven year old may feel that the library is a space where he or she feels as if they are going back to pre-school. Children generally aspire to be older than they are, and libraries must recognize this, as it is very difficult to make a library that is designed for under-fives feel cool to eight and ten year olds. It is always easier to bring out extra furniture – rugs, cushions, soft toys – in order to make an older environment feel welcoming to toddlers and then to put them away again when they are not needed. For this reason, it is always better to design your space with older children in mind. This may affect your choice of colours and furniture, what you see from the door and the stock that is displayed at key turns. It is also important to work across gender. Many children's libraries are staffed by women, and there is a strong tendency for the ambience to become distinctly female, without anyone consciously intending this; indeed, this is evidenced through the proliferation of teddy bears, fabrics, fiction promotion and storytimes. Where are the displays of car books or the activities based on discovery, rather than empathy?

Applying principles of universal design helps the majority of library users, not just those with special needs: step-free access benefits buggy-pushers and elderly grandparents, as much as it does wheelchair users; clear text and strong contrasts in signage make navigation easier for everyone. Heights of shelves, however, will always make books easily reachable by some children and adults and not others. A dynamic approach to stock management and display is the best way to overcome this; regularly changing what can be seen and reached in different places in the space will widen choice and increase the access to books for everyone.

Offering choice and variety

For children, the challenge in library design is to find ways of appealing across age group and gender. Where there is enough space in a library, you can make dedicated areas, but more often than not this won't be possible. What is important is to offer a variety of experiences, so there is a degree of choice. These don't need to be branded for particular age groups, rather, it is important to let children choose their own preferences. At Djanogly City Academy in Nottingham, for example, height is used to differentiate areas and offer choice (see Figure 12.1). Some examples of this are a tablet bar for stand-up use, face-forward book displays and bar-height tables with stools are situated in the entrance; standard tables for group study and individual chairs with study arms are embraced mid-floor, by curved island shelving; and there is a big, relaxed sofa seating-area window, which looks inviting, without obscuring the view beyond. The range of three heights gives a lot of variety in a small space and provides an ambience, which is consciously different from a classroom. The height range also makes a pleasant and equal environment for mixed ages of users. This part of the Academy building is for the 11 to 14 age group, when children vary in height and growth more than any other age. The shortest and tallest students can choose whether they prefer to sit low, medium or high.

Look at how you can manage the library in order to meet different needs through time, as well as space. A seating area for young mums and babies in the morning can change to a space for eight to ten year olds after school, if you can manage the stock effectively and change a couple of displays in key positions.

Figure 12.1 *Djanogly City Academy. Notice the librarian in the top left; she is out in the space of the library and not tied to the help desk.*

Teenagers do like a space of their own, and they prefer it to be separate from the younger children, but in small libraries this creates an empty space for half of the year, when they are in school. At Wickersley Library in Rotherham (see Figure 12.2), the teenage area is branded with brightly coloured *Imagine* graphics, which don't mention age. Eleven to fourteen year olds use the space after school, but in the mornings adults are quite comfortable using the teen computers, and consequently have borrowed a lot of teenage fiction, as well.

Figure 12.2 *Imagine area at Wickersley Library, Rotherham*

From child-friendly to family-friendly

As well as the different age groups, space must be managed for different kinds of activity – for example, individuals browsing or studying; families or groups of friends using the space socially; and larger events, such as storytimes, homework clubs and author presentations. Public libraries were child-centred, before the term became fashionable, and are deservedly proud of this. Becoming family-centred is the new challenge. Must adults perch uncomfortably on tiny toddler chairs, because there is no adult-sized furniture to sit in? Do parents have to make a choice between getting their own books and prioritizing the needs of their children? The childcare books are often the only adult reading on offer in the children's space, but many parents long for something which is not related to children at all. Families come in many shapes and sizes. How do we cater for a parent with three children of different ages, a grandparent with fading eyesight bringing a toddler in a buggy, and a teenager looking after their younger sibling? We need to be a lot more flexible in the way that our services meet these needs.

Children's libraries have a long tradition of organizing events and activities. The influence of reader development has sharpened the focus in recent years, so connections to books and library resources are key. Involving parents and carers, creating social networking opportunities, as well as promoting reading and the library, have replaced the sometimes rather uninspiring craft sessions, which some parents were inclined to treat as a free childcare service. The success of event programmes requires an understanding with staff and users of adjacent spaces in the library. If 30 people attend a Baby Bounce and Rhyme session, that means at least 30 adults, as well as 30 babies, and probably 30 buggies, too. The event cannot be contained in the children's area - noise and belongings will spill out. It is, however, quite short. All it needs is polite adult library staff to mention to anyone who looks disturbed by what's going on that this happens every Wednesday for 45 minutes, and if they prefer a quiet space, they could perhaps consider visiting at a different time.

Children's librarians love large, open areas, as this makes special events easy to manage. However, not enough attention is paid to the everyday experience of visiting at other times of day - that big, open space in the centre is actually quite intimidating for a shy parent to cross, as it feels as if you and your child are on display. And, of course, the larger the space, the bigger the physical activity and the noise will be. Underhill (2009) - the guru of observational market research - has shown how adults walk faster and talk louder in open spaces, and this is just as true of children. If you want to calm children down, you need smaller, more intimate spaces.

One solution is to make all the shelving moveable, but in practice this is often expensive, less safe and less attractive. Putting everything on castors can be an indication of a desire to keep all your options open and avoid making the difficult design decisions, which would successfully shape your space. Tables, chairs and smaller freestanding furniture items are much easier to move than shelving, so design your layout with this in mind. Think hard about which shelving bays will need to be mobile and invest in top-quality systems, which won't wear out, seize up or become dangerous.

In many younger children's libraries, it is well recognized that a play area makes the space more attractive. The problem is that often the play feature - a train or a castle, for example - is presented as the most enjoyable activity. The message, therefore, becomes: 'here's where you climb, hide, role play and have fun'. Children immediately run to it on entering and regard it as the best bit of the experience. Meanwhile, the books sit firmly spine-out on the shelves, passive and inert. The message is: 'here's the boring bit that you only go to when you're made to'. Well designed furniture for libraries brings the books and the play elements together, so that the magic of books is an integral part of the enjoyable experience.

Promotion, not process

Seeing through the eyes of your users will change the physical appearance of the library space and the atmosphere that you create. Just as importantly, however, is the fact that it will change the organization and presentation of your collections. This is where children's libraries in the UK have fallen behind their adult counterparts. Adult libraries have been experimenting with all kinds of reader-centred approaches to stock promotion, while children's libraries have largely stuck to the traditional Dewey and alphabetical sequences. A reader-centred approach to library design looks at how to make reading an attractive experience, how to open up reading choices and how to offer opportunities to share reading experiences (see the wealth of examples of reader-centred work with adults, documented in *The Reader-Friendly Library Service* (Van Riel, Fowler and Downes, 2008)). This takes priority over organizing the library for traditional use. Tempting a child to pick up a book is far more important than teaching them to understand library organization.

Of course, the stock needs to be organized, so that books can be found, but complicated systems of coloured stickers to signify categories are often less than helpful. The example of a children's library guiding explanation, as shown in Figure 12.3, is typical of how good intentions can go astray – a plethora of fonts, capitals and underlines, with no consistency, colours which are hard to distinguish (light pink, dark pink, pink spots), some categories with two alternative names, some categories inexplicably without labels, the category 'All about me' denoted by the colour and word 'white'. How is a child meant to remember all this information from the wall at the entrance, where the sign is displayed, when they walk through the shelving layout in the children's section? The whole effect is terrifyingly complex and intimidating; if you have to understand all of this information before you can choose a book, nobody would ever borrow anything.

The architect and library designer Aat Vos tested library signage against commercial signage, with a group of ten year olds (Vos and de Boer, 2005). Regular library users, they were asked to find a book on dinosaurs in their own children's library. Then they were given a Rawlplug and asked to locate the identical size and style in a DIY store. The process of looking for signs, working out the categories and the organization, and checking on the shelf has similarities in both cases. All the children located the Rawlplug in a fraction of the time that

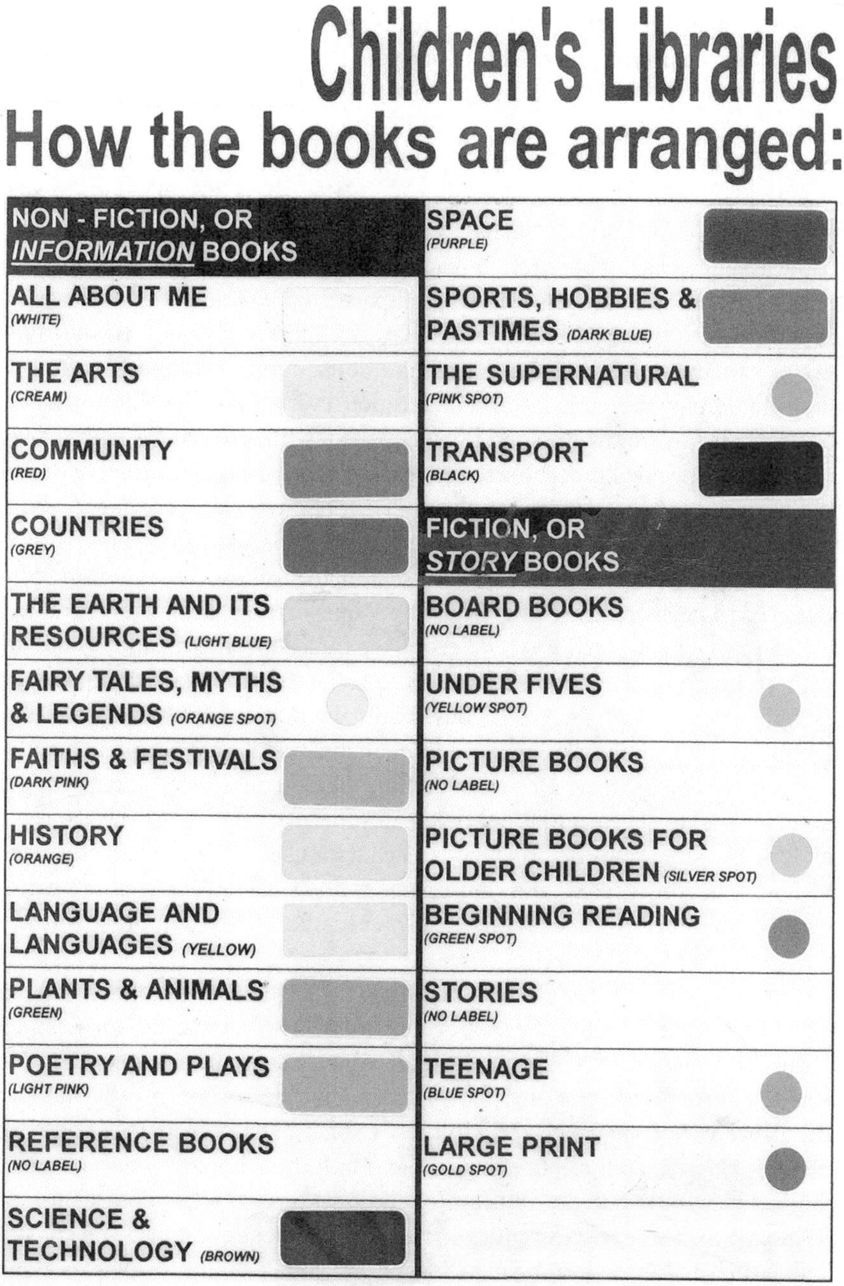

Children's Libraries
How the books are arranged:

NON - FICTION, OR *INFORMATION* **BOOKS**	**SPACE** (PURPLE)
ALL ABOUT ME (WHITE)	**SPORTS, HOBBIES &** **PASTIMES** (DARK BLUE)
THE ARTS (CREAM)	**THE SUPERNATURAL** (PINK SPOT)
COMMUNITY (RED)	**TRANSPORT** (BLACK)
COUNTRIES (GREY)	**FICTION, OR** *STORY* **BOOKS**
THE EARTH AND ITS **RESOURCES** (LIGHT BLUE)	**BOARD BOOKS** (NO LABEL)
FAIRY TALES, MYTHS **& LEGENDS** (ORANGE SPOT)	**UNDER FIVES** (YELLOW SPOT)
FAITHS & FESTIVALS (DARK PINK)	**PICTURE BOOKS** (NO LABEL)
HISTORY (ORANGE)	**PICTURE BOOKS FOR** **OLDER CHILDREN** (SILVER SPOT)
LANGUAGE AND **LANGUAGES** (YELLOW)	**BEGINNING READING** (GREEN SPOT)
PLANTS & ANIMALS (GREEN)	**STORIES** (NO LABEL)
POETRY AND PLAYS (LIGHT PINK)	**TEENAGE** (BLUE SPOT)
REFERENCE BOOKS (NO LABEL)	**LARGE PRINT** (GOLD SPOT)
SCIENCE & **TECHNOLOGY** (BROWN)	

Figure 12.3 *Overly complex stock arrangement in a children's library*

it took them to find the dinosaur book, even though the Rawlplug was an unfamiliar object to many of them. There are painful lessons to learn here.

It is worth thinking hard about how far the library is organized for the convenience of the staff, rather than the customers. I have observed that children's libraries in Sweden and Norway typically organize all their picture books in alphabetical order in kinderboxes – a practice which was abandoned many years ago in the UK. When challenged on how many three year olds choose a story by the first letter of the author's surname, it quickly emerged that this had nothing to do with encouraging children to read. Rather, it was a way of coping with the demands of specific parents, who wanted particular well known authors, most frequently those they had loved themselves as children. It's not difficult to find ways of managing this, which are less time-consuming and less off-putting for young children. Staff in one library made a note every time a specific author was asked for, a list was drawn up and books by the ten most asked for authors were stored in two specific kinderboxes, where they were easy to find, leaving the rest to be managed in more creative and child-friendly ways.

Most children, like most adults, never get to grips with the Dewey system. Today's students also have little call to use alphabetical order, as they are much more used to keyword searching. Bright and able learners, achieving A grades at GCSE level (General Certificate of Secondary Education in England, Wales and Northern Ireland) have to make an effort to recite the alphabetical sequence, as it's simply not part of their everyday world. In this environment, librarians' attempts to enforce the learning of traditional library skills are bound to backfire. There's no problem using Dewey or Library of Congress as a hidden support system for staff to shelve and find books. All supermarkets do just the same with barcodes. But supermarkets don't try to teach their users what the barcode means and how it is constructed, and you certainly don't have to be lectured on the barcode system before you can buy a carton of milk. The system of organization is invisible, if it's working well.

Creative stock management can also help to solve spatial problems. Where the children's area is small in proportion to the whole building, for example, instead of trying to cram too much in, look at how a shared stock space might be created, instead. Wickersley Library is a new build in a suburb of Rotherham, with a lovely, but small, glazed children's space. The solution was to allow children's stock to spill out of the space and into the adult area, with the result being a successful shared adult and children's non-fiction section. Children's books often make the best introductions to a subject for adults, too, if you consider subjects such as natural history, machines and various scientific principles. Books on topics such as pets can be shared across a wide age range, with ten year olds sometimes wanting more detail and depth than most adults. The 'Discover' wall, shown in Figure 12.4, does not say anything about age; it simply mixes attractive books together, displaying them in ways which tempt both adults heading for the quick choice and children and families going through to the children's library.

Figure 12.4 *The 'Discover' wall at Wickersley Library*

Mind and body

In a reader-centred library the books are presented as easy to grab, glance over and browse, wherever you are in the space. You should never have to make an effort to go to the books, the books must be brought to you. If you are relaxing in a soft seat, using a computer to check something or sitting with friends at a table, there should be books within reach to tempt you. School libraries often separate study tables from shelves. When a class arrives, the tables are full of people and chatter, and the shelves are unvisited. It is much better to mix the two together, and splitting tables up will also reduce the overall noise. Many libraries separate computers and books, forcing users to choose one way to go. It makes much more sense to present computers and books together, as complementary routes to the same end. We live in a hybrid world, where everyone uses both print and digital, and library spaces should express this.

Tempting children to pick up a book involves a mix of psychological and physical factors, the brain and the body. We must create the desire in the mind to look, feel and turn the pages and, at the same time, make it easy to physically see, touch and take. It is surprising, when you examine libraries objectively, how poor the equipment is that is tasked to do this job. Take the ubiquitous kinderbox as an example. A simple box on legs or wheels, it is often the wrong height for the age group that it is aimed at; half of the book cover is obscured by the boxing; books are displayed so that only one cover can be seen at a time; and the movement to flip through books is not easy for small hands, as the weight can trap fingers. Next, there is the spinner – a unit which pretends to display, but often has more spine-on focus than face-on display, plus a mechanism which is either too stiff to turn or so fast that the books fly off it altogether. Finally, there is the shelving – sometimes too high for young children, often the wrong height and depth for the size of the books on it and lacking any clear signage which is easy to change. Put simply, if libraries are to compete successfully for children's attention, a major change is needed.

We need to have the quality and impact of bookshop presentation, but libraries are not bookshops, so techniques cannot be transferred wholesale. The basis of most retail display is the multiple products – same size, colour and format – which can be easily stacked to give a high impact from a distance. Libraries do not have large numbers of multiple copies; if they have bought multiples of one book, it is because the book is very popular, and, therefore, copies will be out on loan or reserved for collection. The challenge in library furniture and display is to make individual titles look good together, while also getting it right psychologically and physically. The photograph in Figure 12.5 shows this is possible, with mixed sizes of picture books – lots of face-forward covers to attract attention from a distance, books and seating at a comfortable height for the target age group and books that are easy to reach, move, choose and take all demonstrate the quality and impact of bookstore-like presentation.

There are now many clever designs on the market, which enable libraries to adapt retail merchandizing techniques into library shelving. It is time to throw out those wobbly book stands, where if a child takes a book, the adjacent ones all fall over. Properly designed acrylics bring books to the front of the shelf and act as tidies to hold other books in place, enabling you to spotlight different titles face-forward, as an aid to navigation or as part of a themed promotion. You can

Figure 12.5 *Picture book wall units at Deanshanger Library, Northamptonshire*

change the look of a shelving bay in two minutes. In a school library, select just a few appropriate titles before a class arrives, and they will think the library is full of books just for them.

Reader to reader

Involve children in choosing which books should be highlighted; it's a great reader-centred exercise to get them thinking and talking about books. Exploit the opportunities to add messages with books; peer recommendation is a powerful promotional tool. On-shelf acrylics can hold a graphic, too, so there's an additional discovery to make, when you lift the book away. You can collect comments about reading from young people and insert these, as shown in the me-to-you message in Figure 12.6 and the colourful, vibrant reader quotations in Figure 12.7 (see next page).

Sustainability

Future-proofing is a major concern, especially when libraries do not get many chances to refurnish their space, and any refurbishment must last a good number

Figure 12.6 *Me-to-you message – comments about reading*

Figure 12.7 *Reader quotations used in on-shelf acrylics, as a surprise for the person who takes the book*

of years. Anticipating the needs of new technology is notoriously difficult, though the trend for miniaturizing suggests that libraries will need less space, not more. Getting it right for print formats is easier, as investing in good design and quality materials always pays off. Also, make sure you choose colours and finishes which depend on classic colour theory and not current fashions. Shelving which can be adapted to suit different product sizes will help to manage format changes, but beware of the 'one size fits all' approach, which is likely to leave you with none of your books looking attractive. Sustainable design is not just about using environmentally friendly materials, it's about creating lasting, flexible equipment, which gives long, trustworthy use. Invest in quality shelving, which gives a lot of flexibility, and then change the look of it every day, with good merchandizing. You do not need to move the shelving in a given space in order to create a new look; learn from retail displays where they move the products and add new graphics and branding, which is a lot cheaper.

The library of the future should be able to integrate digital and print much more successfully than we do at present. Most public libraries in the UK do not have enough of a budget to be creative with electronic media, and libraries often have no access or influence over digital content, which is managed corporately in local government. Education may well give the lead here. Learners have their own e-mail accounts throughout their education, and their sense of the institution that they are part of is created as much by their online experience as by the physical buildings. How might this influence library design of the future?

Conclusion

This chapter has discussed the concept of a reader-centred approach to library design and is based on personal experiences of designing more than 80 library interiors. It makes the case that a radical shift in thinking and practice needs to occur in order to keep UK children's libraries relevant and valued in the 21st century. The challenge is to make the physical space attractive and appealing across age groups. Innovative examples can be seen on the Designing Libraries website. It is important that libraries in the future integrate digital and print resources much more successfully than we do at present. At the moment, there is a complete disconnect between physical and virtual, bridged only by basic functions, such as the online catalogue, but in the future I would like to see library buildings which are a reflection of online experience, rather than the other way round. As stated in my introduction, this integration is highlighted as one of the radical shifts in thinking and practice that are needed in order to make children's libraries fit for the future.

References

Underhill, P. (2009) *Why We Buy: the science of shopping*, Simon & Schuster.

Van Riel, R., Fowler, O. and Downes, A. (2008) *The Reader-Friendly Library Service*, Society of Chief Librarians.

Vos, A. and de Boer, M. (2005) *How Children Search*, Artmiks.

Wilkins, G. and Jenkins, M. (2002) *Off the Shelf – a survey of non-users of Kent libraries*, Kent County Council internal report.

Website

Designing Libraries, www.designinglibraries.org.uk/.

13 Case study. Imagine, explore, discover – welcome to The Trove at White Plains Public Library, New York

Sandra Miranda

Introduction

The Trove Children's Library in White Plains, New York, USA, opened in October 2005. It exemplifies an unusual trend in public library design for children - a theatrical space, more like a bookstore or children's museum. This library model generated a multitude of questions. Namely, what was the point of this particular design? How has it worked? How can traditional library services stand out in a digital world? And, finally, what has technology got to do with it?

A new library, or space within a library, is a huge opportunity to recast your purpose and reinvent your image. When we decided to renovate, so as to expand our children's library, some parents were surprised. It's already so nice, they said – so cheerful, so many books and such wonderful staff. We smiled and told them that it would be even better, and then thought hard about what that would mean. Some of us worry about the future of libraries, reading, cultural literacy and educational attainment. It is easy to see that a bright future in these areas has a logical connection to children who love reading, and who become adults and parents, who continue the cycle. But how do we make this happen? How do we compete in today's world?

Well, first, we reasoned, we have to get, and keep, their attention. Computers and electronic devices rule, and the younger you are, the truer this is, but maybe it is not all about technology. When you are little, it is all about curiosity and discovery, which can happen every which way. When you are little, you depend upon your parents to take you places, and you put pressure on your parents to take you back to your favourite ones. Getting the attention of families in a big way brought us back to our image, as expressed in our name, our appearance and the experience that we offer. It is all connected. We have the best tools –

trained professionals and terrific resources – but we are competing with a complex, busy and well marketed world.

And, so, The Trove (definition: a collection of valuable items discovered or found) was born. As our children's manager said, during the decision over whether to take the leap of adopting this new name: 'We can always be the children's library.' After the new name came the new The Trove logo, tag line and story; we broke through a wall of bookshelves and discovered a magical place beyond. The story determined the look of the entrance to the space, and from there our ideas for the various environments took over. We are grateful to our branding firm for the brilliant creative work that provided these basic building blocks of identity.

Figure 13.1 *The entrance to The Trove*

The day that The Trove opened, a little girl was overheard telling her mother that it was the best day of her life. That made it ours, too. The way that book illustrations entice and engage, so, too, does an imaginative physical environment (see Figure 13.1). It is a real setting that children can live in and own and not just see on a screen, as part of something remote, unattainable and make-believe. That's an important part of the magic. Every child in our community can experience this environment first-hand, again and again.

So how, where and why do we use technology in The Trove? Our children's librarians, or Trovettes, as they have named themselves, tend to be self-critical about their knowledge and skills in this area. They are rightfully proud, however, that they are using technology as a powerful backdrop to leverage their best work: working one-on-one with children and parents, offering imaginative programmes, keeping extensive book displays fresh and welcoming one family after another.

Here is how we view the virtues of technology, as they were incorporated into the space. For the patrons, technology should:

- increase feelings of welcome, familiarity, comfort and excitement
- promote resources for both in-house and take-home use
- enable exploration, discovery, education and entertainment
- work on a variety of levels for different ages
- facilitate a wide variety of services
- make the library more convenient to use
- add to the beauty and interest of the physical space.

For the staff, technology should:

- serve important purposes, such as those outlined above
- be easy to manage
- be well chosen, located and supported
- increase safety and security.

We accomplished all of these goals in multiple ways. Our entrance features three flat screens, with multiple options for display. One is tied into a security camera, which captures the images of the people walking in and out. What child does not want to be on TV? Another flat screen displays information messages and the third shows a children's story, so that illustrations from children's literature are often the first thing you see as you walk in the door. During fundraisers, we have used the screens to showcase donors and the services that they support. One parent confessed that her little boy did not want to come to the library, but relaxed when he saw the TV screens.

Galaxy Hall, the main activity room, works for traditional services, such as showing films, but it is also set up to record programs. We use it for webinars and presentations, too. In this room, a closet is the central hub that manages all the technology in The Trove. Our CyberPool technology centre features 16 computers and a SmartBoard. In the CyberPool centre, children can use the internet, a local selection of software and games, the catalogue, databases and online services, such as live homework help. At scheduled times, librarians use this room to teach technology classes for adults. This kind of instruction space was something we otherwise lacked, so we planned for it carefully here.

In the centre of The Trove, a service desk, The Compass, sits under a dome, which is painted like the seven seas. Most of the desk area belongs to patrons. All checkout and check-in at The Trove is self-service; staff are always nearby to help. People can pay for their bills with cash or credit cards, both on the spot or remotely. Another part of The Compass houses a copier for patrons and staff. Librarians are located there to answer questions of all kinds. Condensing all of these services into a central space and allowing patrons to help themselves keeps things convenient, fast-moving and efficient.

OPACs are sprinkled throughout the space, along with a couple of computers, for use when the CyberPool is being used for adult instruction. Free wireless is available for those with their own laptops. For our littlest visitors and their parents, there are computers and software designed especially for toddlers. Recently, we have added laptops that are loaded with literacy software, which can be signed out for use in the library, largely by families learning English.

For casual entertainment, there is a partially enclosed viewing area – The Cave – which seats ten to 12 children. Three sound domes contain the noise; from anywhere but right in The Cave, you cannot hear that a movie is playing. We are usually showing an endless loop of children's stories, but we change this for special occasions (an author celebration, going into kindergarten advice, movies made by local children, and so on.). This space has come in handy for overflow audiences, when Galaxy Hall is packed for a popular feature film, and we've used it during fund-raisers, in order to broadcast presentations.

Also sprinkled throughout The Trove are unobtrusive security cameras. The space, about 12,000 square feet, gets busy; we typically see several hundred people a day. The cameras give staff and patrons a stronger sense of safety and control. In practice, we aren't constantly watching, but they serve as a deterrent and give us the means to go back and check something if necessary, so as to follow up on the rare occasion theft or other serious incidents occur.

We can't please everyone, and we've had some complaints over the years about our use of technology. Why do we have computer screens at the entrance? Why do we have a viewing area, with movies constantly showing? Why do the toddlers need to bang on keyboards or the older kids play computer games? The general drift of the complaint is that some adults want the library experience to be exclusively about books and literature, and they want a respite from technology. These complaints are few, and we have many good answers. Learning takes place in every way imaginable, and technology is one of them. Technology is everywhere, and children recognize it. We need children to feel at home. Technology implies excitement, entertainment and fun to most children, and we want the library to be perceived that way, too.

We also want people to experience the depth and quality of our resources – too often they simply gravitate to the popular and obvious. Our Cave viewing area only features the literature that people aren't discovering themselves. Technology sometimes just helps us get their attention. The idea for The Cave actually came from a tour of popular retail stores for children. We need to pay attention to people who know what attracts customers. More importantly, we are acutely aware of how many families depend on what we offer. Our computers for tots and older children and our free internet access fill a critical gap for those who do not have those resources at home. In our rush to assume that the whole world is connected, this cannot be underestimated.

We should also not forget that successful technology is not always high-tech. One mother told us that her daughter, barely two, toddled into Galaxy Hall, attracted by the theatrical lights that wash the walls with stencilled shapes. As she pressed her finger to the lit-up shape on the wall, part of a spiral galaxy, she said, 'star'. Every day, we see children mesmerized by the kinetic sculpture in our Copper Beech Garden, watching the marbles leap and play through an acrobatic maze. They love our wall puzzles, sand puzzles and our regular puzzles, too. How do we know what will trigger the imagination of a future inventor, teacher or researcher?

Our goal is to offer a learning environment that is layered with opportunity, and we achieve a piece of that goal with technology. Librarians have come from near and far to visit our children's library. We agree that it is a very cool, unique place, and we hope that they leave inspired. However, we remind them that every community library is a trove, with its own unique treasures. Every library can create an attractive and diverse learning environment, on a scale that is right for its unique staff, building and community.

PART 4
Issues for professional practice

14 The importance of service evaluation in libraries for children and schools

Lucy Gildersleeves

Introduction to the evaluation context

Today, libraries for children and young people and their connected adults are constantly challenged, by changing expectations, financial pressures and the need to forge new relationships, both within our parent organizations and with external partners. These library services operate within a context of accountability: to the tax-payer, to local authorities, to school governing bodies, to parents and to grant-funding bodies. Perhaps least emphasized, but most important, should be our accountability to children and young people themselves. This chapter will discuss the situation in the UK for both public library services for children and young people (hereafter referred to as CYPS) and learning resource centres in schools (LRCs)

This chapter will outline the evaluation process, identify a range of resources to support practitioners and offer suggestions for the future.

There is no single set of standards for CYPS or LRCs in the UK, against which to evaluate services. The Public Library Service Standards for England were abolished in 2008 (DCMS, 2008). While the Welsh Public Library Standards continue, using a three-yearly framework, and Northern Ireland works with *Delivering Tomorrow's Libraries* (DACL, 2006), embedding ten service standards, the content addressing children's services is severely limited. Scotland, on the other hand, has a more developed Public Library Quality Improvement Matrix (SLIC, 2007). Of more significant use is the UK Children's Public Library User Survey (C-PLUS) – a voluntary tool, intended for periodic, normally triennial, user consultation. Scottish schools have *Improving Libraries for Learners* (SLIC, 2009) – an evaluation framework, agreed with and recognized by the Scottish schools inspectorate. In England and Wales, school libraries may choose to use the optional self-evaluation toolkit *Improve Your Library* (DfES, 2004).

How we shape relevant services and, thus, communicate our value to management, councils and partner bodies is critical. Libraries have much to offer in furthering local and national agendas for literacy, digital and information confidence and in providing access to services supporting employment and cultural engagement. Yet, this contribution is infrequently spelled out in any detail, if at all, in government policy documents, in a way that makes it easy to recognize and test. Currently, both public and school library services have been vulnerable to cuts and de-professionalization. If CYPS and LRCs are to be recognized as important, evidence is needed at national, local and individual organization levels, in a form which is seen as relevant for those making policy and strategic decisions.

What is evaluation?

Evaluation is the systematic use of evidence to inform the development of services. It allows us to understand the context within which we operate, see patterns in performance, make decisions on priorities and, crucially, show how our activity makes a difference to our communities. It is important for those who are driving forward CYPS and LRCs to connect to the strategic process of parent, partner and political organizations. This is necessary to understand and acknowledge *their* priorities, in order to show how shared agendas can be achieved.

Fulfilling Their Potential (The Reading Agency, 2005) is a useful example of how this might be managed. This is a practical framework of service objectives, graded across three levels of achievement and specifically mapped to the former Labour government's Every Child Matters set of outcomes. As an approach, it is clear, practical and well supported by further resources; the essential service benefits that are identified have enduring value, but the close link to a particular political agenda means that any such framework needs to be recast, in the light of new political language and priorities. It also demonstrates the importance of collaboration between key interested bodies, if an evaluation framework is to have wide application, and included, among these interested bodies, the Reading Agency, the Association of Senior Children's and Education Librarians (ASCEL) and the National Youth Agency.

The LRC toolkit, *Improve Your Library* (DfES, 2004), developed to map into English and Welsh schools' self-evaluation processes, is a suite of frameworks for primary and secondary LRC use, focusing on service quality across a range of learning, development, engagement and management aspects; the frameworks are backed by in-depth advice on the use of relevant evidence. However, despite this detailed scaffolding of processes and links to the wider school performance context, *Improve Your Library* was not officially adopted by either Ofsted or Estyn - the key bodies in English and Welsh school evaluation, and, as evidenced through ongoing research in schools, there is little recognition of the toolkit amongst school senior managers and limited implementation within LRCs.

How does evaluation work?

There are five core aspects of service performance:

- environmental data: information on our community and context (e.g. demographics, government agendas, school profile and policies)
- inputs: the resources needed to deliver services (e.g. staff time, budgets, facilities)
- outputs: the services accomplished with these resources (e.g. stock, reader development and education activities, outreach)
- outcomes: the effectiveness of outputs (how users rate our services)
- impact: the extent to which the service affects or benefits the individual and the community served.

Depending on what we wish to evaluate, we explore chosen aspects, by a process of:

- profiling: building up a picture of the context and current activity of our service
- monitoring: measuring and checking activity against service plans and targets, at given times and over extended periods
- interpreting: analysing combinations of data collected, in order to understand its implications and identify areas for action.

To do this, we collect quantitative data (statistics) and qualitative feedback (comment), which are *measures* of the service. By comparing relevant aspect measures against each other and over time, we create *indicators*, which act as pointers towards opportunities for development. Indicators are never answers in themselves, but are alerts to areas of concern and prompts for further investigation or stimulus for innovation (see, especially, Brophy, 2006; Crawford, 2000, 2006; Markless and Streatfield, 2006).

Historically, library services have been judged on volume and numbers, for example, the proportion of young adult members set against local population, frequency of playgroup visits, books borrowed per pupil by year group, children completing the 'Summer Reading Challenge', etc. Much of this data is available through the considerable statistics accumulated via library management systems and event summaries. Because it appears relatively straightforward to calculate money invested in the service, in the form of staff time, stock purchased, etc., and to set this against units of service generated, there is a superficial appeal in judging the cost-benefit of our services, in terms of such *inputs* and *outputs*. There is value in such data, in terms of building up trends and patterns. However, raw count data generally tells us little about how or why our consumers use a service or what benefit they gained from doing so.

Interestingly, Ofsted's review of what makes good school libraries concluded that even with such statistical data on tap, staff often 'did not make sufficient use of library data as a starting point' or apply to it 'the kind of analysis that might generate important insights' (Ofsted, 2006, 12). Thus, the crude statistical picture needs to be fleshed out, by consulting users on their experience and perspectives (*outcomes*).

Today, the emphasis has shifted to demonstrating the *impact* of services. Survey instruments, such as C-PLUS, allow a simple combination of quantitative and qualitative responses. More detailed information can be collected via observations, through focus groups and conversation with individual children, and by consultation with carers and teachers (see Clark, 2010; Clark and Hawkins, 2011; Poinier and Alevy, 2010). This can be complemented by documentary evidence of CYPS and LRC policies, activities and community profiling, providing the necessary background detail. Brophy (2006), Markless and Streatfield (2006), Connaway and Powell (2010) and Pickard (2007) all provide useful advice on a range of research methods, which can be exploited to plan, capture and analyse the performance information that is needed for impact evaluation.

Structuring the evaluation process

Everything we do in providing library services is potentially worthy of evaluation, whether there is the most effective use of space, library involvement in teaching and learning programmes, running reading groups, how e-books are used or reprioritizing funding to target an excluded group. Similarly, we might be concerned with trends in routine service performance, the scoping and trialling of new initiatives or determining the impact of a promotion or identifying staff development needs. As a result, it is likely that we will be involved in several different reviewing activities at any one time, some of which may be ongoing and others which may be one-off. As evaluation is a time-consuming process, and the findings need to be meaningful to be useful for action, it is important to prepare carefully.

Deciding what to evaluate

The first step is identifying what *we* wish to achieve from an evaluation. In examining how librarians used the *Improve Your Library* toolkits, Gildersleeves (2006) identified three approaches. It became apparent that some chose to examine a particular service aspect, because they felt that it was inadequate; by scrutinizing this service and submitting a report supported by evidence to school management, a need for greater funding was demonstrated. In this, evaluation was used to find relevant evidence, in order to support a case. In contrast to this, others chose to look at why an area of strength was working well. Here, the librarians were using evaluation to identify critical success factors that could be adapted for other areas of the service or could be used to communicate the value of the LRC to teachers. A third group started by identifying a key goal in the school development priorities and selected LRC activities, which contributed towards this; this evaluation tested how effectively the LRC was a part of the whole-school plan. Therefore, it is apparent that all three approaches have their distinct uses.

This provides a link to the importance of auditing the culture of evaluation within the parent and partner organizations to discover what is valued as evidence and why. This can help to identify whom to target with information, which types of approach and examples are politically attractive, or what will be particularly useful in collaboration on shared evaluation. The toolkit *Inspiring Learning for All* (MLA, 2008), for assessing strengths and weaknesses of libraries, museums and archives, offers an example of a framework that is applicable across sectors and is, therefore, a useful starting point in considering evaluation of inter-agency activity, albeit, now requiring retuning to the political language of the Coalition government.

Planning the approach

The next step is to establish a framework or timetable of evaluation activities. This should, ideally, involve a broad scheme across the medium term (one to three years) of the areas to be addressed and a set of sub-frameworks covering key priorities. The broad scheme follows core service aims and activity and is refined to focus on the selected areas. For each framework, specific objectives, outcomes and performance measures are identified and a list prepared, detailing the target evidence to be collected. The frameworks mentioned above are all helpful in developing this approach, and public library organizations and schools are both used to working within medium-term and annual planning, so CYPS and LRCs are connecting into an established process. Practical considerations include, for example, asking:

- Do standards exist, to which we must aspire?
- What criteria are relevant?
- What types of evidence are needed to inform the evaluation?
- What is the best time to carry out the evaluation?
- What is the most effective way of reaching lapsed users or those who never access the service?
- If comparisons are to be made over a period of time, how easy is it to replicate the process?
- If benchmarking against other services is used, how appropriate is the comparison?
- What are the risk factors, which might compromise the evaluation?
- How will we act on the findings?

It is necessary, therefore, to be focused about which areas it is worthwhile to examine, and for which we will genuinely use the information gained, and to concentrate on the *impact*: understanding not only the quantity of use, but what *qualitative difference* the service makes to users and non-users and, also, to the interested organizations. Balancing these beneficiaries can create tensions: for example, a public library targeting time and money towards selected non-users may have a smaller, but proportionately greater, impact on those children than the difference achieved by concentrating services on existing youngsters, but it may incur corresponding negative feedback from some users. Will local politicians be more swayed by the outreach benefit or the voice of the 'core' membership?

An LRC, promoting its after-school homework support, aimed towards weaker students, succeeded in meeting target recruitment numbers, in line with the school's development plan, but found that former regulars left, discouraged by the change in atmosphere and level of attention (evidence for this was gained from a school librarian, in conversation with the author at the School Library Association Conference, June 2010). This example raises questions of intended and subsidiary benefit. Testing library impact on children's learning is notoriously difficult, and it involves close collaboration with teaching colleagues, so as to monitor skills acquisition and use, performance in assignments and the consequential confidence to transfer skills across different study contexts (Williams and Wavell, 2001; York, 2004). Whilst these might be primary benefits of homework support, there could also be social benefits, including the space to study or improvement in interpersonal skills and increased family confidence in the library. When planning for evaluation, it is important to define, at the outset, what it might be desirable to include, in the scope of measurement, in order to meet different user needs, and to establish how much 'before and after' evidence is needed, so as to be able to inform critical assessment of the various changes.

Markless and Streatfield (2001) offer insight into the issues involved in using impact measures.

A key caveat here is the importance of establishing whether the performance criteria that are chosen are capable of generating evidence, tied to the activities that we wish to examine. It is also important to avoid self-fulfilling evaluation – the danger of setting up criteria and testing processes, which bias towards the desired findings. A further problem, noted from preliminary findings of national research into school library impact (Gildersleeves, 2012), is that children – and adults, too – often find it very hard to articulate just how they perceive libraries can contribute to their learning or wider social achievement.

These issues are closely connected to deciding who should be involved in the process and why. Clearly, those to be surveyed, interviewed or observed contribute as participants, but it is also important to involve some of these individuals in the construction of any surveys or evaluation activities. This will ensure that the instruments that are used are effective and will help to engage participants and partners in feeling a sense of ownership of the process, and through that of the public library or LRC.

To evaluate impact, it is, therefore, important to use a 'mixed method' approach, combining statistical and qualitative techniques and building in a range of cross-checks to test evidence. This *triangulation* addresses two concerns:

1   First, the use of multiple strategies to collect and examine data allows us to see if consistent results emerge from the investigation. In this case, we can be reasonably confident that interpretation will have a valid basis. Differences in findings should alert us to re-examining both the methodology used and the criteria selected and demand further investigation.
2   Second, by combining different approaches, a richer picture of the use and benefits of services is developed. Portfolios of evidence, including lesson plans, children's creative and school work, reading logs, event write-ups, photos, videos and testimonials, should all be collected, as part of both overall and specific targeted evaluation. It is important to get into the habit of recording the 'golden moments' – comments, pupil achievements, community interactions – that crop up outside the formal evaluation process and which bring the service impact to life through personal stories.

As impact is concerned with long-term benefits, we also need to monitor services over time, in order to identify trends. Everhart's observations (1998) on the value of structured, regular reflection remain relevant. The Library and Information

Statistics Unit (LISU) report series, up to 2006 (Creaser and Maynard, 2006), show annual data summaries, contributing to five-year trend overviews. This has implications for how we ensure consistency in data collection, analysis and context, if the trend picture is to be an accurate reflection and of practical use in informing future decisions. Both Connaway and Powell (2010) and Pickard (2007) give practical guidance on how to make best use of different research methodologies.

Acting on the evaluation: decision making, communication and advocacy

There is absolutely no point in going through the evaluation process unless the information that is gained will be used to inform future action. The findings, therefore, need to be shared with colleagues involved in service planning, and decisions need to be made on how to adjust or direct public library or LRC activity. This will have implications for resource deployment and service priorities. Where changes are then made, it is likely that after a suitable period these will, in turn, need to be revisited, in order to evaluate what impact has resulted. The final step in the process is to communicate findings, decisions taken and service value to all involved in, or affected by, public libraries and LRCs. This delivers the evidence underpinning choices to decision-makers and provides users with feedback on problems, actions taken and future priorities. This shares the evaluation experience with others who might benefit and ensures a better understanding of what we are about.

This communication of evaluation-based findings and action is a key part of service advocacy and helps to build a relationship with communities. Reporting needs to be tailored and disseminated, according to the target audience. Annual reports are framed within the context of organizational mission and goals, and these provide a formal overview of service delivery on core agendas and can highlight selected achievements in line with key priorities. Annual plans set out the objectives and the performance criteria which will shape the next round of evaluation. Progress updates and final project reports are an important part of publicizing initiatives, as well as meeting the needs of funders. They may also form part of further funding bids. Public libraries are accustomed to such reporting. The picture is more variable in LRCs. In the course of interviewing librarians, during research into LRC use of the *Improve Your Library* toolkits (2005–2006), and, more recently, school management and librarians, for the 'Do School Libraries Make an Impact' research (2011–2012), the author found that many LRC staff – usually those not closely involved with senior management or policy teams – were making little use of qualitative reports to management, governors and teaching staff to draw out the contribution of the LRC to their work. Arguably, it is the library staff, who are excluded from presenting at management meetings, who most need to provide regular evaluation feedback reports and to find other ways of building the LRC relationship with colleagues.

The Ofsted research found that insufficient head teachers understood, or were even aware of, the evidence for LRC effectiveness; the same could be said for children and their carers, whether they might be consumers of public or school library services. Public library services now regularly use websites and local media to report on activities, and many are beginning to exploit social media tools to reach a wider audience – in particular, children and young people, including those who might not normally choose to visit the library. Thus, the Royal Borough of Kensington and Chelsea uses Facebook to encourage participation in its C-PLUS survey, and Northamptonshire has reported, on its website, the service strengths and weaknesses identified by children and, crucially, what action it has taken in response to them. This could be developed even further. LRCs could also look for creative ways of engaging with their wider community. In addition to school magazines and e-newsletters, perhaps we could be radical and use existing pupil progress reporting, so as to offer an opportunity for librarians to give critical feedback on engagement and achievement, thus providing another dimension to LRC involvement in evaluation.

Current evaluation research for children's and school libraries

As part of public library and LRC engagement in advocacy and evaluation, it is worth considering the impact evidence afforded from national research. Since the demise of the LISU annual digest of CIPFA statistics on children's and schools services (Creaser and Maynard, 2006), there has been a gap in the UK trend picture. A 'state of the nation' survey, commissioned by the School Libraries Group of CILIP (Streatfield, Shafer and Rae-Scott, 2010), fills this overview in respect of secondary school LRCs, finding that against a background of financial cuts much good work is still being done in reader development and information literacy, particularly where there is a qualified librarian in post. Complementing this, the first UK-wide secondary school library impact study, Do School Libraries Make a Difference?, is being carried out from 2011 to 2012, focusing on the perceptions of pupils and teaching staff, in relation to the contribution of the LRC to the learning experience. There is some evidence from the initial piloting of the research that findings will be similar to the picture in the substantial body of impact research from the US School Libraries Work! (Scholastic, 2008), where the presence of a well resourced LRC and a trained librarian have been identified as key to children's learning.

In contrast, there has been no substantial impact evaluation of CYPS, since Elkin and Kinnell's A Place for Children (2000) and the report Start with the Child

(CILIP, 2002), despite the latter's recommendation that the research should be updated every three years. The issues that were addressed remain relevant, although the context is, obviously, dated. There is, at present, no national correlation of findings from locally run C-PLUS evaluations.

The National Literacy Trust (NLT) is a UK-based organization that conducts research into children's reading behaviours. Based on a 2009 survey of children's reading and writing, it published reports on school libraries and literacy (Clark, 2010) and on public libraries and literacy (Clark and Hawkins, 2011), which both discovered a clear correspondence between library use and children's reading engagement. Booktrust (n.d.), the NLT and the Reading Agency all report on evaluations of their reader development programmes, but there is, as yet, no one central gateway to this type of research similar to the set of links to useful school library research provided on the CILIP website.

Challenges and opportunities for the future

Libraries are faced with a constant remapping exercise to demonstrate value, as national and local government policy and curricula change. With the Museums, Libraries and Archives Council being discontinued and funding cut from charities such as the NLT and Booktrust, there is likely to be greater reliance on organizations such as CILIP, ASCEL and the School Libraries Association collaborating, in order to update the policy context of evaluation frameworks and to develop examples to support public library services and LRCs. These groups are already working closely with bodies such as the School Library Commission to collect evidence and case examples. In doing this, they are taking note of the findings from the study of the use of the toolkit *Improve Your Library*, which identified a need for case banks to contain a broad range of examples, from the basic to outstanding, as some librarians were easily discouraged by the gap that they perceived between their own service performance and the 'best case' models.

The Ofsted study found that 'few [schools] are confident about self-evaluation, as far as the library is concerned' (Ofsted, 2006, 12), and this was corroborated by these findings, which suggested that school librarians worried about carrying out evaluations and were overwhelmed by the level of detail in the toolkits on offer (Gildersleeves, 2006). With the loss of many school library support services and public libraries under pressure, there is a need for more, and different, ways of offering training in how to simplify and maximize evaluation and advocacy, in order to address these concerns and to equip library staff to use multiple approaches in communicating value to educationalists, councillors and communities. We also need to find innovative ways to calculate the cost of *not* providing CYPS and LRCs.

Carpe diem!

We have an opportunity to capitalize on the present focus on school libraries, highlighted by developments such as Alan Gibbons' Campaign for the Book, the School Libraries Commission and the Scottish and Welsh Information Literacy Projects. The challenge, here, will be to take the combined strength of the research evidence and the individual case examples beyond the library audience and into the political and education zone. Work is already being done by the School Library Association, ASCEL and individual school librarians towards communicating impact evaluation at, for example, teacher conferences, but we need to publish on library impact in education journals, as well as in information service literature.

Conclusion: share more!

There are many interesting examples, which could be used as evidence and to inspire initiatives, assessment approaches and advocacy, but these are often hidden, because they are not reported; they are scattered across the literature and different websites and often there is a lack of sufficient funding for evaluation to be carried out. Activities that we now regard as core offers, such as the Summer Reading Challenge, out-of-hours study support and book-gifting schemes, would not have achieved national roll-out without the accompanying research, proving their positive impact. There is room for greater collaboration between public libraries, LRCs and the academic community, on co-ordinated evaluation of projects across multiple centres. As practitioners, we need to get into the habit of not only reflecting on our activities, but converting this thought into case material to be shared, as part of a national picture. The MLA research and case bank was a useful starting point, especially for public library material, but it is, sadly, no longer updated. In parallel with the 'Do School Libraries Make a Difference?' research, the Department of Information Studies at UCL is developing an open-access bank for LRC and public library case studies, including evaluations, models and templates, but the challenge for any such practitioner resource is ensuring sustainability in the long term. Perhaps, next, we need to evaluate how practitioners and policy-makers are actually using this body of research and case evidence, to ensure that it is a meaningful resource.

References

Booktrust (n.d.), www.booktrust.org.uk/Research.

Brophy, P. (2006) *Measuring Library Performance: principles and techniques*, Facet Publishing.

CILIP (2002) *Start with the Child: report of the CILIP Working Group on library provision for children and young people*, Chartered Institute of Library and Information Professionals.

Clark, C. (2010) *Linking School Libraries and Literacy*, National Literacy Trust.

Clark, C. and Hawkins, L. (2011) *Public Libraries and Literacy*, National Literacy Trust.

Connaway, L. and Powell, R. (2010) *Basic Research Methods for Librarians*, 5th edn, Libraries Unlimited.

Crawford, J. (2000) *Evaluation of Library and Information Services*, 2nd edn, ASLIB.

Crawford, J. (2006) *The Culture of Evaluation in Library and Information Services*, Chandos.

Creaser, C. and Maynard, S. (2006) *A Survey of Library Services to Schools and Children in the UK*, Library and Information Statistics Unit, www.lboro.ac.uk/departments/dils/lisu/pages/publications/scho-chil06.html.

DACL (2006) *Delivering Tomorrow's Libraries: principles and priorities for the development of public libraries in Northern Ireland*, Department of Arts, Culture and Leisure, www.dcalni.gov.uk/final_delivering_tomorrow_s_libraries_document-july-2007 _1mb_document_for_website.pdf.

DCMS (2008), *Public Library Service Standards*, 3rd edn, Department for Culture, Media and Sport, http://webarchive.nationalarchives.gov.uk/+/http://www.culture.gov.uk/ images/publications/PulbicLibraryServicesApril08.pdf.

DfES (2004) *Improve Your Library: a self-evaluation process for school libraries*, Department for Education and Skills, www.teachernet.gov.uk/teachingandlearning/resourcematerials/schoollibraries.

Elkin, J. and Kinnell, M. (eds) (2000) *A Place for Children: public libraries as a major force in children's reading*, British Library Research and Innovation Report 117, Library Association Publishing.

Everhart, N. (1998) *Evaluating the School Library Media Center: analysis techniques and research practices*, Libraries Unlimited.

Gildersleeves, L. (2006) Evaluating Evaluation: introducing a research project on the impact of Improve Your Library: a self-evaluation process for school libraries, *Aslib Proceedings*, **58** (1/2), 73–88.

Gildersleeves, L. (2012) Do School Libraries Make a Difference?: some considerations on investigating school library impact in the United Kingdom. In Hall, I., Thornton, S. and Town, S. (eds), *Proving Value in Challenging Times: Proceedings of the 9th International Northumbria Conference on performance measurement in library and information services held on 22–25 August 2011, University of York.*

Markless, S. and Streatfield, D. (2001) Developing Performance and Impact Indicators and Targets in Public and Education Libraries, *International Journal of Information Management*, **21** (2), 167–79.

Markless, S. and Streatfield, D. (2012) *Evaluating the Impact of your Library*, 2nd edn, Facet Publishing.

MLA (2008) *Inspiring Learning for All*, Museums, Libraries and Archives Council, http://inspiringlearningforall.org/.

Ofsted (2006), *Good School Libraries: making a difference to Learning*, Office for Standards in Education, www.ofsted.gov.uk/Ofsted-home/Publications-and-research/Browse-all-by/Education/Leadership/Governance/Good-school-libraries-making-a-difference-to-learning.

Pickard, A. (2007) *Research Methods in Information*, Facet Publishing. New edition to be published 2013.

Poinier, S. and Alevy, J. (2010) Our Instruction DOES Matter! Data collected from students' works cited speaks volumes, *Teacher Librarian*, **37** (3), 38–9.

Scholastic (2008) *School Libraries Work!*, 3rd edn, Research Foundation Paper, Scholastic, www.scholastic.com/content/collateral_resources/pdf/s/slw3_2008.pdf.

SLIC (2007) *Public Library Quality Improvement Matrix*, Scottish Library and Information Council, www.scottishlibraries.org/activities-qse-plqim.

SLIC (2009) *Improving Libraries for Learners*, Scottish Library and Information Council, www.slainte.org.uk/files/pdf/slic/schoollibs/ImprovingLibsForLearners.pdf.

Streatfield, D., Shaper, S. and Rae-Scott, S. (2010) *School Libraries in the UK: a worthwhile past, a difficult present – and a transformed future?*, Chartered Institute of Library and Information Professionals, www.cilip.org.uk/get-involved/special-interest-groups/school/Documents/full-school-libraries-report.pdf

The Reading Agency (2005) *Fulfilling their Potential*, www.readingagency.org.uk/young/fulfilling-their-potential/.

Williams D. A. and Wavell C. (2001) *Impact of the School Library Resource Centre on Learning*, Resource: the Council for Museums, Archives and Libraries.

York, S. (2004) Elbowing in on the Evaluation Process, *Library Media Connection*, **22** (5), 38–40.

The rights of the child and youth advocacy – issues for professional practice in the library setting

Edward Halpin, Philippa Trevorrow, Laura Topping and Carolynn Rankin

Introduction

Arts Council England has the responsibility for championing, developing and investing in libraries in England and states that access to knowledge, experiences and treasures within libraries is every child's birth right (Arts Council England, 2011). Children have a basic need to find out information, and the information that they gain is essential for individual development. They can use the information they obtain to change their circumstances, function better in society and be informed individuals, who can contribute to social change:

> Libraries deal with human values protected by human rights. This basic truth
> seemed to have been somewhat forgotten or put aside by more conventional talk
> about all kinds of professional matters. But the notion of human rights as
> fundamental to libraries' aspirations and core activities is increasingly receiving
> attention.
> (Koren, 2000, 273)

Koren makes a valuable and worthwhile point, in reminding us of the importance of libraries and the close relationship that they have with fundamental human rights. In this chapter, the primary consideration will be the rights of the child and youth advocacy and their relationship to professional practice in the library setting. This is not a new issue for the professional librarian, though the issue might well be considered as such, in view of the complexity of a global society, with internet access and the opportunity for instant communication, particularly through social networking. The ethical, moral and philosophical conundrums daily faced by librarians in schools, public libraries and in supporting and advising on work with children and young people provide constant operational and practical questions.

The reality for the professional librarian is that in carrying out their daily duties, they have to consider access, stock management, purchasing management, censorship, the cultural and social make-up of the community that they serve, professional ethics, the values and policies of their organization and myriad of small, daily interventions in their workplace. On a day-to-day basis, these are just part of the job, and the professional skills and personal judgement that are applied are, also, simply parts of the job. Historically, there have been tensions concerning the types of collection that should be available to the public or that should be stored behind closed doors, debates about censorship and freedom of speech and the ever-nagging question of what was suitable or appropriate for children. Thomas Bowdler became famous, or, perhaps, infamous, for his publication of *The Bowdler Shakespeare* (1853) and *Gibbon's 'History of the Decline and Fall of the Roman Empire'* (1923), in which he expunged material thought to be too racy or unsuitable for women or children, thus giving his name to a form of censorship known today as Bowdlerization. Today, the decisions on what should, and should not, be accessed and, in particular, what children and young people should, or should not, be allowed to access, remains firmly in the mind of librarians and managers. The difficulty relates to how librarians should respond. What should they base their decisions on? What influence should the local community or campaigns against particular groups/issues have on their work? While these decisions face the librarian every day, particularly in relation to websites and website material, are decisions really made or are they more often avoided?

Decisions are subject to a variety of daily drivers – professional judgement, policy, stakeholder interventions, to name a few – but they are also informed by professional codes of practice, and, beyond these, it is possible to view in the distance human or child rights' declarations as a final guiding tool. For example, there is guidance from professional bodies, such as the American Library Association (ALA) or the Chartered Institute of Library and Information Professionals (CILIP) in the UK, which set parameters. There are also international human and child rights' conventions (UNICEF, 2012), which are recognized international law. Koren, in her paper 'Children's Rights and Library Best Practices', reminds us that:

> For all who are concerned with children and young people, the United Nations
> Convention on the Rights of the Child offers support in library policy and practice.
> (Koren, 2003, 1)

The declarations on human rights and child rights, along with national government legislation and policy, form the framework for decisions for librarians, but can also create problems for them. The United Nations Convention on the Rights of the Child (CRC) (UN, 1989) provides a universal framework on the rights of the child, building on and explicating the United Nations Universal Declaration of Human Rights (UNUDHR) (UN, 1948), in respect to children. These universal rights' statements create a framework to guide the expectations that we have for children in our society. Within the articles of these conventions are some that are specific to the library and the librarian, which will be considered within this chapter, alongside the professional practice and individual judgement of librarians in their daily work. The *Public Library Manifesto* of the International Federation of Library Associations and Institutions (IFLA) and The United Nations Educational, Scientific and Cultural Organization (UNESCO) (IFLA/UNESCO, 1994) forms another central point of reference. In light of these frameworks, and in view of the content, it is also important to consider how we view children and young people, affording them the rights and expectations of young citizens; there is, therefore, a need to understand what this status could be and the implications that this has for both them and the librarian.

The chapter will consider some of the key legal codes outlining children and human rights, offers a framework on youth citizenship and considers how some examples of professional practice relate to the library.

Human rights, child rights and professional codes

The provisions of the UNUDHR (UN, 1948) and the CRC (UN, 1989) provide an international framework of protection for people throughout the world and accord specific rights to children. In Articles 18 and 19 of the UNUDHR, there is provision for freedom of thought, freedom of expression and the freedom to hold opinion, with the Declaration stating that: 'this right includes freedom to hold opinions without interference and to seek, receive and impart information and ideas through any media and regardless of frontiers' (UN, 1948). The CRC (UN, 1989) reinforces these general codifications, with some specific to children, providing a full range of human rights for all children - civil and political, social, economic and cultural. Hick and Halpin (2001), in considering children's rights and the internet, state, 'The underlying values - or guiding principles - of the CRC guide the way in which each right is fulfilled and respected and serve as a reference for the implementation and monitoring of children's rights' (2001, 63-4). The CRC outlines, in 41 articles, the human rights to be respected and protected for every child under the age of 18. The four guiding principles are as follows:

1 Article 2 - on non-discrimination - states that no child should be injured, privileged, punished by or deprived of any rights, on the grounds of his or her race, colour or gender; on the basis of his or her language, religion or national, social or ethnic origin; on the grounds of any political or other opinion; on the

basis of caste, property or birth status; or on the basis of disability.

2 Article 3 – on the best interests of the child – states that in all circumstances concerning the child, they should be the primary focus, whether this is within public or private institutions, legal or administrative settings. In each and every circumstance, in each and every decision affecting the child, the various possible solutions must be considered and due weight given to the child's best interests. 'Best interests of the child' means that the legislative bodies must consider whether laws being adopted or amended will benefit children in the best possible way.

3 Article 6 – on survival and development – addresses children's right to life, survival and development. The survival and development principle is in no way limited to a physical perspective, rather, it emphasizes the need to ensure the full and harmonious development of the child, including at the spiritual, moral and social levels, where education will play a key role.

4 Article 12 – on participation – is the principle affirming that children are full-fledged persons, who have the right to express their views in all matters affecting them and requires that those views be heard and given appropriate consideration, in relation to the child's age and development. This article recognizes the potential of children to enrich decision-making processes, to share perspective and to participate as citizens and actors of change.

Very specific articles follow these guiding principles, which have relevance to the library and librarian; also, in Article 12, the need to see the child or young person as a citizen becomes apparent. The CRC fact sheet then describes Articles 13 to 17 thus:

1 Article 13 (Freedom of expression): Children have the right to get and share information, as long as the information is not damaging to them or others. In exercising the right to freedom of expression, children have the responsibility to also respect the rights, freedoms and reputations of others. The freedom of expression includes the right to share information in any way they choose, including by talking, drawing or writing.

2 Article 14 (Freedom of thought, conscience and religion): Children have the right to think and believe what they want and to practise their religion, as long as they are not stopping other people from enjoying their rights. Parents should help guide their children in these matters. The Convention respects the rights and duties of parents in providing religious and moral guidance to their children. Religious groups around the world have expressed support for the Convention, which indicates that it in no way prevents parents from bringing their children up within a religious tradition. At the same time, the Convention recognizes that

as children mature and are able to form their own views, some may question certain religious practices or cultural traditions.

3 Article 15 (Freedom of association): Children have the right to meet together and to join groups and organizations, as long as it does not stop other people from enjoying their rights. In exercising their rights, children have the responsibility to respect the rights, freedoms and reputations of others.

4 Article 16 (Right to privacy): Children have a right to privacy. The law should protect them from attacks against their way of life, their good name, their families and their homes.

5 Article 17 (Access to information; mass media): Children have the right to get information that is important to their health and well-being. Governments should encourage mass media - radio, television, newspapers and internet content sources - to provide information that children can understand and to not promote materials that could harm children. Mass media should particularly be encouraged to supply information in languages that minority and indigenous children can understand. Children should also have access to children's books.

The right to information

For many hundreds of years, information providers have been surrounded by proponents of various kinds of censorship, including banning books and editing them to remove content that was believed to be unsuitable. The librarian has, as a matter of course, had to deal with this issue, either directly (for example, when limiting access to special collections, such as erotica) or indirectly (for example, when selecting books). Current concerns relate to a new mode of information delivery and emphasize questions about access to information in a broader context. The key issue facing public libraries delivering information and services via the internet continues to be censorship. Some argue that librarians have always acted as censors (Brophy, 2001). The advent of ICT, however, has introduced a new mechanism for censoring. With the implementation of filter systems on public access computers, the issue of stock selection or special access is no longer a professional choice. The type of material that is filtered includes that which might be of public interest or of political or personal value. The internet does not create a new question of access and censorship, but returns us to old questions in a new context. In blocking content - for example, books and films - censorship, in fact, restricts the action of civil participation, as well. Citizens have rights that are codified and legitimized in the UNUDHR (UN, 1948). The Declaration sets out a framework for freedom and dignity in society (Hick and Halpin, 2001), however, these rights are not absolute or distinct. Sometimes individual rights conflict with each other. Therefore, each right needs to be balanced with other rights. These freedoms and rights apply to all citizens and countries that are signatories to the Declaration and are deemed to apply equally to adults and young people.

Young people have been recognized by the UN to be in need of specific protection. The UN CRC (UN, 1989) incorporates the right of young citizens to have access to information from a range of different sources, which gives rise to the question - how do we define young citizens?

Young people as citizens

If we take the various codifications of the rights of children and young people, we can clearly see that the rights affirm them as citizens, but we then need to consider how they may be defined as such. Through research funded by the European Union, Trevorrow, Orange and Halpin (2006) have developed a model of active youth citizenship (see Figure 15.1).

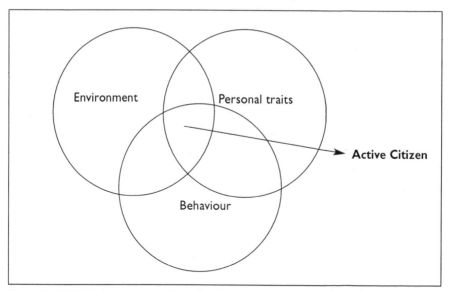

Figure 15.1 *Model of active youth citizenship (Trevorrow, Orange and Halpin, 2006).*

According to this model, there are three dimensions of active youth citizenship: environment, personal traits and behaviour practices. The model is a graphical representation of the major dimensions that contribute to active youth citizenship. Each dimension will have some degree of impact upon the others, but what we are interested in is how each influences the overall active participation of young citizens. The model was developed on an extensive review of literature and was critiqued, via information gathered and analysed from a questionnaire (40 responses) distributed to youth organizations in five countries (namely, Cyprus, Greece, Italy, Romania and the UK). Other models published in the literature, although with different representation and focus, corroborated many aspects and elements of the one that is displayed here. Hart's (1992) model includes much of the information comprising the environment dimension, with a focus on the requirement of sub-systems. The personal traits dimension is corroborated by models such as ACT (2003), Osler and Starkey (1999) and Woyach and Cox (1997), which show that certain skills are necessary to becoming an active participant in society and that knowledge of one's rights is a requirement. Finally, elements of the behaviour dimension can be observed in Hart's (1992) model and also in Treseder's (1997) model, with the idea of empowerment as a significant factor.

Environment

The environment dimension consists of the external factors that affect individuals, as they strive to become participating citizens – a concept that, as we move towards a society dominated by digital technologies, includes the notion of e-citizenship (Becta, 2003). This dimension can be further divided into sub-systems – needs, aspects and resources – that influence the individual in some way.

Young peoples' experiences will undoubtedly affect their later life levels of participation (Frazer and Emler, 1997). Experiences with societal conditions and structures can act as enablers for, or constraints on, individual participation (Jones and Wallace, 1992; Morch, 1997). The environment dimension includes the sub-systems to which the individual may be exposed, for example, public libraries, school, youth clubs and parental guidance. An individual's degree of engagement with these sub-systems determines the material, intellectual and cultural resources and information that is available to him or her (Frazer and Emler, 1997).

Public libraries are a valuable resource for young people, and they were given prominence by both the People's Network (MLA, 2004) and Framework for the Future (DCMS, 2003). They are seen as offering a neutral, welcoming, community space and supporting active citizenship, in addition to being public anchors for neighbourhoods and communities (DCMS, 2003). The National Lottery has provided funding to equip nearly all public libraries with ICT infrastructure, thereby offering internet access to the public. Thus, the public library is seen as a significant element of the environment dimension, as it is a place where there should be access, in abundance, to information, resources and knowledge.

Trevorrow, Orange and Halpin (2006) identify basic needs that must be fulfilled, if individuals are to become active members of the community. One of these is the need for autonomy: recognizing one's own identity and having the skills, knowledge and freedom to act as a self-governing individual (Alderson, 2000; Coles, 1995). Support from the sub-system of members of the community – such as friends, family and professional practitioners – is required to facilitate satisfactory fulfilment of these needs (Harris, 1998; Sinclair and Franklin, 2000). According to Jones and Wallace (1992), there are three aspects of citizenship: civil, political and social. The civil determines the right to individual freedom and justice. The political determines the right to participate in political power. The social determines the right to well-being and a civilized life. In addition to this, an understanding of the nature of the state and of legal, political and social systems is believed to help the individual participate fully in society (Williamson, 1997).

Personal traits

This dimension includes the competencies and attitudes that a young person needs in order to become an active participant in society. Embedded in the competencies are a number of skills and beliefs and a good deal of knowledge. People require certain skills to act as self-governing individuals, and these include being able to open their minds to alternatives, being able to make decisions (Hill, Pike and Selby, 1998) and being able to gather the extensive information that is necessary for making informed judgements (ACT, 2003; Parsons, 2002). Most young people who actively participate in society, do so because they like to be involved – to have the opportunity to debate issues, to be listened to and not to be dictated to (Harris, 1998; Mohamed and Wheeler, 2001). Knowledge and understanding play significant roles in youth becoming active citizens. Knowing their rights and understanding and appreciating the community in which they live will encourage young citizens to participate. 'Knowledge is a source of power' (Cairns, 2001, 356), and young people need to have a diversity of information, in order to be able to contribute to the full.

Behaviour practices

This dimension includes the actions that individuals take and represents the degree to which they may engage as active citizens. This is an important dimension, and the feelings of desire, wanting to be involved and wanting to take action need to be considered. Having the appropriate knowledge, skills and attitudes 'does not imply a dynamic, committed, engaged citizen' (Hall, Williamson and Coffey, 2000, 464), if the individual does not want to act on those competencies. Individuals may choose not to engage, if they have a negative view of the organization or product with which they are asked to involve themselves. Such negativity sometimes comes from personal experience and sometimes from personal perception (Lowndes, Pratchett and Stoker, 2001). Young people need to feel empowered; this can be achieved through having appropriate information, making decisions and having responsibilities. A secondary benefit of such empowerment can be that it encourages future participation (Milburn, 2000; Osler and Starkey, 1999; Sinclair and Franklin, 2000).

Access to, and enjoyment of, information, choice in information and knowledge attainment, as well as the development of literacy, form a fundamental part of development as a citizen and inevitably add to the dilemmas already faced by the librarian. Some of these issues are now discussed in more detail.

Issues for library practitioners in their professional practice

Moral questions about children's literature have a long historical context. With the invention of books for children, as a result of the invention of 'the child', what was appropriate for those children to see and read started to become an issue. In the Victorian era, this was moral literature and cautionary tales. Children's literature reflects the views of the society that it is created in. For example, it was appropriate in the 1950s and earlier for children to be given a clear view of gender roles, which would fit them for the society that they were living in, as a man or a woman. The British Empire was reflected, particularly in the war eras.

In the 1960s, a changing society led to a change in children's books and a rise in presenting alternative models to children. Feminists began to write about children's literature, and alternative views of children's literature were presented, including the definition of gender roles. As political correctness grew in the 1980s, there was an expansion in this kind of children's literature. One such book was *Jenny Lives with Eric and Martin* (Bösche, 1983) – a matter-of-fact picture book about a girl with two fathers, which was held in a London children's library. There was a reaction against this book from those who disapproved strongly of homosexuality. Legislation was introduced amid calls for greater censorship from councils (including schools and public libraries), which stated:

A local authority shall not:

(a) intentionally promote homosexuality or publish material with the intention of promoting homosexuality;
(b) promote the teaching in any maintained school of the acceptability of homosexuality as a pretended family relationship.

(Section 28, Local Government Act, 1988)

There was considerable debate on both sides of this question, and the Act was not removed from the statute books until 2003. The Act caused school and public libraries to self-censor, for fear of reprisals. For public librarians, the question of whether ethical standpoints should be something to follow in obedience to, or in defiance of, the law was evident. It might appear, from our current standpoint in history, that what is classed as appropriate literature for children is a question on which we are all united, but, in fact, censorship continues. One book which caused controversy more recently is *And Tango Makes Three* (Parnell and Richardson, 2005). Reported by the ALA as top of the list of banned books for 2008 (2009), this is the true story of two male penguins, who become a family of three at a zoo.

When children's librarians choose stock for their libraries, they will be well aware of the possible reactions that some books might get, and they may also hold personal views of their own on the matter. As such, there are considerable ethical issues involved, for example, the rights of the state balanced against the rights of the parents or the individual rights of the child. There is little direct guidance on this issue. Public libraries often have policies on providing stock that is representative of other cultures and races, which promotes inclusion, not discrimination.

There is current debate about children's rights and the changing nature of the child in the information age, for example, the concerns about what children can and cannot access online, and whether the nature of being a child is changing (Trevorrow et al., 2005). The effect of the recession and reductions in budgets means that children's librarians are decreasing, and stock selection is increasingly being outsourced; this has, perhaps, been done without fully considering the ethical issues that are involved in the decision. It is important for public libraries to feel secure in their decisions, particularly in times of political uncertainty and confusing guidelines.

Picture books are popular, with lots of encouragement for children and parents to use them from campaigns and charities, such as The Reading Agency, the National Year of Reading, Bookstart and The Big Picture. Because of the young age of children when reading picture books, they have no freedom to choose books independently of parents and carers, but, at this age, their opinions are being formed about how the world works and their place in it. If these opinions are formed solely by reference to the parents, they may not be rounded ones or they may fail to broaden the child's perspectives. Public librarians can hold considerable influence for change:

> As stewards of information, library and information professionals are indeed instrumental in the facilitation of knowledge and thus power.
>
> (Buchanan and Henderson, 2009, 99)

Gardner's (2007) writing on civic and social responsibility is relevant to the tension between deciding what is best for the librarians and library and what is best for the community or society as a whole. 'Civic' refers to one's responsibility for those one works with, such as colleagues and the library itself, safeguarding them from possible danger. Avoiding stocking books that might lead to complaints that threaten the library's existence would be a moral imperative, if one followed this theory. 'Social' means one's duty to society, i.e. responsibility for those who are served by one's own work, which, in this case, would be the community that is served by the library. This is particularly relevant to public libraries, as they are funded by local government chosen by the people, thus, they clearly have a primary responsibility to the people in their area. The dilemma of the librarian choosing stock is whether their responsibility is mostly a civic one – to protect their colleagues from accusations of either moral lassitude or censorship – or a social one – to serve society by providing a stock that promotes tolerance.

Child rights

> We owe it to the children in our lives to make sure they have choices in what they read and learn. (Tillotson, 2006, 4)

The idea of the child having rights is a crucial one. We are used to thinking of children as unformed extensions of their parents, and it is easy to overlook that they have rights, which may differ from those of their parents, particularly when considering the early years and the right to access books and information.

Wall argues for 'a new childism', which ensures that human rights covers humans of all ages (2008, 524.) He discusses the different theories that have existed in the past about the moral status of children (ranging from children as naturally bad to children as naturally good). He feels that all of these standpoints 'dehumanize' children, by reinforcing them as 'not yet full social citizens', who are not yet entitled to human rights (2008, 527). He places children in the role of the 'other', or the marginalized, and points out that we are morally responsible towards them and that adults have a duty to fight for the rights of children, who are too young to fight for themselves. This suggests a moral imperative for librarians to advocate on behalf of the rights of the child to access a range of literature that is for his or her good. However, in the world of professional ethics and in the world of libraries, children are often considered a separate case, and the guidelines may often be different from those for adults.

Child rights in practice

As discussed previously, the rights of the child are highlighted by the CRC, which states that children should be protected from discrimination; they should have the right to freedom of expression and, in particular should benefit from:

> The preparation of the child for responsible life in a free society, in the spirit of understanding, peace, tolerance, equality of sexes, and friendship among all peoples, ethnic, national and religious groups and persons of indigenous origin.
>
> (UN, 1990, Article 29)

This would suggest that child rights, in terms of stock selection, involve access and exposure to literature, which promotes the above, by displaying difference in a positive, healthy way. Scolnicov considers that a: 'child's identity is formed relative to, but separate from, his or her family. Identity has many facets, including those of gender, family membership, nationality, and moral outlook' (2007, 251). She weighs up the right of the child to choose his or her own religion, against the right of the parent to choose a religion for their child, and considers the possibility that education should be neutral, in order to allow for the child's right to choose. She describes how the argument has usually been divided between parents and the state, battling for the choice of what to teach children, but that this division totally ignores the rights of children themselves and suggests that parents hold rights over children only 'in trust', until children are old enough to make choices.

This suggests a world in which we have a duty to ensure that young children do have some exposure to difference, because we live in a society that contains difference, and a child may, him or herself, be different. This would mean that all children have a right to experience, for example, literature that refers to alternative families and stories that come from different cultures and backgrounds.

Children's rights in libraries

Rankin and Brock discuss the rights of children and summarize the consensus of the library community, that:

> . . . libraries can change children's lives. Books can inspire imagination, help emotional growth and develop understanding of the world and our place in the local and global community, past and present.
>
> (2009, 4)

Camicia and Saavedra (2009) describe how the civic education system in the USA fails children by not teaching them more about multiculturalism, thereby failing children who live in a multicultural world. They explain the danger of restricting children's outlook: 'this silencing constructed and maintained the hegemony of an undemocratic educational environment' (2009, 512). The argument for child rights clearly favours librarians ensuring that the widest possible range of books are made available to children. Every child has a right to grow up with tolerance for others and in an environment that welcomes his or her own differences. Publishers such as Tamarind are clear on this stance; in its catalogue Tamarind states that children need to see people like themselves, so that they know that success is possible. Less recognized by society, currently, is the need for books that avoid gender stereotyping, display alternative families or present ways of life that are outside the experience of middle-class families.

Community rights

Professional literature for librarians has discussed how to meet the needs and requests of the community. For example, Benne (1991) discusses the problem of dealing with the community and parental rights, but falls back on the need for an official policy, without discussing at any length how that is made. Rankin and Brock (2009) raise the issue of responding to the community's needs through community profiling and targeting the service to the local population. This makes sense, but raises the issue of needs weighed against wishes. Only providing books that are requested may not provide enough information to fully develop the readers. Libraries need to widen views, rather than just meet them. This might even be considered to be an underlying need of the community that is not always recognized.

Much has been written on how to distinguish selection from censorship. Benne sums up the most common argument, that 'selection must be a positive action – acquiring materials for a service programme and for users – rather than a negative one – keeping out titles that might become controversial in the community' (1991, 130). This implies that the right of sections of the community to access certain books outweighs the right of other sections of the community to exclude certain books. This places the responsibility firmly with the judgement of the individual librarian.

Stannard (2008) considered, in her Sheffield study, who should be the main guardian of children – the parents or the state (in the form of librarians). She looked at the views of librarians and parents and concluded that they believed that: 'the parents should be the guardians of children's fiction in a public library' (2008, 2). She found that parents felt that they would prefer a wider range of books available, from which they could personally choose those which were appropriate for their own children and that they were resistant to the idea of librarians deciding this. This backs up Benne's point, assuming that all parents are happy to censor, where they see fit.

An exchange between Almond and Blum, in the June 2010 issue of *Journal of Moral Education* (Blum, 2010), explored the difficulty of balancing a range of very different viewpoints, with regard to 'education for tolerance'. A clear argument is that it is better for a society to have children brought up to be tolerant of different beliefs, cultures and backgrounds. This would mean that the picture book collection, for example, should display all these different beliefs as equal and thus available. Cole's (2000) UK study found that censorship was common amongst librarians, with the values of the community often being cited as the reason behind the censorship. Cole suggests that if library associations want librarians to act in accordance with the professional values of intellectual freedom, they will need to be more 'proactive' in promoting the need for this.

Librarians, as professionals, are uniquely empowered to make ethical choices in stock selection. Buchanan and Henderson discuss how a professional's decision affects many people, and, therefore, decisions have to be made from a position of knowledge:

> Professionals] understand the difference between selection and censorship. We understand our community. . . . We think differently than a parent does, for instance, where banning books or selecting a 'controversial' resource is concerned . . . we must consider our community's values and we must understand our profession's values, while realizing the two may be at odds. A professional negotiates those odds.
> (2009, 95-6)

Official guidance for librarians

There is ample professional guidance for librarians on censorship in children's literature. For example, the Museums, Libraries and Archives Council's (MLA) *Guidelines on Controversial Materials* (2009) provides some advice regarding young people. The broad guidance is that a wide range of opinions and views should be reflected in the library stock and online accessible materials, and all communities that are served by the public library should have representation in the stock. The main restriction indicated by the *Guidelines* is that of legality. The general trend is that, where not constrained by law or local authority, items should not be excluded just because they might offend some people. Racial and religious hatred is one example of an illegal practice that is relevant in this case. The *Guidelines* explicitly state that selection should not depend on 'the personal view of library staff, suppliers or other partners' (2009, 9) and that outsourcing of selection involves training those who are responsible for this task. It refers to the rights and responsibilities of parents, indicating that parents are responsible for what their children view online at the library.

Further guidance is provided in the CILIP Code of Practice (2009b). For example, the 'responsibility to society' section states that the general 'public good' should be a priority for librarians. There is an ethical argument that can be made that what we believe to be good for society in general can, and even must, be a part of a child's upbringing. For example, if we desire a more tolerant and fairer society, this would back up the argument for ensuring the availability of books about other races and sexual orientations, and the promotion of feminist ideas. However, this is clearly dependent on what we view as a good society, which, essentially, comes down to relying on one's individual beliefs. It also holds the ethical principle of defending access to information.

The IFLA guidelines for library services to babies and toddlers flag up the fact that books should be selected that are 'age appropriate . . . non-biased and non-sexist' (2007, 7). For the stock selector, this does not elucidate as much as is first thought, since the term 'age-appropriate' means different things to different people. For example, the age and content of sexuality education is a popularly debated topic, with some claiming that the age of seven is too early and others discussing the inclusion of same-sex parenting (Byrd, 2011). The term 'sexist' is also seen differently by different people – 'princess' books are ubiquitous, especially within the Disney context, but many feminists would strongly object to them.

There is clearly a flaw in relying predominantly on the professional objectivity of guidelines:

> One way in which individuals limit their responsibility is by conforming to the consensus of the domain. In other words, they follow established professional norms without giving much thought to competing responsibilities. . . . Other professionals carefully weigh competing professional responsibilities and make difficult choices among these responsibilities.
>
> (Gardner, 2007, 248)

This is realistic, in the sense that where people feel one position or the other is ethically correct, they will not go against their instincts. It is also true to say that the ethical codes can be used in many varying cases, in order to justify more than one viewpoint.

Buchanan and Henderson view codes of ethics as a foundation and framework on which to build. Codes of ethics do not always provide answers, and they, of course, do not operate on levels of deep specificity; they provide guidelines, not rules, which is probably best, and, certainly, they are not laws (2009). As Benne (1991) discusses, the librarian has a difficult choice to make when selecting texts and being able to consciously justify the inclusion, or not, of specific material.

The question then becomes what kind of positive action might be appropriate to take. Blanshard (1998) points out the need for proactively selecting multicultural stock and avoiding racist texts. She also points out that sexist books should not be selected and that the books that are chosen should not be 'didactic or propagandist' (165). She considers the issue of controversial books and states that the stock should display well reasoned tendencies and not specifically avoid sensitive or controversial texts. McMenemy, Poulter and Burton raise the point that librarians may disagree with the government on this particular issue:

> occasionally [politicians] may need to be reminded of their responsibilities by professional organisations. It is a core role of librarians to campaign vigorously for free speech and counter any attempt at censorship.
>
> (2007, 50)

There is certainly a case for intervention on the grounds of social inclusion. Tied together with the rights of the child, there is a strong case for proactively selecting books which positively show many different ways of life, including, but not restricted to, people from different racial and social backgrounds, less stereotypical families, for example, single parents, same-sex parents, polyamorous parents, different religions/non-religious backgrounds and people with disabilities, and challenging gender stereotypes. The question that remains is how the librarians who are responsible for choosing stock are negotiating all these ethical issues and whether they would feel comfortable (or would wish) to be 'radical' or proactive in their stock selection of picture books.

Ethical issues and professionalism

The decisions that a professional makes affects large numbers of people - our patrons, our stakeholders and our societies - and this clearly differentiates professionals from lay persons (Buchanan and Henderson, 2009, 95). As mentioned earlier, Gardner (2007), discussing professional ethics, identifies two main forms of responsibility: civic and social. A professional's ethical practice is dependent on professional knowledge acquired through education, qualification and experience, which will have generated specific skills, values and beliefs (Brock, Rankin and Swiniarski, 2011). Gorman (2000) proposes eight values that offer foundational support to librarianship: stewardship, service, intellectual freedom, rationalism, literacy and learning, equity of access, privacy and democracy. One of the hallmarks of a profession is the framework of values that underpin the work of practitioners; IFLA has compiled a collection of professional guidelines for librarians and other library employees adopted by national library or librarians associations or implemented by government agencies. CILIP has developed a set of 12 Ethical Principles and a Code of Professional Practice for Library and Information Professionals in the UK. The introduction to the CILIP Code states that library and information professionals are frequently the essential link between information users and the information or piece of literature which they require, and, therefore, they occupy a privileged position, which carries corresponding responsibilities (CILIP, 2009a).

The purpose of the Principles and Code is to provide a framework to help library and information professionals who are members of CILIP to manage the responsibilities and sensitivities that figure prominently in their work. A consideration of ethical issues is an essential quality of the 'reflective' practitioner. McMenemy, Poulter and Burton (2007) point out that ethical codes are useful documents for two specific reasons. First, they offer members of the professional association a model of behaviour that is expected of them, establishing the parameters of acceptable behaviour. Second, they communicate a set of values to the wider world, including employers and other stakeholders. However, although ethical codes are in place for librarians in the UK, it is not known how useful and relevant they are in supporting and guiding the everyday work of practitioners, when facing ethical dilemmas.

Hauptman states:

> Codes, rules, regulations and even laws do not create or foster an ethical environment; a true commitment on the part of the organization and its individual members is mandatory if we are to operate fairly, and offer all patrons and clients the service that they deserve while avoiding social harm.
>
> (Hauptman, 2002, 135)

Conclusion

This chapter has discussed how the librarian, as a professional, makes decisions on a daily basis that are fundamental to child development, children's rights and the reflection of the individual, culture and society within which they work. Children are citizens, as established by rights. However, these rights are constrained by children's own ability to make informed decisions and change as they develop as citizens. In the interim, in relation to rights in respect of information, both the state and parents, alongside the librarian, exercise interventions. There are many examples of practice, guidance and codes, but other professions have gone further in valuing and applying the moral and ethical processes. We can ask the question: is it time for the library profession to do the same? And, in the process, is it time to consider the impact on the individual professional and, also, on the child as reader and young citizen?

References

ACT (2003) *Cycle of Change, Institute for Citizenship*, Active Citizenship Today, www.crf-usa.org/active-citizenship-today-act/active-citizenship-today-act-online.html.

ALA (2009) Attempts to Remove Children's Book on Male Penguin Couple Parenting Chick Continue, press release, American Library Association, www.ala.org/ala/newspresscenter/news/pressreleases2009/april2009/nlw08bbtopten.cfm.

Alderson, P. (2000) *Young Children's Rights: exploring beliefs, principles and practice*, Jessica Kingsley.

Almond, B. (2010) Education for Tolerance: cultural difference and family values, *Journal of Moral Education*, **39** (2), 131-43.

Archard, D. (2004) *Children: rights and childhood*, 2nd edn, Routledge.

Arts Council England (2011) *Culture, Knowledge and Understanding: great museums and libraries for everyone*, Arts Council England.

Becta (2003) *Becta ICT Advice: ICT advice for teachers*, British Educational Communications and Technology Agency, http://webarchive.nationalarchives.gov.uk/20110130111510/ http://www.becta.org.uk.

Benne, M. (1991) *Principles of Children's Services in Public Libraries*, American Library Association.

Blanshard, C. (1998) *Managing Library Services for Children and Young People*, Library Association Publishing.

Blum, L. (2010) Secularism, Multiculturalism and Same-sex Marriage: a comment on Brenda Almond's 'Education for Tolerance', *Journal of Moral Education*, **39** (2), 145-60.

Bösche, S. (1983) *Jenny Lives With Eric and Martin*, Gay Men's Press.

Bowdler, T. (ed.) (1853) *The Bowdler Shakespeare: in six volumes*, Cambridge University Press.

Bowdler, T. (ed.) (1923) *Gibbon's History of the Decline and Fall of the Roman Empire, Repr. with the Omission of all Passages of an Irreligious or Immoral Tendency*, BiblioBazaar.

Brock, A., Rankin, C. and Swiniarski, L. (2011) Are we Doing it By the Book? Professional ethics for teachers and librarians in the early years. In Campbell, A. and Broadhead, P. (eds), *Working with Children and Young People: ethical debates and practices across disciplines and continents*, Peter Lang.

Brophy, P. (2001) *The Library in the Twenty-First Century: new services for the information age*, Library Association Publishing.

Buchanan, E. and Henderson, K. (2009) *Case Studies in Library and Information Science Ethics*, McFarland.

Byrd, A. D. (2011) Same-Sex Marriage and the Schools: potential impact on children via sexuality education, *Brigham Young University Education & Law Journal*, **2**, 179-203.

Cairns, L. (2001) Investing in Children: learning how to promote the rights of all children, *Children and Society*, **15** (5), 347-60.

Camicia, S. and Saavedra, C. (2009) A New Childhood Social Studies Curriculum for a New Generation of Citizenship, *International Journal of Children's Rights*, **17**, 501-17.

CILIP (2009a) *Ethical Principles for Library and Information Professionals*, Chartered Institute of Library and Information Professionals, www.cilip.org.uk/get-involved/policy/ethics/pages/principles.aspx.

CILIP (2009b) *Code of Practice*, Chartered Institute of Library and Information Professionals, www.cilip.org.uk/get-involved/policy/ethics/pages/code.aspx.

Cole, N. (2000) The Influence of Attitudes on Public Library Stock Management Practise, *Libri*, **50**, 37-47.

Coles, B. (1995) *Youth and Social Policy: youth citizenship and young careers*, UCL Press Limited.

DCMS (2003) *Framework for the Future: libraries, learning and information in the next decade*, Department for Culture, Media and Sport, http://webarchive.nationalarchives.gov.uk/+/http:/www.culture.gov.uk/reference_library/publications/4505.aspx.

Frazer, E. and Emler, N. (1997) Participation and Citizenship: a new agenda for youth politics research? In Bynner, J., Chisholm, L. and Furlong, A. (eds), *Youth, Citizenship and Social Change in a European Context*, Ashgate Publishing.

Gardner, H. (2007) *Responsibility at Work*, Jossey-Bass.

Gorman, M. (2000) *Our Enduring Values: librarianship in the 21st century*, ALA Editions.

Hall, T., Williamson, H. and Coffey, A. (2000) Youth People, Citizenship and the Third Way: a role for the youth service, *Journal of Youth Studies*, **3** (4), 461-72.

Harris, B. (1998) The Inside Story, *UK Youth*, **91**, Spring, 30-3.

Hart, R. A. (1992) Children's Participation: from tokenism to citizenship, UNICEF Innocenti Research Centre.

Hauptman, R. (2002) *Ethics and Librarianship*, McFarland.

Hick, S. and Halpin, E. (2001) Children's Rights and the Internet, *The Annals of the American Academy of Political and Social Science*, May, 56-70.

Hill, B., Pike, G. and Selby, D. (1998) *Perspectives on Childhood: an approach to citizenship education*, Cassell.

IFLA (2007) *Guidelines for Library Services to Babies and Toddlers*, International Federation of Library Associations and Institutions, http://archive.ifla.org/VII/d3/pub/Profrep100.pdf.

IFLA and UNESCO) (1994) *Public Library Manifesto 1994*, International Federation of Library Associations and Institutions and United Nations Educational, Scientific

and Cultural Organization,
http://archive.ifla.org/VII/s8/unesco/eng.htm.

Jones, G. and Wallace, C. (1992) *Youth, Family and Citizenship*, Open University Press.

Koren, M. (2000) Children's Rights, Libraries Potential and the Information Society,
IFLA Journal, **26** (4), 273-9.

Koren, M. (2003) Children's Rights and Library Best Practices, *World Library and Information Congress, 69th IFLA General Conference and Council: Proceedings from an International Conference held on 1-9 August 2003, Berlin*, International Federation of Library Associations and Institutions.

Local Government Act (1988), Section 28,
www.opsi.gov.uk/acts/acts1988/Ukpga_19880009_en_5.htm.

Lowndes, V., Pratchett, L. P. and Stoker, G. (2001) Trends in Public Participation: part 2 - citizens' perspectives, *Public Administration*, **79** (2), 445-55.

McMenemy, D., Poulter, A. and Burton, P. (2007) *A Handbook of Ethical Practice*, Chandos.

Milburn, T. (2000) Connecting with Young People and Youth Issues, *Youth and Policy*, **68**, 46-57.

MLA (2009) *Guidelines on Controversial Materials*, Museums, Libraries and Archives Council.

Mohamed, I. A. and Wheeler, W. (2001) *Broadening the Bounds of Youth Development. Youth as Engaged Citizens*, The Ford Foundation.

Morch, S. (1997). Youth and Activity Theory. In Bynner, J., Chisholm, L. and Furlong, A. (eds), *Youth, Citizenship and Social Change in a European Context*, Ashgate Publishing.

Osler, A. and Starkey, H. (1999) Rights, Identities and Inclusion: European action programmes as political education, *Oxford Review of Education*, **25** (1&2), 199-215.

Parnell, P. and Richardson, J. (2005) *And Tango Makes Three*, Simon and Schuster.

Parsons, R. (2002) *The National Youth Agency Experience: making a success of youth action*, The National Youth Agency.

Rankin, C. (2011) The Early Years Librarian - a key partner in promoting early language and literacy. In Brock, A. and Rankin, C. (eds), *Professionalism in the Interdisciplinary Early Years Team Supporting Young Children and their Families*, Continuum Publishing.

Rankin, C. and Brock, A. (2009) *Delivering the Best Start: a guide to early years libraries*, Facet Publishing.

Scolnicov, A. (2007) The Child's Right to Religious Freedom and Formation of Identity, *International Journal of Children's Rights*, **15**, 251-67.

Sinclair, R. and Franklin, A. (2000) Youth People's Participation, *Quality Protects Research Briefing*, Department of Health.

Stannard, T. (2008) *The Guardians of Children's Literature? A study into the attitudes of public library staff and parents regarding issues of censorship of children's books*, MA thesis, University of Sheffield.

Tamarind (2010) *Books Catalogue*, Tamarind.

Tillotson, L. (2006) Editorial, *Book Links*, September, 4.

Treseder, P. (1997) *Empowering Children and Young People: training manual*, Save the Children.

Trevorrow, P., Griffin, D., Halpin, E. and Wootton, C. (2005) The Effect of Internet Filtering on Active Youth Citizenship in the Information Age: experience from public libraries in the United Kingdom, *The Canadian Journal of Information and Library Science*, **29** (4), 437–70.

Trevorrow, P., Orange, G. and Halpin, E. (2006) Developing a Model of Active Youth Citizenship, Research in Progress Paper, www.imresearch.org/RIPs/Index_RIPs.htm.

UN (1948) Universal Declaration of Human Rights, United Nations, www.un.org/en/documents/udhr/.

UN (1989) *Convention on the Rights of the Child*, United Nations, www.unesco.org/education/pdf/CHILD_E.PDF.

UN (1990) *UN Convention on the Rights of the Child*, United Nations, www2.ohchr.org/english/law/crc.htm.

UNICEF (2012) *Convention on the Rights of the Child*, United Nations Children's Fund, www.unicef.org/crc/.

Wall, J. (2008) Human Rights in Light of Childhood, *International Journal of Children's Rights*, **16** (4), 523–43.

Williamson, H. (1997) Youth Work and Citizenship. In Bynner, J., Chisholm, L. and Furlong, A. (eds), *Youth, Citizenship and Social Change in a European Context*, Ashgate Publishing.

Woyach, R. B. and Cox, K. J. (1997) Principles for Youth Leadership Development Programs. *Leadership Link*, The Ohio State University Leadership Center.

Index